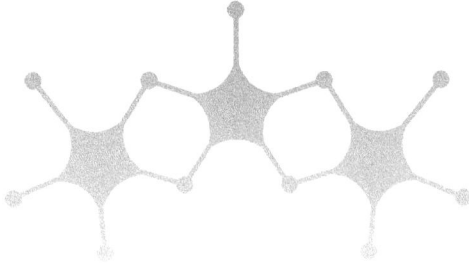

NEUROPOWER

LEADING WITH NEUROINTELLIGENCE

THIRD EDITION
APPENDICES

PETER BUROW

The material contained in this book is not intended as medical advice. If you have a medical issue or illness, consult a qualified physician.

NeuroPower Appendices

Published by;

Copernicus Publishing Pty Ltd
10 Grosvenor Street, Blackburn North VIC 3130 Australia
PO Box 125, Balwyn North VIC 3104 Australia
Ph +61 3 9017 3162
Fx +61 3 9923 6632

Proofing by Amanda Banhidi
Desktop Publishing by Wade McFarlane

Contents

Overview of the Appendices

This book of Appendices contains supplementary information to NeuroPower: Leading with Neurointelligence and should be read in conjunction with it.

This book of appendices contains the following content:

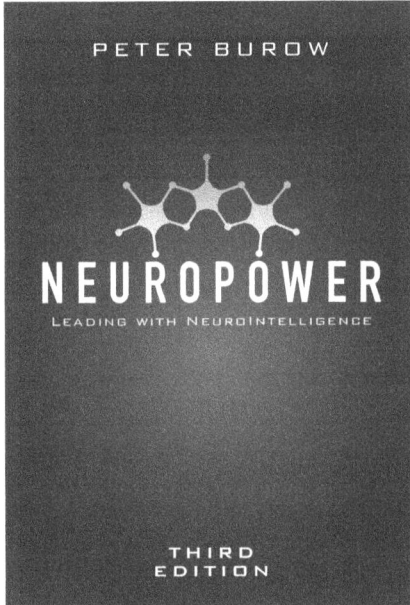

APPENDIX 1 - HOW THE CORE BELIEFS AND ARCHETYPES WORK TOGETHER

Appendix 1 details and explains the complete roadmap of your personality from Neuro-Limbic Type (Core Beliefs) to Neuro-Rational Type (Archetype) to Patron Leader.

APPENDIX 2 – NEURO-RATIONAL TYPE TEST

Appendix 2 is the Master Profile questionnaire which enables readers to 'best guess' their Master Neuro-Rational Type.

APPENDIX 3 – NEURO-RATIONAL TYPE MATRIX

Appendix 3 is a table that summarises the key attributes of the Master Neuro-Rational Types such as their noble qualities, their personal code of conduct, contribution to the team culture, and first steps of integration or disintegration.

APPENDIX 4 – PROCESS OF INTEGRATION AND (DIS)INTEGRATION

Appendix 4 summarises, for each of the Master Neuro-Rational Types, the steps of integration towards enlightenment and the steps of disintegration towards ignorance and death.

APPENDIX 5 – EXPLORATION OF THE MIRROR

In order to find personal internal harmony and to have full awareness of others' behaviours, it is critical to understand the role and character of both the Mirror and Master. Appendix 5 discusses Dr Fredric Schiffer's research which showed the presence of the Mirror, what can happen when we are blind to our Mirror, and some techniques which enable us to find harmony between our Mirror and Master. This also aligns with the Maya Lenca mythology of the duality of being and it is from here that we have borrowed the term 'Mirror' and key Maya medicine integration techniques.

APPENDIX 6 – INTELLIGENCE COMPATIBILITY MATRIX

Appendix 6 identifies the level of compatibility between different Intelligences. This can assist in identifying the sources of interpersonal conflict.

APPENDIX 7 – THE PATH OF INTEGRATION FOR EACH NEURO-RATIONAL TYPE

Appendix 7 tables the human nobility that each Neuro-Rational Type has access to at the different levels of consciousness.

APPENDIX 8 – NEUROPOWER AND ITS SYNERGY WITH MAYA LENCA PHILOSOPHY OF PERSONALITY, WELLNESS AND ILLNESS

This paper, authored by Leonel Chevez, the grandson of the last remaining Royal Maya Lenca, compares Maya philosophy and mythology with *NeuroPower*.

APPENDIX 9 – THE CELTIC CROSS

Appendix 9 discusses the Celtic Cross, its metaphoric meanings and symbols, and how these relate to the *NeuroPower* framework.

APPENDIX 10 – ONE OF THE GREATEST STORIES EVER TOLD

Appendix 10 tells the story of Camelot, King Arthur and the Round Table. Each character aligns with one of the Neuro-Rational Types. The story shows how the Archetypes act and interact, and how they grow and develop as their life unfolds.

APPENDIX 11 – THE NEUROPOWER ASSUMPTIONS

The *NeuroPower* framework is most effective when used in an environment that is supported by the thirty three *NeuroPower* assumptions. These 33 assumptions provide the philosophical platform for the *NeuroPower* framework.

APPENDIX 12 – APPLYING THE NEUROPOWER INSIGHT TO MAKE YOU A BETTER LEADER

Appendix 12 discusses how applying knowledge of the people's Intelligences and NLTs is critical to good leadership.

APPENDIX 13 – THE NEUROSCIENCE OF THE SIX INTELLIGENCES

Appendix 13 details the neuroscience of each of the six Intelligences in terms of evolutionary social brain function, and somatic, feeling and thinking aspects.

APPENDIX 14 — NEURO-LIMBIC TYPE BODY SHAPES

Appendix 14 depicts how a person's body shape can be linked to their NLT (Diversi, 2006).

APPENDIX 15 - ARTICLE: WHEN GOOD TEAMS MAKE BAD DECISIONS

Complex strategic decisions involving judgement, interpretation and complex trade-offs are at the centre of effective teamwork at senior levels of organisations. Yet leadership teams find it difficult to get it right. Perhaps this is because our brains have developed problem-solving processes that rely heavily on past experiences which significantly bias our beliefs today. This article explains how Cognitive Bias and 'group think' undermine judgement.

APPENDIX 16 - ARTICLE: BUILDING TRUST WITH THE NINE CORE BELIEF TYPES

Becoming a good advisor takes more than having good advice to offer. There are additional skills involved, ones that no one ever teaches you, that are critical to your success. Most importantly, we have learned the hard way that you don't get the chance to employ advisory skills until you can get someone to trust you enough to share their problems with you. No one ever taught us how to do that either. Yet we had to learn it. Somehow. This article explains how to build trust with the nine NLTs (Core Belief Types).

APPENDIX 1

How the Core Beliefs and Archetypes Work Together

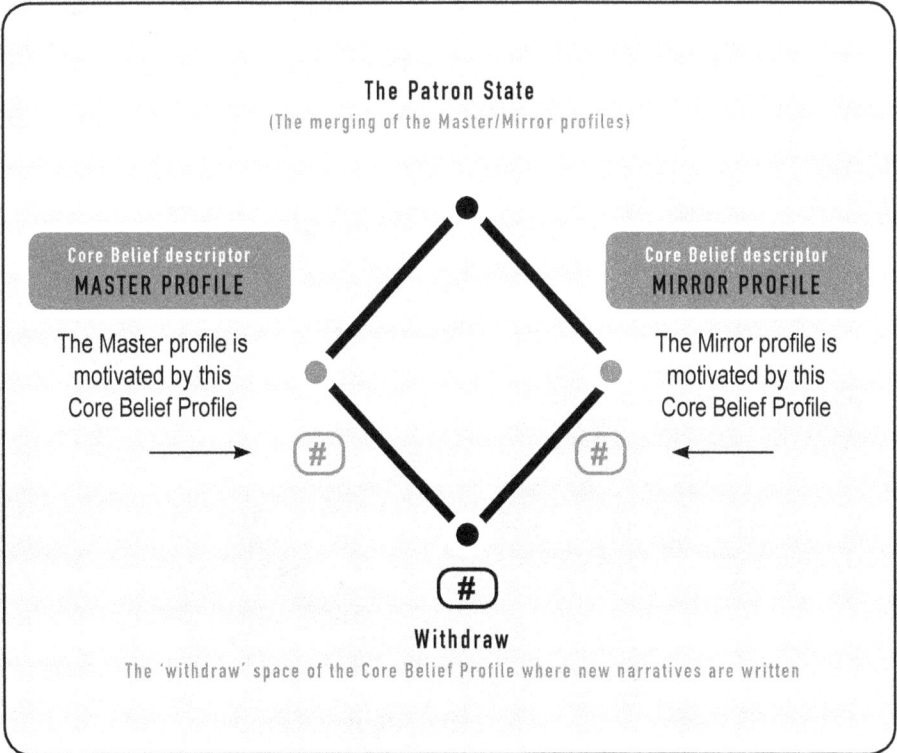

The Patron State
(The merging of the Master/Mirror profiles)

Core Belief descriptor		Core Belief descriptor
MASTER PROFILE		**MIRROR PROFILE**

The Master profile is motivated by this Core Belief Profile

→   #

The Mirror profile is motivated by this Core Belief Profile

←

#

Withdraw
The 'withdraw' space of the Core Belief Profile where new narratives are written

Introduction – How to Interpret this Section

INNATE CHARACTER

- The 'Innate Character' is the personal Code of Conduct for this profile

TEAM ROLE (FOR EXAMPLE; JUDGE)

The 'Team Role' is the personal strength for this profile. It is also the Master personality

Cognitive Strengths

- The strength of the Master profile (in the sample shown opposite - Judge)

Threats to their Leadership Credibility

- What can threaten Leadership Credibility when the Master profile becomes too aggressive

Opportunities for Development

- Opportunities for the Master profile to develop

Cognitive Weaknesses

- The blindspot of the Master profile (in the sample shown opposite - Architect)

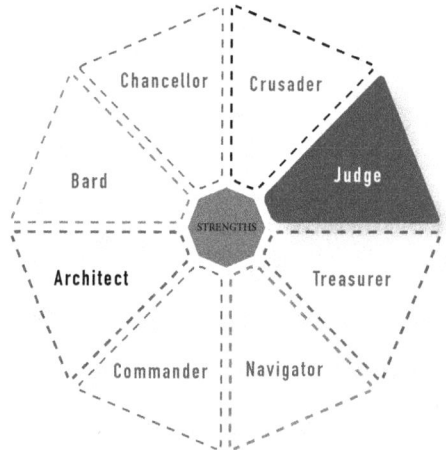

Chancellor | Crusader
Bard
Judge
STRENGTHS
Architect | Treasurer
Commander | Navigator

How the profile thinks under pressure (Core Belief Profile)

The explanation of how the profile thinks under pressure is a description of the Core Belief Profile of the person at their worst and under extreme pressure.

SUGGESTED DEVELOPMENTAL AREAS FOR THIS PROFILE

MANAGE YOUR HABITUAL LIMBIC REACTIONS:

- Hints for managing the Core Belief Profile

LOOK OUT FOR THE SIGNS OF DISINTEGRATION

The first step of the spiral down of the Master profile when triggered by an event, thought, association or deed interpreted through the perspective of the Core Belief.

Draw on the strengths of your Alter Ego

The Alter Ego is the repressed part of the self and is referred to as the Mirror profile. It is the opposite of the Master profile.

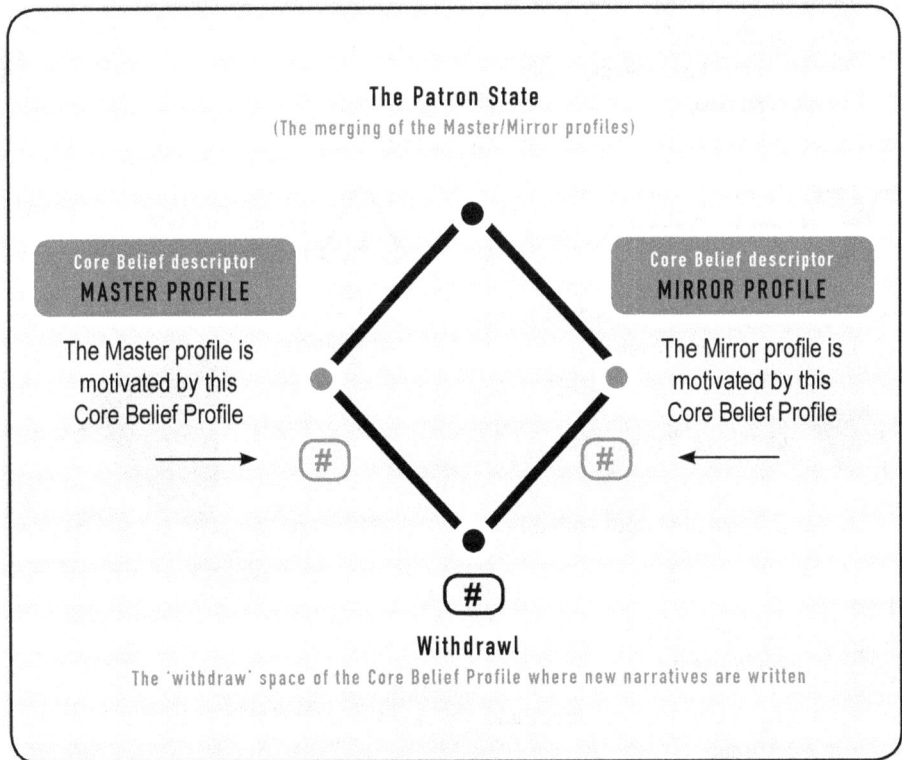

The Patron State
(The merging of the Master/Mirror profiles)

Core Belief descriptor
MASTER PROFILE

The Master profile is motivated by this Core Belief Profile

Core Belief descriptor
MIRROR PROFILE

The Mirror profile is motivated by this Core Belief Profile

#

#

#

Withdrawl
The 'withdraw' space of the Core Belief Profile where new narratives are written

Crusader: Groupies Triad

INNATE CHARACTER

- Always keeps sensitive information that has been shared in confidence to themselves
- Acts ethically in their dealings with others
- Spends time to make sure there is agreement about roles - both theirs and others
- Corrects others - clearly, constructively and professionally
- Speaks directly to the person they have an issue with without unnecessarily involving other unrelated people
- Provides other team members with a sense of purpose

TEAM ROLE (CRUSADER)

The Crusader will do whatever it takes to achieve their vision. They are very high energy and motivational by nature, often aspiring with the highest principles. The Crusader is a persuasive communicator, knows lots of people, is excellent at securing resources for their vision and filling team members with the hope, energy and enthusiasm to get the job done. Focus on clarity of role and keeping team members accountable.

Cognitive Strengths

- Able to break through virtually any barrier to achieve results

Cognitive Weaknesses

- Needs to learn how not to offend

Opportunities for Development

- Can be totally task-oriented and suffer burnout

Threats to their Leadership Credibility

- Can create many enemies who retaliate

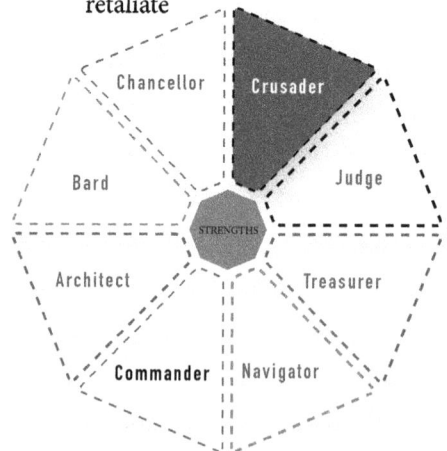

How this Core Belief Profile (CBP) thinks under pressure

The deceit of the CBP3 that is most easily seen is self-deceit. However, it is also the deception of others. Since the CBP3 is constantly changing themselves to be consistent with the most successful image of whatever group or individual they are participating with, they deceive themselves and others that they are actually what it is that they are doing. This deceit can manifest itself as simply putting one's best foot forward by just placing a little spin on the facts to sound good, charm or to self-promote. Deceit is a desire for approval measured by material success.

SUGGESTED DEVELOPMENTAL AREAS FOR THIS PROFILE

MANAGE YOUR HABITUAL LIMBIC REACTIONS:

- Recognise that success is not proof of virtue.
- Recognise that there is a difference between who you are and what you do, and learn to value both independently.
- Note your automatic tendency to take over, whether it is a good idea or not. Allow others to lead and see where they go.
- Take time in your schedule for other people – without an agenda or need for results!
- Develop the ability to be honest about how you feel.
- Develop the capacity to make a personal connection with those around you.

LOOK OUT FOR THE SIGNS OF DISINTEGRATION

If the commitment of others to the Crusader, despite their lack of integrity, is not forthcoming, the Crusader will begin to bully and blame others. This bullying comes in the form of cutting words, strong emotions, mood highs and lows and a focus on personal attacks. The Crusader delusionally convinces themselves that they are 'in the right' and that others need 'reprimanding' to justify their own position. At this stage the Crusader develops and tells elaborate stories that blame others for their own lack of integrity.

Draw on the strengths of your Alter Ego

When the Crusader's Mirror, the Commander, is in control the Crusader loves having fun, breaking the rules, being disorderly, talking loudly, behaving badly and generally doing all the things the Crusader abhors.

When integrated into the personality, the Commander gives the Crusader patience, acceptance, warmth, generosity and the ability to solve problems patiently. It even gives them the ability to enjoy life and amuse themselves.

Crusader Groupies – Diamond of Personality

Whole of Personality

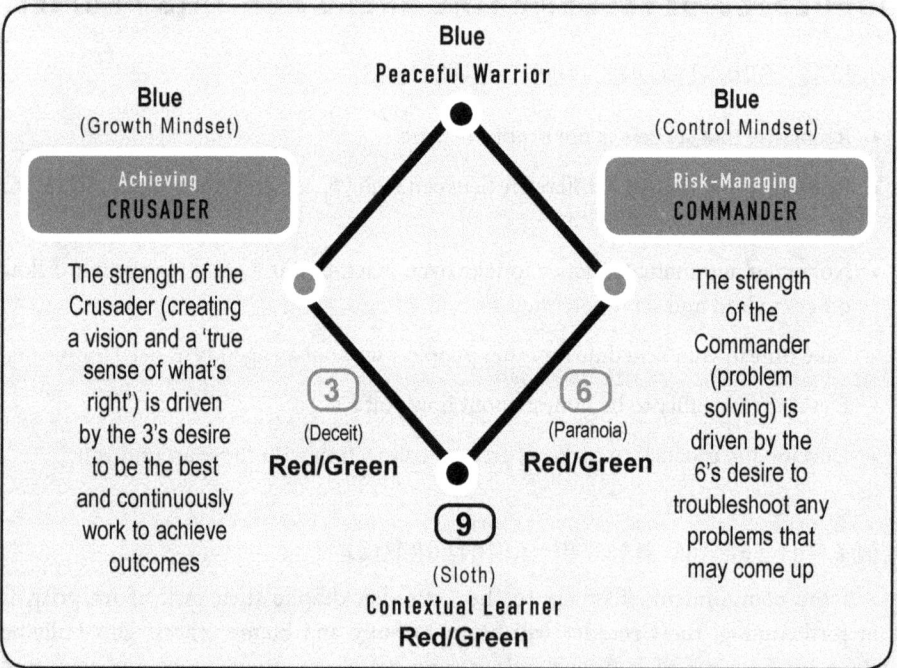

Blue
Peaceful Warrior

Blue
(Growth Mindset)

Blue
(Control Mindset)

Achieving
CRUSADER

Risk-Managing
COMMANDER

The strength of the Crusader (creating a vision and a 'true sense of what's right') is driven by the 3's desire to be the best and continuously work to achieve outcomes

The strength of the Commander (problem solving) is driven by the 6's desire to troubleshoot any problems that may come up

3
(Deceit)
Red/Green

6
(Paranoia)
Red/Green

9
(Sloth)
Contextual Learner
Red/Green

Crusader: Idealist Triad

INNATE CHARACTER

- Always keeps sensitive information that has been shared in confidence to themselves
- Acts ethically in their dealings with others
- Spends time to make sure there is agreement about roles - both theirs and others
- Corrects others - clearly, constructively and professionally
- Speaks directly to the person they have an issue with without unnecessarily involving other unrelated people
- Provides other team members with a sense of purpose

TEAM ROLE (CRUSADER)

The Crusader will do whatever it takes to achieve their vision. They are very high energy and motivational by nature, often aspiring with the highest principles. The Crusader is a persuasive communicator, knows lots of people, is excellent at securing resources for their vision and filling team members with the hope, energy and enthusiasm to get the job done. Focus on clarity of role and keeping team members accountable.

Cognitive Strengths

- Able to break through virtually any barrier to achieve results

Cognitive Weaknesses

- Needs to learn how not to offend

Opportunities for Development

- Can be totally task-oriented and suffer burnout

Threats to their Leadership Credibility

- Can create many enemies who retaliate

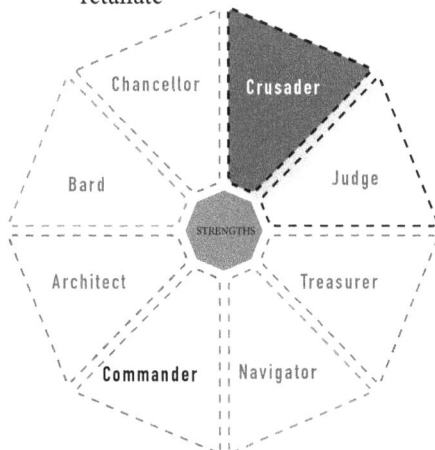

How this Core Belief Profile (CBP) thinks under pressure

In the presence of being trapped or controlled the emotions of the CBP7 will force them to move quickly from one thing to another, sampling but never deepening any particular experience. This is particularly true if the experience could result in emotional pain. CBP7 manifests as gluttony for new, fun and enjoyable experiences. Life is like a smorgasbord and is experienced as a range of experiences rather than a single experience repeated often. At their worst, they will seek absolute freedom without responsibility or commitment.

SUGGESTED DEVELOPMENTAL AREAS FOR THIS PROFILE

MANAGE YOUR HABITUAL LIMBIC REACTIONS:

- Be aware of your tendency to rationalise, to explain away failure and ethical violations without taking responsibility.
- Develop the skill of really listening rather than trying to think of something clever to say later.
- Work! Actually get your work completed rather than thinking about what else you could be doing.
- Practise mental sobriety. Do not just become drunk on ideas.

LOOK OUT FOR THE SIGNS OF DISINTEGRATION

If the commitment of others to the Crusader, despite their lack of integrity, is not forthcoming, the Crusader will begin to bully and blame others. This bullying comes in the form of cutting words, strong emotions, mood highs and lows and a focus on personal attacks. The Crusader delusionally convinces themselves that they are 'in the right' and that others need 'reprimanding' to justify their own position. At this stage the Crusader develops and tells elaborate stories that blame others for their own lack of integrity.

Draw on the strengths of your Alter Ego

When the Crusader's Mirror, the Commander, is in control the Crusader loves having fun, breaking the rules, being disorderly, talking loudly, behaving badly and generally doing all the things the Crusader abhors.

When integrated into the personality, the Commander gives the Crusader patience, acceptance, warmth, generosity and the ability to solve problems patiently. It even gives them the ability to enjoy life and amuse themselves.

Crusader Idealist Diamond of Personality

WHOLE OF PERSONALITY

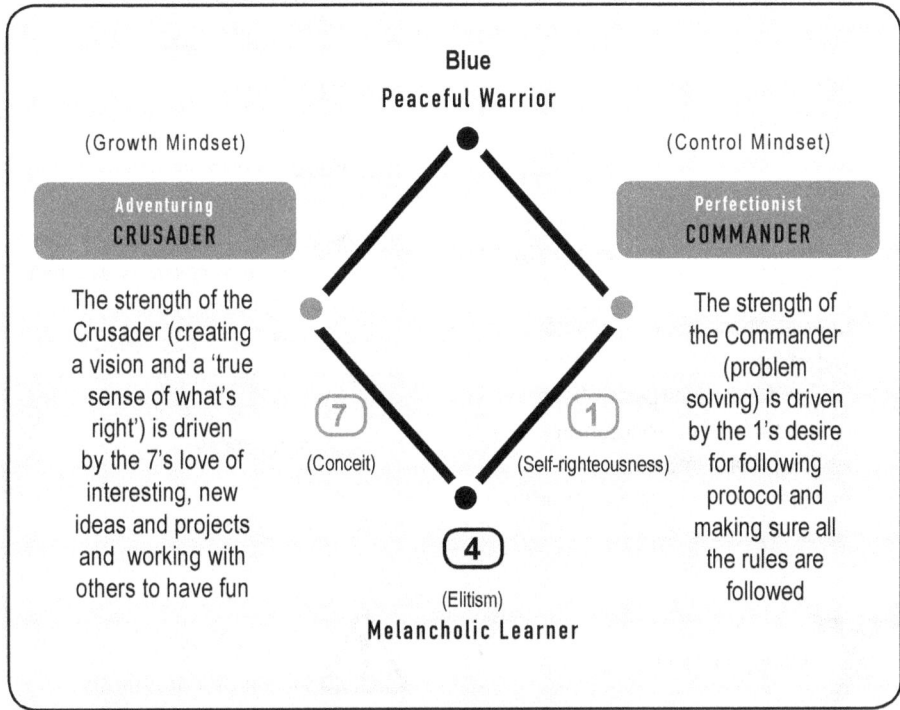

Blue
Peaceful Warrior

(Growth Mindset)   (Control Mindset)

Adventuring
CRUSADER

Perfectionist
COMMANDER

The strength of the Crusader (creating a vision and a 'true sense of what's right') is driven by the 7's love of interesting, new ideas and projects and working with others to have fun

⑦
(Conceit)

①
(Self-righteousness)

The strength of the Commander (problem solving) is driven by the 1's desire for following protocol and making sure all the rules are followed

④
(Elitism)
Melancholic Learner

Crusader: Power Triad

INNATE CHARACTER

- Always keeps sensitive information that has been shared in confidence to themselves
- Acts ethically in their dealings with others
- Spends time to make sure there is agreement about roles - both theirs and others
- Corrects others - clearly, constructively and professionally
- Speaks directly to the person they have an issue with without unnecessarily involving other unrelated people
- Provides other team members with a sense of purpose

TEAM ROLE (CRUSADER)

The Crusader will do whatever it takes to achieve their vision.

They are very high energy and motivational by nature, often aspiring with the highest principles. The Crusader is a persuasive communicator, knows lots of people, is excellent at securing resources for their vision and filling team members with the hope, energy and enthusiasm to get the job done. Focus on clarity of role and keeping team members accountable.

Cognitive Strengths

- Able to break through virtually any barrier to achieve results

Cognitive Weaknesses

- Needs to learn how not to offend

Opportunities for Development

- Can be totally task-oriented and suffer burnout

Threats to their Leadership Credibility

- Can create many enemies who retaliate

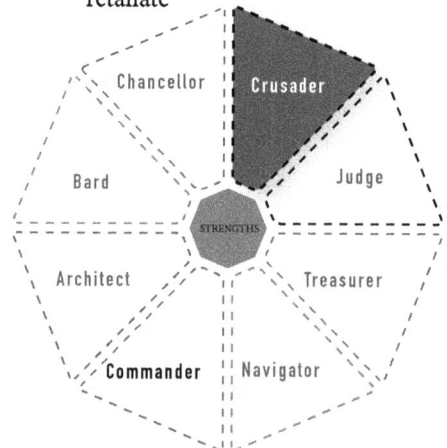

How this Core Belief Profile (CBP) thinks under pressure

At their worst the CBP8 will entertain an enormous lust for life. They will seek intensity in all things as the hallmark of a fulfilling life. If they enjoy something, then there can never be enough. They always want more. Moderation is death when the emotion of the CBP8 is high. Always they want more, better, faster and louder. This sometimes leads to difficulty with people or friends who cannot 'keep up' with their energy. This intensity is used to control others through the creation of physical, material or emotional dependence. Intensity sorts out the strong from the weak. This CBP reports that most people fall into two categories – those that can't help being weak and those that can..

SUGGESTED DEVELOPMENTAL AREAS FOR THIS PROFILE

MANAGE YOUR HABITUAL LIMBIC REACTIONS:

- Feeling as if someone is taking advantage of you is not the same as someone actually taking advantage of you. Check the details before you automatically retaliate.

- Choose your battles. Constantly ask yourself, 'Is this fight worth it?'

- Before you totally attack someone, ask yourself whether you are willing to deal with the consequences.

- For many people, your threats and tirades are not effective, no matter how much you may enjoy putting them on.

- When giving instructions, be very specific about the behaviour that will satisfy your expectations.

- Find ways to use others' talents and give them a sense of ownership and empowerment rather than just being a hired hand.

LOOK OUT FOR THE SIGNS OF DISINTEGRATION

If the commitment of others to the Crusader, despite their lack of integrity, is not forthcoming, the Crusader will begin to bully and blame others. This bullying comes in the form of cutting words, strong emotions, mood highs and lows and a focus on personal attacks. The Crusader delusionally convinces themselves that they are 'in the right' and that others need 'reprimanding' to justify their own position. At this stage the Crusader develops and tells elaborate stories that blame others for their own lack of integrity.

Draw on the strengths of your Alter Ego

When the Crusader's Mirror, the Commander, is in control the Crusader loves having fun, breaking the rules, being disorderly, talking loudly, behaving badly and generally doing all the things the Crusader abhors.

When integrated into the personality, the Commander gives the Crusader patience, acceptance, warmth, generosity and the ability to solve problems patiently. It even gives them the ability to enjoy life and amuse themselves.

Crusader Power Diamond of Personality

Whole of Personality

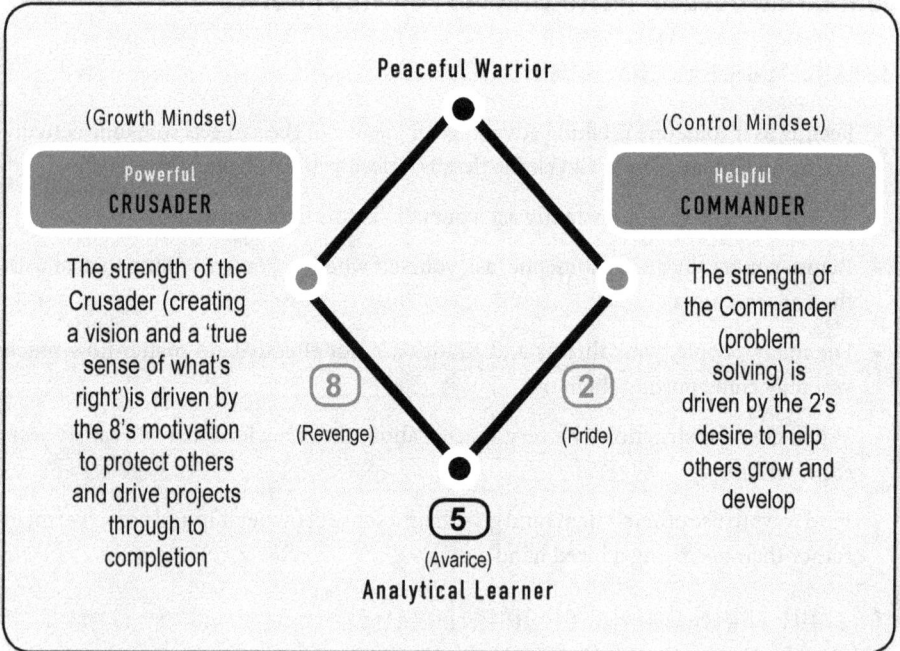

Peaceful Warrior

(Growth Mindset)   (Control Mindset)

Powerful
CRUSADER

Helpful
COMMANDER

The strength of the Crusader (creating a vision and a 'true sense of what's right')is driven by the 8's motivation to protect others and drive projects through to completion

8 (Revenge)

2 (Pride)

The strength of the Commander (problem solving) is driven by the 2's desire to help others grow and develop

5 (Avarice)

Analytical Learner

Commander: Idealist Triad

INNATE CHARACTER

- Stands up for what they believe is right
- Stands by their actions without fear of reprisals or consequences
- Acts justly and fairly in all dealings with colleagues
- Solves problems as they arise without fuss and drama
- Encourages the team to innovate or adapt if necessary to ensure a quality result
- Encourages other team members to be courageous in thought and deed

TEAM ROLE (COMMANDER)

The Commander is able to solve problems that are complex, undefined or constantly changing. They are excellent at managing groups of people in high stress, dangerous or crisis situations. The Commander is practical and creative and can solve things 'on the hop'. The Commander is the natural leader when the right emergency action is needed without preparation.

Cognitive Strengths

- Excellent at creating structure and processes

Cognitive Weaknesses

- Tends to see people as cogs, rather than people

Opportunities for Development

- Needs to keep the big picture in mind! Needs to reconnect

Threats to their Leadership Credibility

- Can lose connection – feel life is pointless and enter into self-defeating behaviour

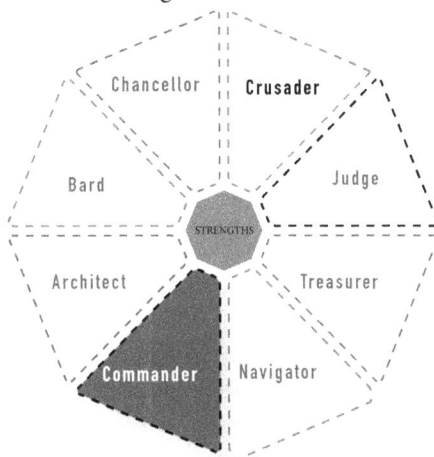

How this Core Belief Profile (CBP) thinks under pressure

At their worst the CBP1 is a hyper-critical, self-righteous individual fixated on adhering to the rules regardless of the situation or circumstance. They can be incapable of giving praise or appreciation for anything or anyone – since nothing ever reaches perfection. At their worst the greatest compliment that a CBP1 can give is, 'There was nothing that I could criticise in the work that you did.'

SUGGESTED DEVELOPMENTAL AREAS FOR THIS PROFILE

MANAGE YOUR HABITUAL LIMBIC REACTIONS:

- Try to model the behaviour that you want to see in others. Do not merely criticise others until they comply with your expectations.
- Appreciate that many of your comments will be taken as criticism, regardless of whether you see them that way.
- Consider the context of any criticism. While it may be appropriate for a specific behaviour, your context may be skewed and may ignore a great deal of relevant information.
- Aspire to your idealism but do not hold yourself and others to attaining it in every area of life.
- Develop realistic expectations for yourself.
- Appreciate and accept that making mistakes is part of the learning process.
- Learn when the given time would be better prioritised on other tasks rather than transforming a workable job to a perfect job.
- Understand that people do not want to be judged. So if you insist on constantly offering criticism you will be shunned and avoided. This will seriously limit your career development.
- Do not adopt the position of moral champion; take a break from the job of policing everyone around you.
- You probably have a tendency to accept and comply blindly with the rules of other people and institutions. You need to develop your own principles and practices based on context.

LOOK OUT FOR THE SIGNS OF DISINTEGRATION

Rather than looking at how they can get on with the job at hand, the Commander will look for the inconsistencies in the behaviour of others and in the systems they are following as a first line of defence against anyone who says they are not doing anything.

During this time, the Commander's professional performance subsides as the procrastination rises. As far as they are concerned, they are okay and everything is working just fine.

Draw on the strengths of your Alter Ego

The Commander's Mirror, the Crusader, is motivated by undertaking crusades that are exciting, adventurous and worthy of their efforts and talents. As the Mirror, the Crusader demands to chase the 'big, hairy, audacious goal' or sets their sights on a mountain so large that it takes everyone's breath away. The Crusader is most likely to take over when the Commander is bored or between helping people in crisis.

Commander Idealist Diamond of Personality

Whole of Personality

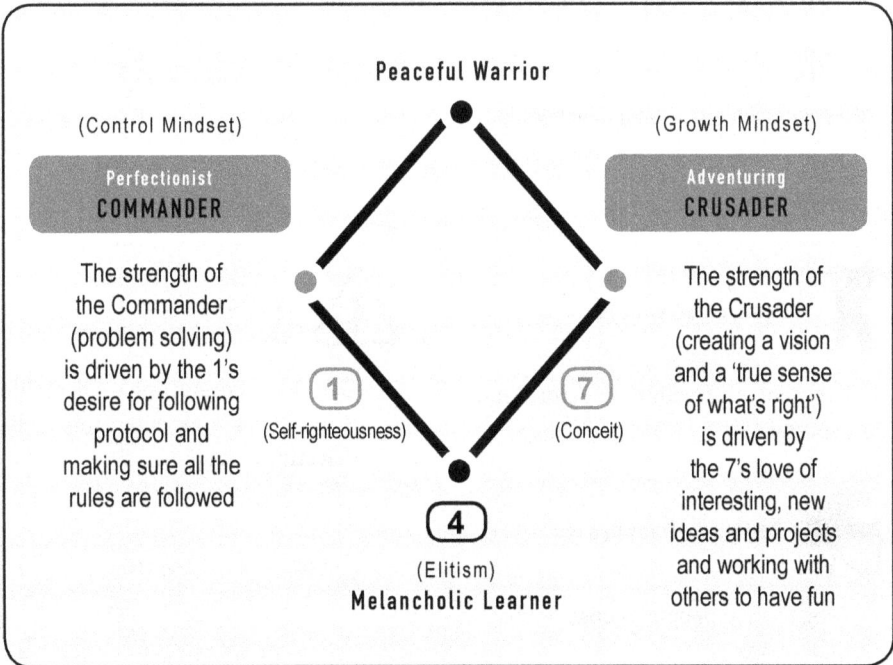

Peaceful Warrior

(Control Mindset)   (Growth Mindset)

| Perfectionist | | Adventuring |
| COMMANDER | | CRUSADER |

The strength of the Commander (problem solving) is driven by the 1's desire for following protocol and making sure all the rules are followed

1

(Self-righteousness)

7

(Conceit)

4

(Elitism)

Melancholic Learner

The strength of the Crusader (creating a vision and a 'true sense of what's right') is driven by the 7's love of interesting, new ideas and projects and working with others to have fun

Commander: Power Triad

INNATE CHARACTER

- Stands up for what they believe is right
- Stands by their actions without fear of reprisals or consequences
- Acts justly and fairly in all dealings with colleagues
- Solves problems as they arise without fuss and drama
- Encourages the team to innovate or adapt if necessary to ensure a quality result
- Encourages other team members to be courageous in thought and deed

TEAM ROLE (COMMANDER)

The Commander is able to solve problems that are complex, undefined or constantly changing. They are excellent at managing groups of people in high stress, dangerous or crisis situations. The Commander is practical and creative and can solve things 'on the hop'. The Commander is the natural leader when the right emergency action is needed without preparation.

Cognitive Strengths

- Excellent at creating structure and processes

Cognitive Weaknesses

- Tends to see people as cogs, rather than people

Opportunities for Development

- Needs to keep the big picture in mind! Needs to reconnect

Threats to their Leadership Credibility

- Can lose connection – feel life is pointless and enter into self-defeating behaviour

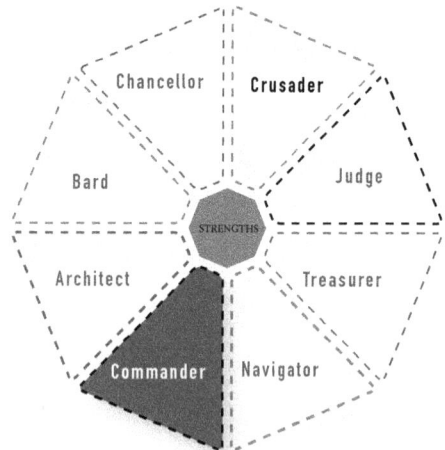

How this Core Belief Profile (CBP) thinks under pressure

When the emotion of pride becomes all consuming then the CBP2 not only avoids their own needs but ceases to be aware that they have any needs at all. The CBP2 is more easily able to recognise the needs of their spouse, family or of the person they are with rather than see their own. This often involves them in transferring their own needs onto other people. For example, if a CBP2 were cold, they may ask someone else, 'Are you cold?' rather than recognising that they themselves are cold. This creates a manipulative tendency where the CBP2 uses the feelings and needs of others to get their own needs fulfilled. Another downside of this tendency is that frequently the help that the CBP2 offers is not the help that is desired or required.

SUGGESTED DEVELOPMENTAL AREAS FOR THIS PROFILE

MANAGE YOUR HABITUAL LIMBIC REACTIONS:

- Turn your compassion onto yourself. Ask yourself, 'What are my real needs? Who really matters to me?' Take time to find out your own feelings, interests and desires.
- Allow people to, sometimes, solve their own problems. Be aware of your tendency to rescue others. Be clear about your roles and responsibilities.
- Appreciate that everyone else is not going to focus on meeting your needs. So have the courage to ask for what you want.
- Ensure that you are performing the content component of your work as well as the interpersonal side.
- Learn to be interdependent rather than dependent. Be realistic in seeing your importance and learn to simply ask for what you want.
- Learn to accept praise without discounting it.
- Learn to deal straight without manipulating.

LOOK OUT FOR THE SIGNS OF DISINTEGRATION

Rather than looking at how they can get on with the job at hand, the Commander will look for the inconsistencies in the behaviour of others and in the systems they are following as a first line of defence against anyone who says they are not doing anything.

During this time, the Commander's professional performance subsides as the procrastination rises. As far as they are concerned, they are okay and everything is working just fine.

Draw on the strengths of your Alter Ego

The Commander's Mirror, the Crusader, is motivated by undertaking crusades that are exciting, adventurous and worthy of their efforts and talents. As the Mirror, the Crusader demands to chase the 'big, hairy, audacious goal' or sets their sights on a mountain so large that it takes everyone's breath away. The Crusader is most likely to take over when the Commander is bored or between helping people in crisis.

Commander Power Diamond of Personality

Whole of Personality

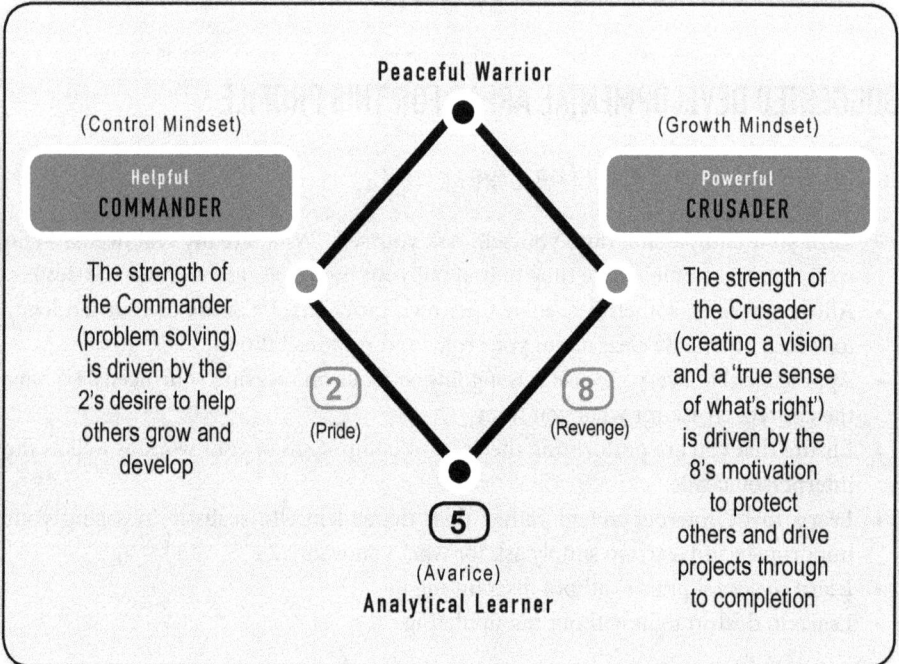

Peaceful Warrior

(Control Mindset) (Growth Mindset)

Helpful
COMMANDER

Powerful
CRUSADER

The strength of the Commander (problem solving) is driven by the 2's desire to help others grow and develop

The strength of the Crusader (creating a vision and a 'true sense of what's right') is driven by the 8's motivation to protect others and drive projects through to completion

2 (Pride)

8 (Revenge)

5 (Avarice)

Analytical Learner

Commander: Groupies Triad

INNATE CHARACTER

- Stands up for what they believe is right
- Stands by their actions without fear of reprisals or consequences
- Acts justly and fairly in all dealings with colleagues
- Solves problems as they arise without fuss and drama
- Encourages the team to innovate or adapt if necessary to ensure a quality result
- Encourages other team members to be courageous in thought and deed

TEAM ROLE (COMMANDER)

The Commander is able to solve problems that are complex, undefined or constantly changing. They are excellent at managing groups of people in high stress, dangerous or crisis situations. The Commander is practical and creative and can solve things 'on the hop'. The Commander is the natural leader when the right emergency action is needed without preparation.

Cognitive Strengths

- Excellent at creating structure and processes

Cognitive Weaknesses

- Tends to see people as cogs, rather than people

Opportunities for Development

- Needs to keep the big picture in mind! Needs to reconnect

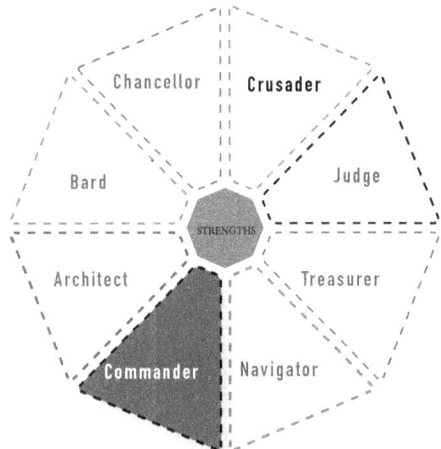

Threats to their Leadership Credibility

- Can lose connection – feel life is pointless and enter into self-defeating behaviour

How this Core Belief Profile (CBP) thinks under pressure

The emotions of the CBP6 are manifested through the continuum of phobic to counter-phobic. The flight form of fear, through retreat or through compliance, is the phobic response while the confrontational and antiauthoritarian response is referred to as counter-phobic. While phobic CBP6's may be very present to their fear and seek to avoid it, the counterphobic CBP6 has absolutely no idea that they are fearful because they attack anything that they fear, flying in the face of the most dangerous situations. At their worst the CBP6 spends a lot of time in preparation for possible disasters. They are often thinking ahead to the worst-case scenario and anticipating it. The need for absolute certainty leads to endless planning and procrastination on the part of the CBP6.

SUGGESTED DEVELOPMENTAL AREAS FOR THIS PROFILE

MANAGE YOUR HABITUAL LIMBIC REACTIONS:

- Practise having confidence. When 6's look for ways to trust others, they will find them.

- Some 6's assume that their leader has all the answers and that they have none. They become completely compliant in order to avoid the constant doubting of no change authority. You must find your own inner sense of authority.

- Do not be afraid to play the role of devil's advocate. After all, it is what you do best anyway. You have developed formidable skill at cutting through pretence and exposing what will not work. Show where the problems and pitfalls are. Learn to give compliments; 6's tend to have a problem with gratitude.

- Define your own positive goals and focus on them just as much as on where you can go wrong.

- To avoid constantly laying blame, focus on the problem and not on the person.

LOOK OUT FOR THE SIGNS OF DISINTEGRATION

Rather than looking at how they can get on with the job at hand, the Commander will look for the inconsistencies in the behaviour of others and in the systems they are following as a first line of defence against anyone who says they are not doing anything.

During this time, the Commander's professional performance subsides as the procrastination rises. As far as they are concerned, they are okay and everything is working just fine.

Draw on the strengths of your Alter Ego

The Commander's Mirror, the Crusader, is motivated by undertaking crusades that are exciting, adventurous and worthy of their efforts and talents. As the Mirror, the Crusader demands to chase the 'big, hairy, audacious goal' or sets their sights on a mountain so large that it takes everyone's breath away. The Crusader is most likely to take over when the Commander is bored or between helping people in crisis.

Commander Groupies Diamond of Personality

Whole of Personality

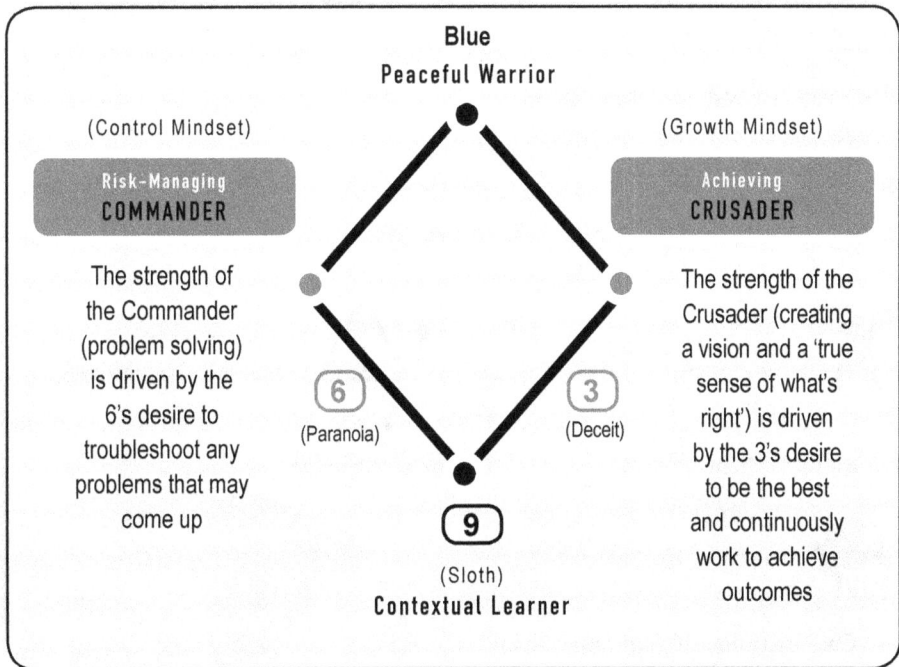

Blue
Peaceful Warrior

(Control Mindset)   (Growth Mindset)

Risk-Managing
COMMANDER

Achieving
CRUSADER

The strength of the Commander (problem solving) is driven by the 6's desire to troubleshoot any problems that may come up

6
(Paranoia)

3
(Deceit)

9
(Sloth)
Contextual Learner

The strength of the Crusader (creating a vision and a 'true sense of what's right') is driven by the 3's desire to be the best and continuously work to achieve outcomes

Chancellor: Groupies Triad

INNATE CHARACTER

- Acknowledges and considers other opinions in a respectful and non-judgemental way
- Considers the opinions of others with an open mind
- Ensures all team members have a say in group decisions
- Seeks out, listens and considers the opposite viewpoint on any given subject
- Offers support to colleagues who may be experiencing difficulties
- Encourages others to show their appreciation

TEAM ROLE (CHANCELLOR)

The Chancellor genius comes from their ability to build bridges between people. As a consequence they develop powerful interpersonal strategies and so they can achieve their objectives with very little disruption. The Chancellor has the ability to influence entire organisations without anybody triggering resistance.

Cognitive Strengths

- Understands people and how to motivate them

Cognitive Weaknesses

- Can focus on self-gain rather than the bigger picture

Opportunities for Development

- Needs to discipline themselves to follow the system

Threats to their Leadership Credibility

- Can fall foul of the system if not careful

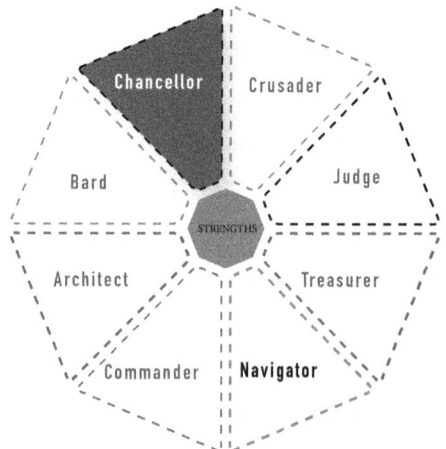

How this Core Belief Profile (CBP) thinks under pressure

The deceit of the CBP3 that is most easily seen is self-deceit. However, it is also the deception of others. Since the CBP3 is constantly changing themselves to be consistent with the most successful image of whatever group or individual they are participating with, they deceive themselves and others that they are actually what it is that they are doing. This deceit can manifest itself as simply putting one's best foot forward by just placing a little spin on the facts to sound good, charm or to self-promote. Deceit is a desire for approval measured by material success.

SUGGESTED DEVELOPMENTAL AREAS FOR THIS PROFILE

MANAGE YOUR HABITUAL LIMBIC REACTIONS:

- Recognise that success is not proof of virtue.

- Recognise that there is a difference between who you are and what you do, and learn to value both independently.

- Note your automatic tendency to take over, whether it is a good idea or not. Allow others to lead and see where they go.

- Take time in your schedule for other people – without an agenda or need for results!

- Develop the ability to be honest about how you feel.

- Develop the capacity to make a personal connection with those around you.

LOOK OUT FOR THE SIGNS OF DISINTEGRATION

Very quickly the Chancellor loses sight of reality and instead disappears into a world of supposition and deceit. Rather than dealing with the causal issues, the Chancellor adopts a form of self-deception in which they avoid having to face their own manipulation and insecurity. Those closest to them become the most suspect and all kinds of conspiracy theories start to emerge in the Chancellor's mind. This delusion can convince the Chancellor that individuals have made statements or discussed them in negative or deriding ways. With a grain of truth and 98% fiction the Chancellor uses their understanding of others to dream up scenarios that will lead to their failure. This paranoia leads to a complete lack of trust and further entrenches the Chancellor in creating an 'us and them', telling the 'us' one thing and the 'them' something else.

Draw on the strengths of your Alter Ego

While the Chancellor is flexible, charming, subtle, creative and intuitive, the Chancellor's Mirror, the Navigator, is inflexible, blunt, direct, obvious and focused on reality. The Chancellor's Mirror, the Navigator, is constantly demanding perfection, structure, details and proof of accomplishment and has a very clear idea where they should be living, to whom they should be married and their income and lifestyle. The challenge is that these expectations are all below the awareness of the Chancellor so even though they work hard and achieve all their objectives, if these don't line up with the unconscious requirements of the Mirror, the Chancellor will not find the satisfaction for which they are searching.

Chancellor Groupies Diamond of Personality

Whole of Personality

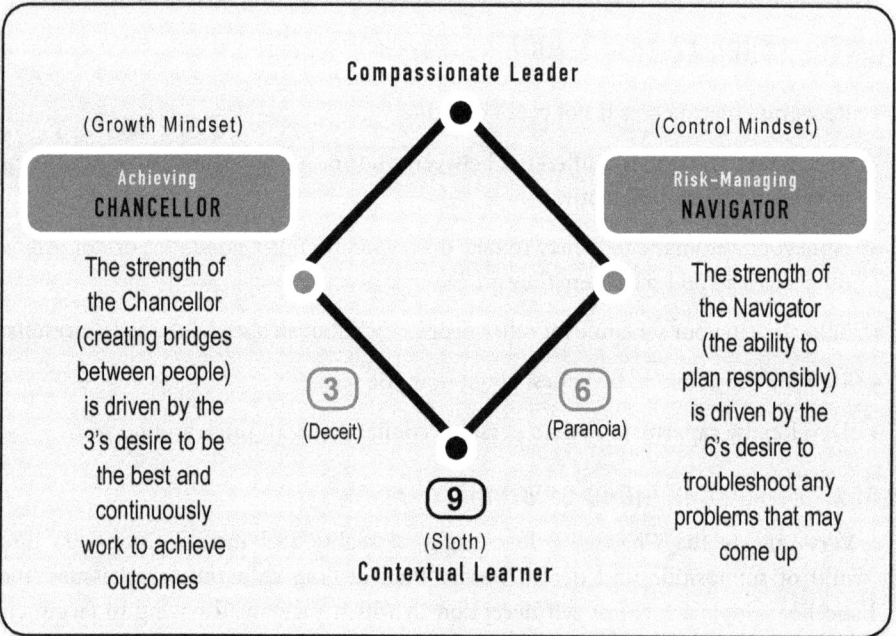

Compassionate Leader

(Growth Mindset)   (Control Mindset)

Achieving
CHANCELLOR

Risk-Managing
NAVIGATOR

The strength of the Chancellor (creating bridges between people) is driven by the 3's desire to be the best and continuously work to achieve outcomes

3
(Deceit)

6
(Paranoia)

9
(Sloth)

The strength of the Navigator (the ability to plan responsibly) is driven by the 6's desire to troubleshoot any problems that may come up

Contextual Learner

Chancellor: Idealist Triad

INNATE CHARACTER

- Acknowledges and considers other opinions in a respectful and non-judgemental way
- Considers the opinions of others with an open mind
- Ensures all team members have a say in group decisions
- Seeks out, listens and considers the opposite viewpoint on any given subject
- Offers support to colleagues who may be experiencing difficulties
- Encourages others to show their appreciation

TEAM ROLE (CHANCELLOR)

The Chancellor genius comes from their ability to build bridges between people. As a consequence they develop powerful interpersonal strategies and so they can achieve their objectives with very little disruption. The Chancellor has the ability to influence entire organisations without anybody triggering resistance.

Cognitive Strengths

- Understands people and how to motivate them

Cognitive Weaknesses

- Can focus on self-gain rather than the bigger picture

Opportunities for Development

- Needs to discipline themselves to follow the system

Threats to their Leadership Credibility

- Can fall foul of the system if not careful

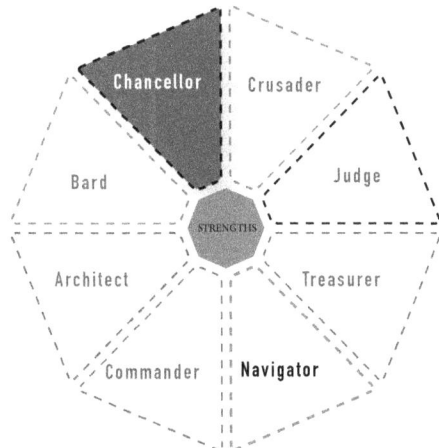

How this Core Belief Profile (CBP) thinks under pressure

In the presence of being trapped or controlled the emotions of the CBP7 will force them to move quickly from one thing to another, sampling but never deepening any particular experience. This is particularly true if the experience could result in emotional pain. CBP7 manifests as gluttony for new, fun and enjoyable experiences. Life is like a smorgasbord and is experienced as a range of experiences rather than a single experience repeated often. At their worst, they will seek absolute freedom without responsibility or commitment.

SUGGESTED DEVELOPMENTAL AREAS FOR THIS PROFILE

MANAGE YOUR HABITUAL LIMBIC REACTIONS:

- Be aware of your tendency to rationalise, to explain away failure and ethical violations without taking responsibility.

- Develop the skill of really listening rather than trying to think of something clever to say later.

- Work! Actually get your work completed rather than thinking about what else you could be doing.

- Practise mental sobriety. Do not just become drunk on ideas.

LOOK OUT FOR THE SIGNS OF DISINTEGRATION

Very quickly the Chancellor loses sight of reality and instead disappears into a world of supposition and deceit. Rather than dealing with the causal issues, the Chancellor adopts a form of self-deception in which they avoid having to face their own manipulation and insecurity. Those closest to them become the most suspect and all kinds of conspiracy theories start to emerge in the Chancellor's mind. This delusion can convince the Chancellor that individuals have made statements or discussed them in negative or deriding ways. With a grain of truth and 98% fiction the Chancellor uses their understanding of others to dream up scenarios that will lead to their failure. This paranoia leads to a complete lack of trust and further entrenches the Chancellor in creating an 'us and them', telling the 'us' one thing and the 'them' something else.

Draw on the strengths of your Alter Ego

While the Chancellor is flexible, charming, subtle, creative and intuitive, the Chancellor's Mirror, the Navigator, is inflexible, blunt, direct, obvious and focused on reality. The Chancellor's Mirror, the Navigator, is constantly demanding perfection, structure, details and proof of accomplishment and has a very clear idea where they should be living, to whom they should be married and their income and lifestyle. The challenge is that these expectations are all below the awareness of the Chancellor so even though they work hard and achieve all their objectives, if these don't line up with the unconscious requirements of the Mirror, the Chancellor will not find the satisfaction for which they are searching.

Chancellor Idealist Diamond of Personality

Whole of Personality

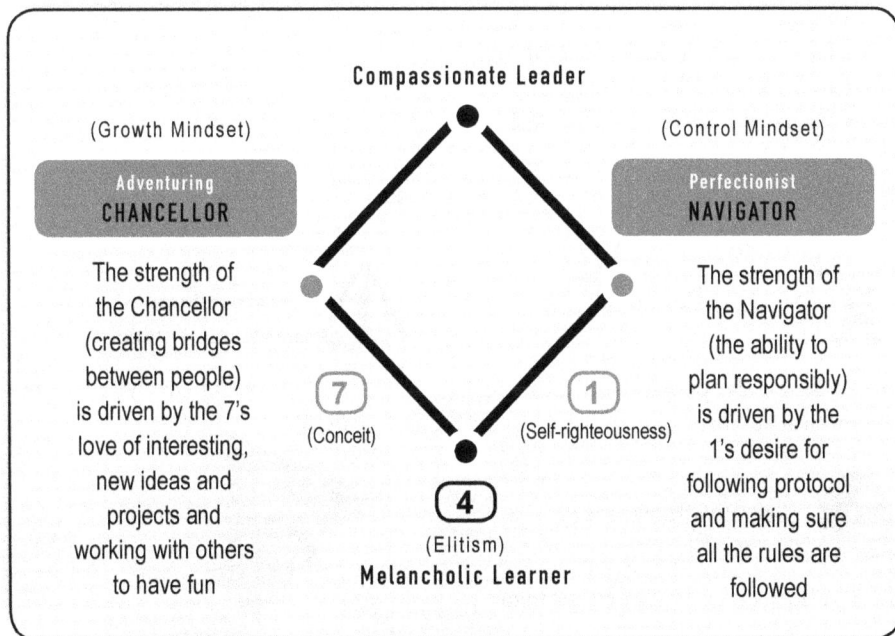

Compassionate Leader

(Growth Mindset)

Adventuring
CHANCELLOR

(Control Mindset)

Perfectionist
NAVIGATOR

The strength of the Chancellor (creating bridges between people) is driven by the 7's love of interesting, new ideas and projects and working with others to have fun

7
(Conceit)

1
(Self-righteousness)

4
(Elitism)
Melancholic Learner

The strength of the Navigator (the ability to plan responsibly) is driven by the 1's desire for following protocol and making sure all the rules are followed

Chancellor: Power Triad

INNATE CHARACTER

- Acknowledges and considers other opinions in a respectful and non-judgemental way
- Considers the opinions of others with an open mind
- Ensures all team members have a say in group decisions
- Seeks out, listens and considers the opposite viewpoint on any given subject
- Offers support to colleagues who may be experiencing difficulties
- Encourages others to show their appreciation

TEAM ROLE (CHANCELLOR)

The Chancellor genius comes from their ability to build bridges between people. As a consequence they develop powerful interpersonal strategies and so they can achieve their objectives with very little disruption. The Chancellor has the ability to influence entire organisations without anybody triggering resistance.

Cognitive Strengths

- Understands people and how to motivate them

Cognitive Weaknesses

- Can focus on self-gain rather than the bigger picture

Opportunities for Development

- Needs to discipline themselves to follow the system

Threats to their Leadership Credibility

- Can fall foul of the system if not careful

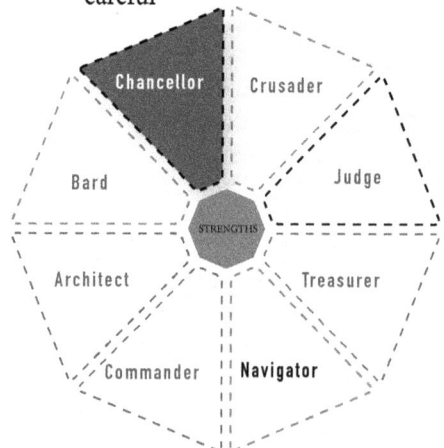

How this Core Belief Profile (CBP) thinks under pressure

At their worst the CBP8 will entertain an enormous lust for life. They will seek intensity in all things as the hallmark of a fulfilling life. If they enjoy something, then there can never be enough. They always want more. Moderation is death when the emotion of the CBP8 is high. Always they want more, better, faster and louder. This sometimes leads to difficulty with people or friends who cannot 'keep up' with their energy. This intensity is used to control others through the creation of physical, material or emotional dependence. Intensity sorts out the strong from the weak. This CBP reports that most people fall into two categories – those that can't help being weak and those that can.

SUGGESTED DEVELOPMENTAL AREAS FOR THIS PROFILE

MANAGE YOUR HABITUAL LIMBIC REACTIONS:

- Feeling as if someone is taking advantage of you is not the same as someone actually taking advantage of you. Check the details before you automatically retaliate.
- Choose your battles. Constantly ask yourself, 'Is this fight worth it?'
- Before you totally attack someone, ask yourself whether you are willing to deal with the consequences.
- For many people, your threats and tirades are not effective, no matter how much you may enjoy putting them on.
- When giving instructions, be very specific about the behaviour that will satisfy your expectations.
- Find ways to use others' talents and give them a sense of ownership and empowerment rather than just being a hired hand.

LOOK OUT FOR THE SIGNS OF DISINTEGRATION

Very quickly the Chancellor loses sight of reality and instead disappears into a world of supposition and deceit. Rather than dealing with the causal issues, the Chancellor adopts a form of self-deception in which they avoid having to face their own manipulation and insecurity. Those closest to them become the most suspect and all kinds of conspiracy theories start to emerge in the Chancellor's mind. This delusion can convince the Chancellor that individuals have made statements or discussed them in negative or deriding ways. With a grain of truth and 98% fiction the Chancellor uses their understanding of others to dream up scenarios that will lead to their failure. This paranoia leads to a complete lack of trust and further entrenches the Chancellor in creating an 'us and them', telling the 'us' one thing and the 'them' something else.

Draw on the strengths of your Alter Ego

While the Chancellor is flexible, charming, subtle, creative and intuitive, the Chancellor's Mirror, the Navigator, is inflexible, blunt, direct, obvious and focused on reality. The Chancellor's Mirror, the Navigator, is constantly demanding perfection, structure, details and proof of accomplishment and has a very clear idea where they should be living, to whom they should be married and their income and lifestyle. The challenge is that these expectations are all below the awareness of the Chancellor so even though they work hard and achieve all their objectives, if these don't line up with the unconscious requirements of the Mirror, the Chancellor will not find the satisfaction for which they are searching.

Chancellor Power Diamond of Personality

Whole of Personality

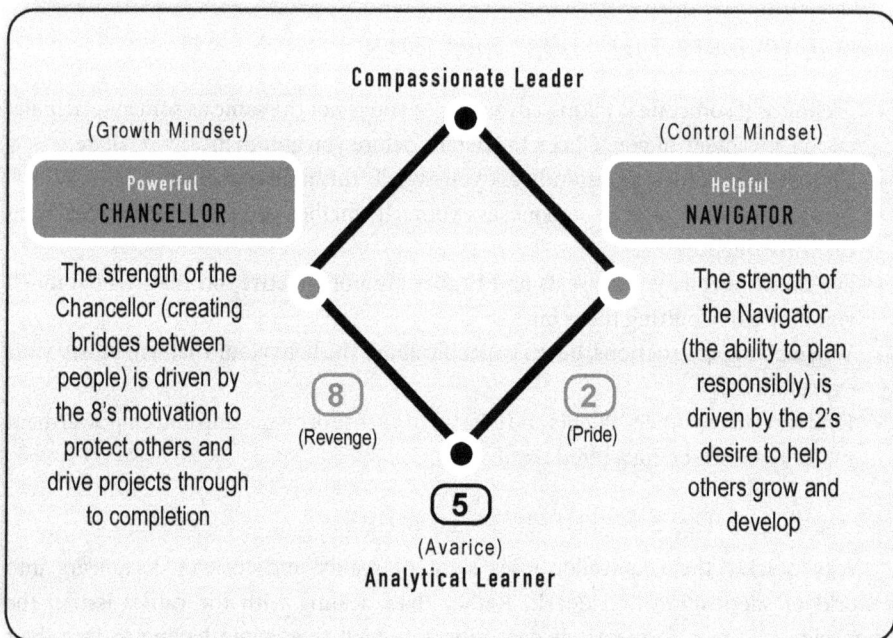

Compassionate Leader

(Growth Mindset)   (Control Mindset)

Powerful
CHANCELLOR

Helpful
NAVIGATOR

The strength of the Chancellor (creating bridges between people) is driven by the 8's motivation to protect others and drive projects through to completion

The strength of the Navigator (the ability to plan responsibly) is driven by the 2's desire to help others grow and develop

8
(Revenge)

2
(Pride)

5
(Avarice)

Analytical Learner

Bard: Groupies Triad

INNATE CHARACTER

- Displays an allegiance to all co-workers (above, below and beside them)
- Shows an understanding of how others are feeling
- Makes others feel valued and important
- Creates a workplace environment where colleagues feel they can try new approaches and take risks
- Looks for the unique contribution all colleagues can make to the team
- Encourages the team to be honest and open

TEAM ROLE (BARD)

The Bard creates an environment where the unique strengths of each individual can be used for the best team outcome. This involves creating a sense of abundance, outlining the principles of team interaction, getting agreement for objectives and facilitating discussion that fosters the best contribution for each team member, while reminding all team members of the team vision and purpose. The Bard's' role is to ensure the team is functioning as a team rather than as a group of individuals.

Cognitive Strengths

- Inspirational and motivational

Cognitive Weaknesses

- Not happy with anything that's not perfect

Opportunities for Development

- Needs to remember to get back in touch with reality

Threats to their Leadership Credibility

- Can become so out of touch their skills and thoughts are irrelevant

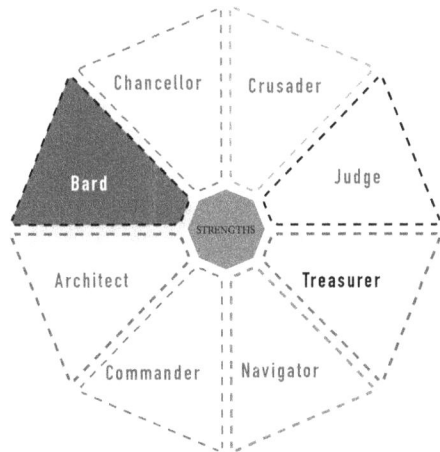

How this Core Belief Profile (CBP) thinks under pressure

The deceit of the CBP3 that is most easily seen is self-deceit. However, it is also the deception of others. Since the CBP3 is constantly changing themselves to be consistent with the most successful image of whatever group or individual they are participating with, they deceive themselves and others that they are actually what it is that they are doing. This deceit can manifest itself as simply putting one's best foot forward by just placing a little spin on the facts to sound good, charm or to self-promote. Deceit is a desire for approval measured by material success.

SUGGESTED DEVELOPMENTAL AREAS FOR THIS PROFILE

MANAGE YOUR HABITUAL LIMBIC REACTIONS:

- Recognise that success is not proof of virtue.
- Recognise that there is a difference between who you are and what you do, and learn to value both independently.
- Note your automatic tendency to take over, whether it is a good idea or not. Allow others to lead and see where they go.
- Take time in your schedule for other people – without an agenda or need for results!
- Develop the ability to be honest about how you feel.
- Develop the capacity to make a personal connection with those around you.

LOOK OUT FOR THE SIGNS OF DISINTEGRATION

The first phase of disintegration sees the Bard feeling insecure about their important relationships because of the deceit they have enacted.

To get the reassurance they believe they need, they use manipulation and persuasion to reassure others that they were not lying and that their honour and good character are still intact.

They can't believe the feedback they receive because they are delusional. This phase can see the Bard lie, exaggerate, change alliances and shamelessly compete for attention. No self-deception is too big. No political game is too ambitious.

Draw on the strengths of your Alter Ego

While Bards see themselves as gentle, visionary, passionate people with an ability to heal the past and create a better world, their Mirror, the Treasurer, is obsessed with order, details, stability and security.

Bards can be confusing because while their language is passionate, optimistic and nurturing, their behaviour, which is influenced by the Mirror Treasurer, suggests they are penny-pinching, controlling and almost obsessive-compulsive.

Bard Groupies Diamond of Personality

Whole of Personality

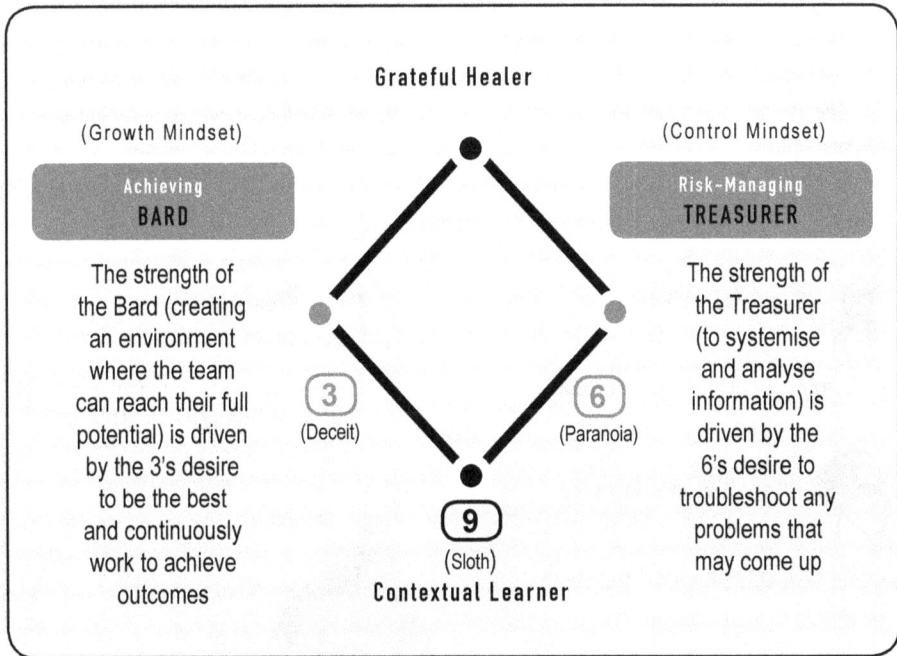

Grateful Healer

(Growth Mindset)

Achieving
BARD

The strength of the Bard (creating an environment where the team can reach their full potential) is driven by the 3's desire to be the best and continuously work to achieve outcomes

3
(Deceit)

(Control Mindset)

Risk-Managing
TREASURER

The strength of the Treasurer (to systemise and analyse information) is driven by the 6's desire to troubleshoot any problems that may come up

6
(Paranoia)

9
(Sloth)
Contextual Learner

Bard: Idealist Triad

INNATE CHARACTER

- Displays an allegiance to all co-workers (above, below and beside them)
- Shows an understanding of how others are feeling
- Makes others feel valued and important
- Creates a workplace environment where colleagues feel they can try new approaches and take risks
- Looks for the unique contribution all colleagues can make to the team
- Encourages the team to be honest and open

TEAM ROLE (BARD)

The Bard creates an environment where the unique strengths of each individual can be used for the best team outcome. This involves creating a sense of abundance, outlining the principles of team interaction, getting agreement for objectives and facilitating discussion that fosters the best contribution for each team member, while reminding all team members of the team vision and purpose. The Bard's' role is to ensure the team is functioning as a team rather than as a group of individuals.

Cognitive Strengths

- Inspirational and motivational

Cognitive Weaknesses

- Not happy with anything that's not perfect

Opportunities for Development

- Needs to remember to get back in touch with reality

Threats to their Leadership Credibility

- Can become so out of touch their skills and thoughts are irrelevant

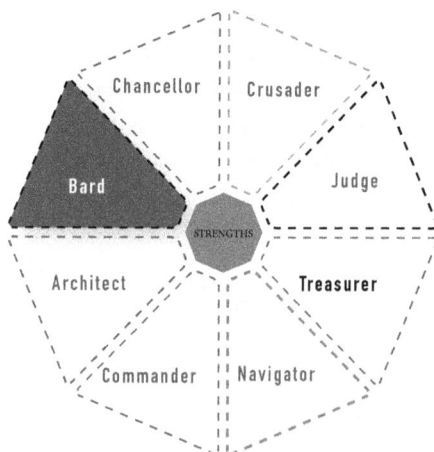

How this Core Belief Profile (CBP) thinks under pressure

In the presence of being trapped or controlled the emotions of the CBP7 will force them to move quickly from one thing to another, sampling but never deepening any particular experience. This is particularly true if the experience could result in emotional pain. CBP7 manifests as gluttony for new, fun and enjoyable experiences. Life is like a smorgasbord and is experienced as a range of experiences rather than a single experience repeated often. At their worst, they will seek absolute freedom without responsibility or commitment.

SUGGESTED DEVELOPMENTAL AREAS FOR THIS PROFILE

MANAGE YOUR HABITUAL LIMBIC REACTIONS:

- Be aware of your tendency to rationalise, to explain away failure and ethical violations without taking responsibility.

- Develop the skill of really listening rather than trying to think of something clever to say later.

- Work! Actually get your work completed rather than thinking about what else you could be doing.

- Practise mental sobriety. Do not just become drunk on ideas.

LOOK OUT FOR THE SIGNS OF DISINTEGRATION

The first phase of disintegration sees the Bard feeling insecure about their important relationships because of the deceit they have enacted.

To get the reassurance they believe they need, they use manipulation and persuasion to reassure others that they were not lying and that their honour and good character are still intact.

They can't believe the feedback they receive because they are delusional. This phase can see the Bard lie, exaggerate, change alliances and shamelessly compete for attention. No self-deception is too big. No political game is too ambitious.

Draw on the strengths of your Alter Ego

While Bards see themselves as gentle, visionary, passionate people with an ability to heal the past and create a better world, their Mirror, the Treasurer, is obsessed with order, details, stability and security.

Bards can be confusing because while their language is passionate, optimistic and nurturing, their behaviour, which is influenced by the Mirror Treasurer, suggests they are penny-pinching, controlling and almost obsessive-compulsive.

Bard Idealist Diamond of Personality

Whole of Personality

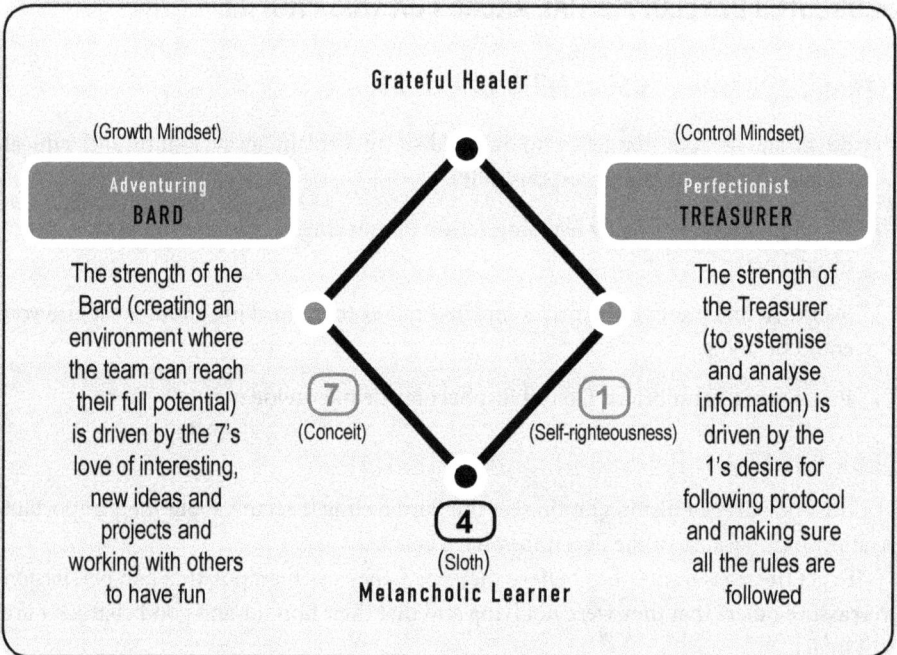

Grateful Healer

(Growth Mindset)

(Control Mindset)

| Adventuring BARD | Perfectionist TREASURER |

The strength of the Bard (creating an environment where the team can reach their full potential) is driven by the 7's love of interesting, new ideas and projects and working with others to have fun

⑦
(Conceit)

① (Self-righteousness)

④ (Sloth)

Melancholic Learner

The strength of the Treasurer (to systemise and analyse information) is driven by the 1's desire for following protocol and making sure all the rules are followed

Bard: Power Triad

INNATE CHARACTER

- Displays an allegiance to all co-workers (above, below and beside them)
- Shows an understanding of how others are feeling
- Makes others feel valued and important
- Creates a workplace environment where colleagues feel they can try new approaches and take risks
- Looks for the unique contribution all colleagues can make to the team
- Encourages the team to be honest and open

TEAM ROLE (BARD)

The Bard creates an environment where the unique strengths of each individual can be used for the best team outcome. This involves creating a sense of abundance, outlining the principles of team interaction, getting agreement for objectives and facilitating discussion that fosters the best contribution for each team member, while reminding all team members of the team vision and purpose. The Bard's' role is to ensure the team is functioning as a team rather than as a group of individuals.

Cognitive Strengths

- Inspirational and motivational

Cognitive Weaknesses

- Not happy with anything that's not perfect

Opportunities for Development

- Needs to remember to get back in touch with reality

Threats to their Leadership Credibility

- Can become so out of touch their skills and thoughts are irrelevant

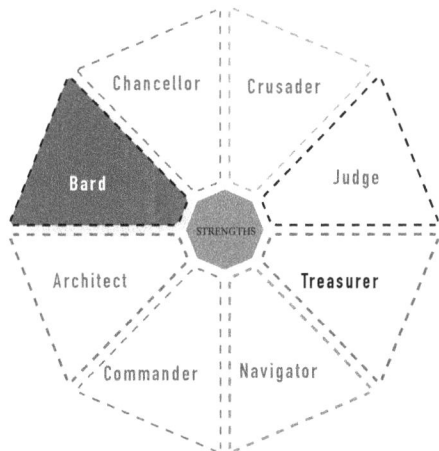

How this Core Belief Profile (CBP) thinks under pressure

At their worst the CBP8 will entertain an enormous lust for life. They will seek intensity in all things as the hallmark of a fulfilling life. If they enjoy something, then there can never be enough. They always want more. Moderation is death when the emotion of the CBP8 is high. Always they want more, better, faster and louder. This sometimes leads to difficulty with people or friends who cannot 'keep up' with their energy. This intensity is used to control others through the creation of physical, material or emotional dependence. Intensity sorts out the strong from the weak. This CBP reports that most people fall into two categories – those that can't help being weak and those that can.

SUGGESTED DEVELOPMENTAL AREAS FOR THIS PROFILE

MANAGE YOUR HABITUAL LIMBIC REACTIONS:

- Feeling as if someone is taking advantage of you is not the same as someone actually taking advantage of you. Check the details before you automatically retaliate.

- Choose your battles. Constantly ask yourself, 'Is this fight worth it?'

- Before you totally attack someone, ask yourself whether you are willing to deal with the consequences.

- For many people, your threats and tirades are not effective, no matter how much you may enjoy putting them on.

- When giving instructions, be very specific about the behaviour that will satisfy your expectations.

- Find ways to use others' talents and give them a sense of ownership and empowerment rather than just being a hired hand.

LOOK OUT FOR THE SIGNS OF DISINTEGRATION

The first phase of disintegration sees the Bard feeling insecure about their important relationships because of the deceit they have enacted.

To get the reassurance they believe they need, they use manipulation and persuasion to reassure others that they were not lying and that their honour and good character are still intact.

They can't believe the feedback they receive because they are delusional. This phase can see the Bard lie, exaggerate, change alliances and shamelessly compete for attention. No self-deception is too big. No political game is too ambitious.

Draw on the strengths of your Alter Ego

While Bards see themselves as gentle, visionary, passionate people with an ability to heal the past and create a better world, their Mirror, the Treasurer, is obsessed with order, details, stability and security.

Bards can be confusing because while their language is passionate, optimistic and nurturing, their behaviour, which is influenced by the Mirror Treasurer, suggests they are penny-pinching, controlling and almost obsessive-compulsive.

Bard Power Diamond of Personality

Whole of Personality

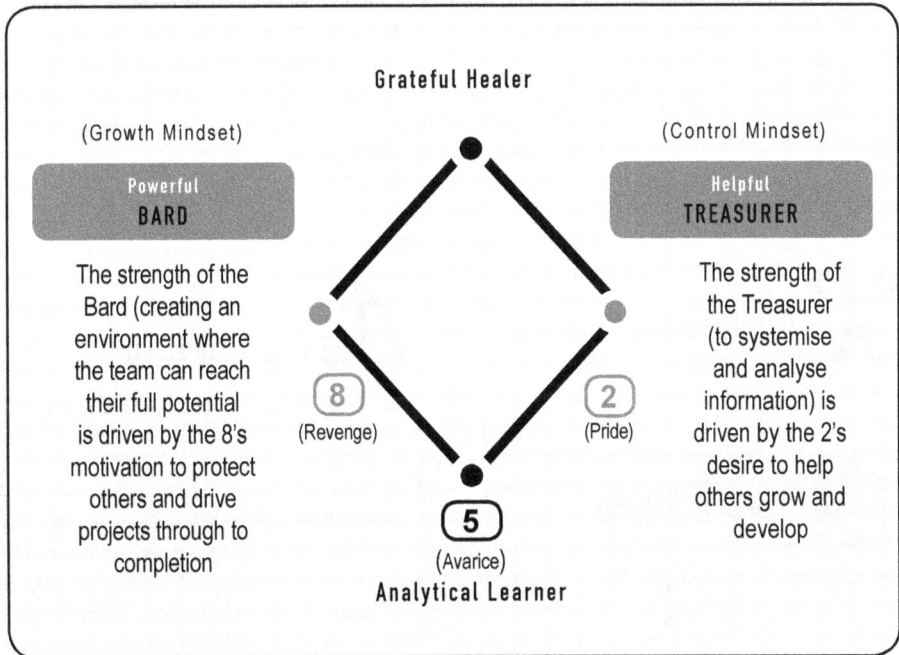

Grateful Healer

(Growth Mindset)   (Control Mindset)

Powerful
BARD

Helpful
TREASURER

The strength of the Bard (creating an environment where the team can reach their full potential is driven by the 8's motivation to protect others and drive projects through to completion

⑧
(Revenge)

②
(Pride)

The strength of the Treasurer (to systemise and analyse information) is driven by the 2's desire to help others grow and develop

⑤
(Avarice)
Analytical Learner

Treasurer: Idealist Triad

INNATE CHARACTER

- Encourages colleagues to develop their technical knowledge and skills
- Creates clear audit trails related to activity or key decisions
- Learns from mistakes and documents this learning so that other team members can benefit
- Shows respect for colleagues' knowledge or expertise
- Rationally considers the facts before making key decisions
- Encourages others to show team members respect

TEAM ROLE (TREASURER)

The Treasurer ensures agreed processes are followed, documents are accurate and quality is maintained. They have a good head for numbers and naturally ensures that finances are documented with fairness and accountability. They are also good at making sure issues around legality are squared off. They focus on learning and analysis and, as part of this process, ensures there is a full audit trail and that records of meetings, agreements and resolutions are accurate and readily available.

Cognitive Strengths

- Excellent, cool head in a crisis

Cognitive Weaknesses

- Can lose energy and interest when there is no pressure

Opportunities for Development

- Needs to learn how to value and empathise with others to fine-tune their approach to persuasion

Threats to their Leadership Credibility

- Can treat people like machines

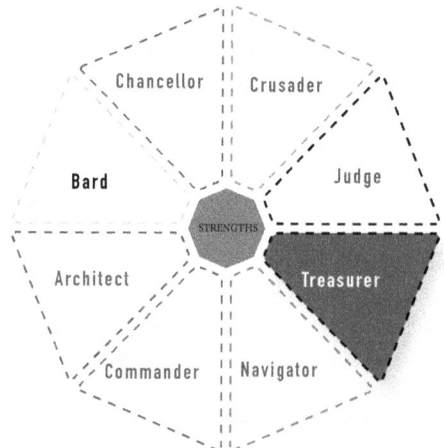

How this Core Belief Profile (CBP) thinks under pressure

At their worst the CBP1 is a hyper-critical, self-righteous individual fixated on adhering to the rules regardless of the situation or circumstance. They can be incapable of giving praise or appreciation for anything or anyone – since nothing ever reaches perfection. At their worst the greatest compliment that a CBP1 can give is, 'There was nothing that I could criticise in the work that you did.'

SUGGESTED DEVELOPMENTAL AREAS FOR THIS PROFILE

MANAGE YOUR HABITUAL LIMBIC REACTIONS:

- Try to model the behaviour that you want to see in others. Do not merely criticise others until they comply with your expectations.
- Appreciate that many of your comments will be taken as criticism, regardless of whether you see them that way.
- Consider the context of any criticism. While it may be appropriate for a specific behaviour, your context may be skewed and may ignore a great deal of relevant information.
- Aspire to your idealism but do not hold yourself and others to attaining it in every area of life.
- Develop realistic expectations for yourself.
- Appreciate and accept that making mistakes is part of the learning process.
- Learn when the given time would be better prioritised on other tasks rather than transforming a workable job to a perfect job.
- Understand that people do not want to be judged. So if you insist on constantly offering criticism you will be shunned and avoided. This will seriously limit your career development.
- Do not adopt the position of moral champion; take a break from the job of policing everyone around you.
- You probably have a tendency to accept and comply blindly with the rules of other people and institutions. You need to develop your own principles and practices based on context.

LOOK OUT FOR THE SIGNS OF DISINTEGRATION

As the Treasurer spirals down, so too will their flexibility. Adherence to plans becomes a clear focus and their management style can become totally closed to any new suggestions. They may become abrupt, disconnected and autocratic. During this phase their personal hygiene may subside and they may become fascinated by tools, weapons or equipment that can help them defend themselves against a vicious world that hates them. At this first step of spiral down they will likely refuse to believe anything is wrong.

Draw on the strengths of your Alter Ego

At work, the Treasurer's Alter Ego, the Bard, can be seen in patient listening, reflective and supportive comments given during tough times, support for the underdog and an interest in creating an inclusive and supportive work environment where everyone is respected, valued and allowed to reach their full potential.

Treasurer Idealist Diamond of Personality

Whole of Personality

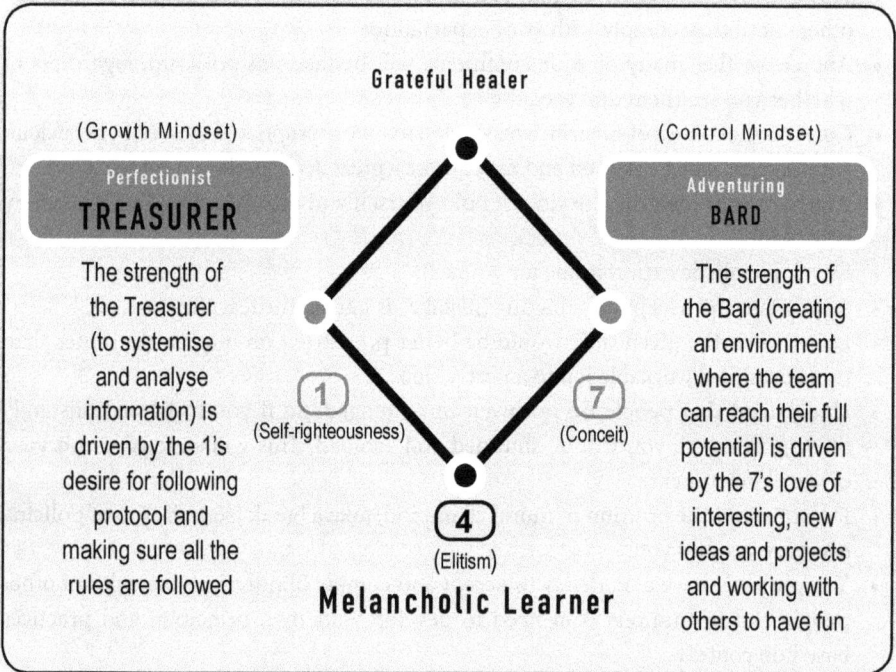

Grateful Healer

(Growth Mindset)   (Control Mindset)

Perfectionist
TREASURER

Adventuring
BARD

The strength of the Treasurer (to systemise and analyse information) is driven by the 1's desire for following protocol and making sure all the rules are followed

(1)
(Self-righteousness)

(7)
(Conceit)

The strength of the Bard (creating an environment where the team can reach their full potential) is driven by the 7's love of interesting, new ideas and projects and working with others to have fun

(4)
(Elitism)

Melancholic Learner

Treasurer: Power Triad

INNATE CHARACTER

- Encourages colleagues to develop their technical knowledge and skills
- Creates clear audit trails related to activity or key decisions
- Learns from mistakes and documents this learning so that other team members can benefit
- Shows respect for colleagues' knowledge or expertise
- Rationally considers the facts before making key decisions
- Encourages others to show team members respect

TEAM ROLE (TREASURER)

The Treasurer ensures agreed processes are followed, documents are accurate and quality is maintained. They have a good head for numbers and naturally ensures that finances are documented with fairness and accountability. They are also good at making sure issues around legality are squared off. They focus on learning and analysis and, as part of this process, ensures there is a full audit trail and that records of meetings, agreements and resolutions are accurate and readily available.

Cognitive Strengths

- Excellent, cool head in a crisis

Cognitive Weaknesses

- Can lose energy and interest when there is no pressure

Opportunities for Development

- Needs to learn how to value and empathise with others to fine-tune their approach to persuasion

Threats to their Leadership Credibility

- Can treat people like machines

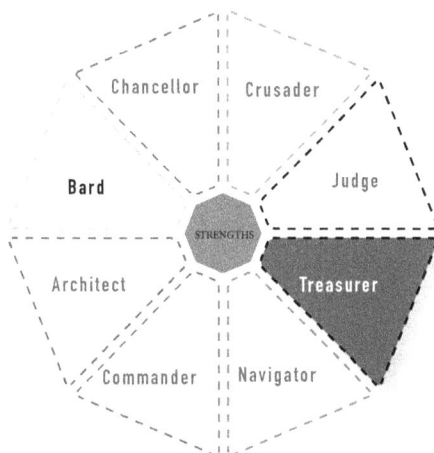

How this Core Belief Profile (CBP) thinks under pressure

When the emotion of pride becomes all consuming then the CBP2 not only avoids their own needs but ceases to be aware that they have any needs at all. The CBP2 is more easily able to recognise the needs of their spouse, family or of the person they are with rather than see their own. This often involves them in transferring their own needs onto other people. For example, if a CBP2 were cold, they may ask someone else, 'Are you cold?' rather than recognising that they themselves are cold. This creates a manipulative tendency where the CBP2 uses the feelings and needs of others to get their own needs fulfilled. Another downside of this tendency is that frequently the help that the CBP2 offers is not the help that is desired or required.

SUGGESTED DEVELOPMENTAL AREAS FOR THIS PROFILE

MANAGE YOUR HABITUAL LIMBIC REACTIONS:

- Turn your compassion onto yourself. Ask yourself, 'What are my real needs? Who really matters to me?' Take time to find out your own feelings, interests and desires.

- Allow people to, sometimes, solve their own problems. Be aware of your tendency to rescue others. Be clear about your roles and responsibilities.

- Appreciate that everyone else is not going to focus on meeting your needs. So have the courage to ask for what you want.

- Ensure that you are performing the content component of your work as well as the interpersonal side.

- Learn to be interdependent rather than dependent. Be realistic in seeing your importance and learn to simply ask for what you want.

- Learn to accept praise without discounting it.

- Learn to deal straight without manipulating.

LOOK OUT FOR THE SIGNS OF DISINTEGRATION

As the Treasurer spirals down, so too will their flexibility. Adherence to plans becomes a clear focus and their management style can become totally closed to any new suggestions. They may become abrupt, disconnected and autocratic. During this phase their personal hygiene may subside and they may become fascinated by tools, weapons or equipment that can help them defend themselves against a vicious world that hates them. At this first step of spiral down they will likely refuse to believe anything is wrong.

Draw on the strengths of your Alter Ego

At work, the Treasurer's Alter Ego, the Bard, can be seen in patient listening, reflective and supportive comments given during tough times, support for the underdog and an interest in creating an inclusive and supportive work environment where everyone is respected, valued and allowed to reach their full potential.

Treasurer Power Diamond of Personality

Whole of Personality

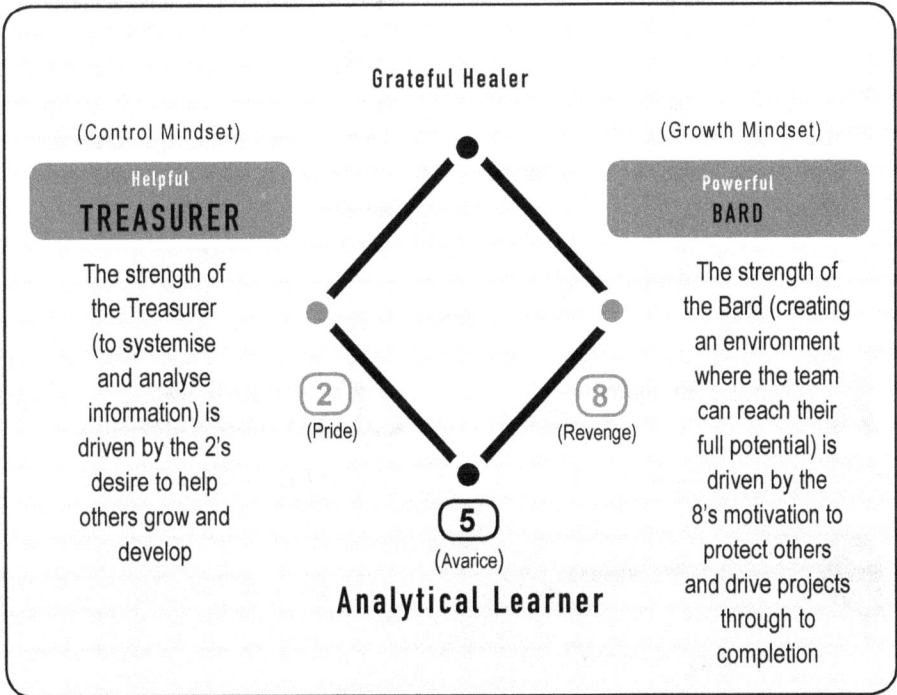

Grateful Healer

(Control Mindset)

(Growth Mindset)

Helpful
TREASURER

Powerful
BARD

The strength of the Treasurer (to systemise and analyse information) is driven by the 2's desire to help others grow and develop

The strength of the Bard (creating an environment where the team can reach their full potential) is driven by the 8's motivation to protect others and drive projects through to completion

2
(Pride)

8
(Revenge)

5
(Avarice)

Analytical Learner

Treasurer: Groupies Triad

INNATE CHARACTER

- Encourages colleagues to develop their technical knowledge and skills
- Creates clear audit trails related to activity or key decisions
- Learns from mistakes and documents this learning so that other team members can benefit
- Shows respect for colleagues' knowledge or expertise
- Rationally considers the facts before making key decisions
- Encourages others to show team members respect

TEAM ROLE (TREASURER)

The Treasurer ensures agreed processes are followed, documents are accurate and quality is maintained. They have a good head for numbers and naturally ensures that finances are documented with fairness and accountability. They are also good at making sure issues around legality are squared off. They focus on learning and analysis and, as part of this process, ensures there is a full audit trail and that records of meetings, agreements and resolutions are accurate and readily available.

Cognitive Strengths

- Excellent, cool head in a crisis

Cognitive Weaknesses

- Can lose energy and interest when there is no pressure

Opportunities for Development

- Needs to learn how to value and empathise with others to fine-tune their approach to persuasion

Threats to their Leadership Credibility

- Can treat people like machines

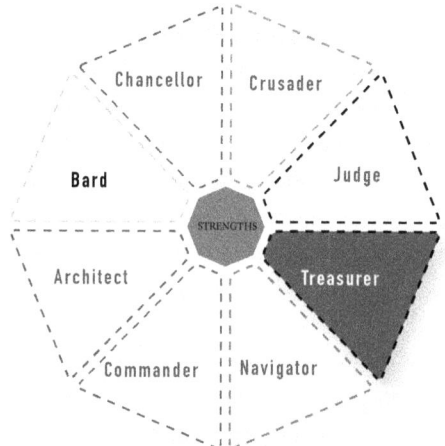

Chancellor | Crusader
Bard | Judge
STRENGTHS
Architect | Treasurer
Commander | Navigator

How this Core Belief Profile (CBP) thinks under pressure

The emotions of the CBP6 are manifested through the continuum of phobic to counter-phobic. The flight form of fear, through retreat or through compliance, is the phobic response while the confrontational and antiauthoritarian response is referred to as counter-phobic. While phobic CBP6's may be very present to their fear and seek to avoid it, the counterphobic CBP6 has absolutely no idea that they are fearful because they attack anything that they fear, flying in the face of the most dangerous situations. At their worst the CBP6 spends a lot of time in preparation for possible disasters. They are often thinking ahead to the worst-case scenario and anticipating it. The need for absolute certainty leads to endless planning and procrastination on the part of the CBP6.

SUGGESTED DEVELOPMENTAL AREAS FOR THIS PROFILE

MANAGE YOUR HABITUAL LIMBIC REACTIONS:

- Practise having confidence. When 6's look for ways to trust others, they will find them.

- Some 6's assume that their leader has all the answers and that they have none. They become completely compliant in order to avoid the constant doubting of no change authority. You must find your own inner sense of authority.

- Do not be afraid to play the role of devil's advocate. After all, it is what you do best anyway. You have developed formidable skill at cutting through pretence and exposing what will not work. Show where the problems and pitfalls are. Learn to give compliments; 6's tend to have a problem with gratitude.

- Define your own positive goals and focus on them just as much as on where you can go wrong.

- To avoid constantly laying blame, focus on the problem and not on the person.

LOOK OUT FOR THE SIGNS OF DISINTEGRATION

As the Treasurer spirals down, so too will their flexibility. Adherence to plans becomes a clear focus and their management style can become totally closed to any new suggestions. They may become abrupt, disconnected and autocratic. During this phase their personal hygiene may subside and they may become fascinated by tools, weapons or equipment that can help them defend themselves against a vicious world that hates them. At this first step of spiral down they will likely refuse to believe anything is wrong.

Draw on the strengths of your Alter Ego

At work, the Treasurer's Alter Ego, the Bard, can be seen in patient listening, reflective and supportive comments given during tough times, support for the underdog and an interest in creating an inclusive and supportive work environment where everyone is respected, valued and allowed to reach their full potential.

Treasurer Groupies Diamond of Personality

Whole of Personality

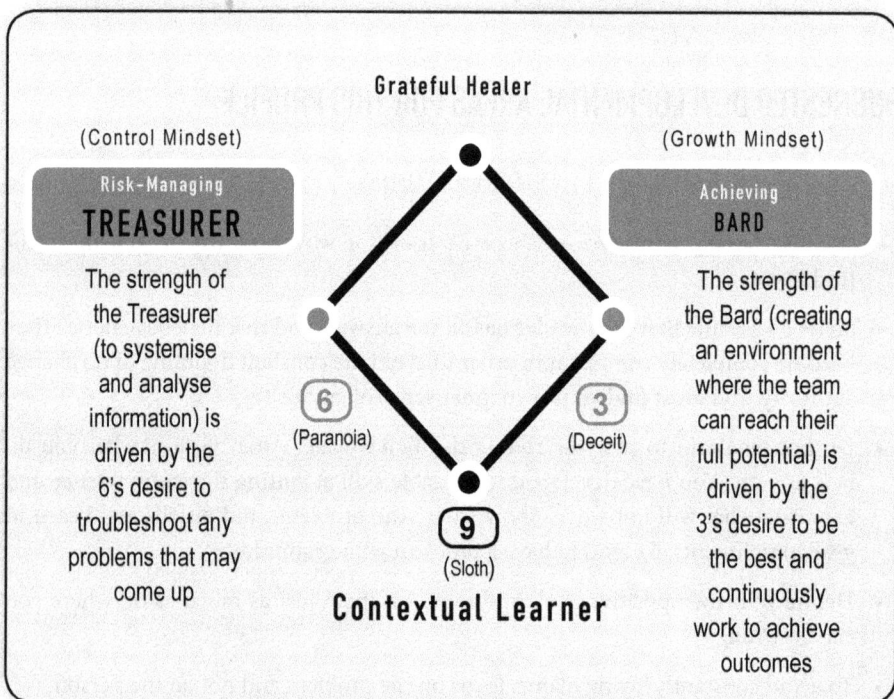

Grateful Healer

(Control Mindset)   (Growth Mindset)

Risk-Managing
TREASURER

Achieving
BARD

The strength of the Treasurer (to systemise and analyse information) is driven by the 6's desire to troubleshoot any problems that may come up

The strength of the Bard (creating an environment where the team can reach their full potential) is driven by the 3's desire to be the best and continuously work to achieve outcomes

6
(Paranoia)

3
(Deceit)

9
(Sloth)

Contextual Learner

Navigator: Idealist Triad

INNATE CHARACTER

- Stands up for what they know is right
- Displays supportive/protective behaviour for their colleagues
- Creates a sense of security and stability within the team
- Effectively plans work with clear milestones and systems of reporting
- Identifies and manages the risks associated with completing individual or team objectives
- Works at giving other team members confidence

TEAM ROLE (NAVIGATOR)

Navigators can see what is ahead for the team, both internally and externally and can create systems and processes that draw on relevant data to achieve the agreed vision. These systems are then documented in a methodical and comprehensive way. The Navigator has an excellent sense of cause and effect and the ability to sequence activities appropriately.

Cognitive Strengths

- Can balance the future vision with immediate practicalities

Cognitive Weaknesses

- Can get stressed always juggling between vision and implementation

Opportunities for Development

- Needs to learn how to be able to change tack midpoint

Threats to their Leadership Credibility

- Can 'close down' and refuse to budge off the agreed plan, even when change is required

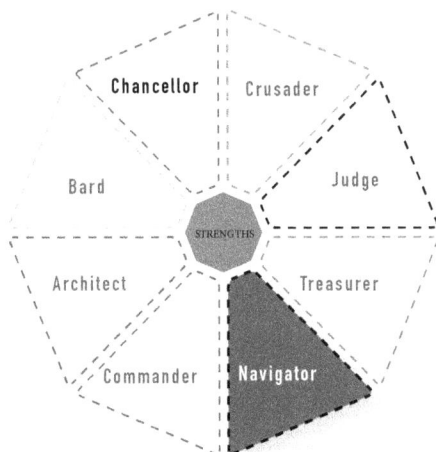

How this Core Belief Profile (CBP) thinks under pressure

At their worst the CBP1 is a hyper-critical, self-righteous individual fixated on adhering to the rules regardless of the situation or circumstance. They can be incapable of giving praise or appreciation for anything or anyone – since nothing ever reaches perfection. At their worst the greatest compliment that a CBP1 can give is, 'There was nothing that I could criticise in the work that you did.'

SUGGESTED DEVELOPMENTAL AREAS FOR THIS PROFILE

MANAGE YOUR HABITUAL LIMBIC REACTIONS:

- Try to model the behaviour that you want to see in others. Do not merely criticise others until they comply with your expectations.
- Appreciate that many of your comments will be taken as criticism, regardless of whether you see them that way.
- Consider the context of any criticism. While it may be appropriate for a specific behaviour, your context may be skewed and may ignore a great deal of relevant information.
- Aspire to your idealism but do not hold yourself and others to attaining it in every area of life.
- Develop realistic expectations for yourself.
- Appreciate and accept that making mistakes is part of the learning process.
- Learn when the given time would be better prioritised on other tasks rather than transforming a workable job to a perfect job.
- Understand that people do not want to be judged. So if you insist on constantly offering criticism you will be shunned and avoided. This will seriously limit your career development.
- Do not adopt the position of moral champion; take a break from the job of policing everyone around you.
- You probably have a tendency to accept and comply blindly with the rules of other people and institutions. You need to develop your own principles and practices based on context.

LOOK OUT FOR THE SIGNS OF DISINTEGRATION

The spiral down for the Navigator is triggered by not effectively playing the role they have been engaged to play. This can fill them with shame and personal disgust. As they spiral down so too does their flexibility. Rigid adherence to plans becomes a clear focus and their management style becomes totally closed to any new suggestions. They could become abrupt, disconnected and autocratic.

Draw on the strengths of your Alter Ego

The Navigator's Alter Ego, the Chancellor, will express itself in humour, a willingness to change tack when new opportunities present themselves and an almost involuntary involvement in the politics of the organisation. The best contribution of the Alter Ego at work, for the Navigator in a leadership position, is the Alter Ego's insistence that their employees are genuinely engaged in understanding, supporting and implementing the strategic direction. The Alter Ego is also responsible for the Navigator's willingness to move jobs and take career advancement opportunities, even if it means moving to another company, city, profession or country.

Navigator Idealist Diamond of Personality

Whole of Personality

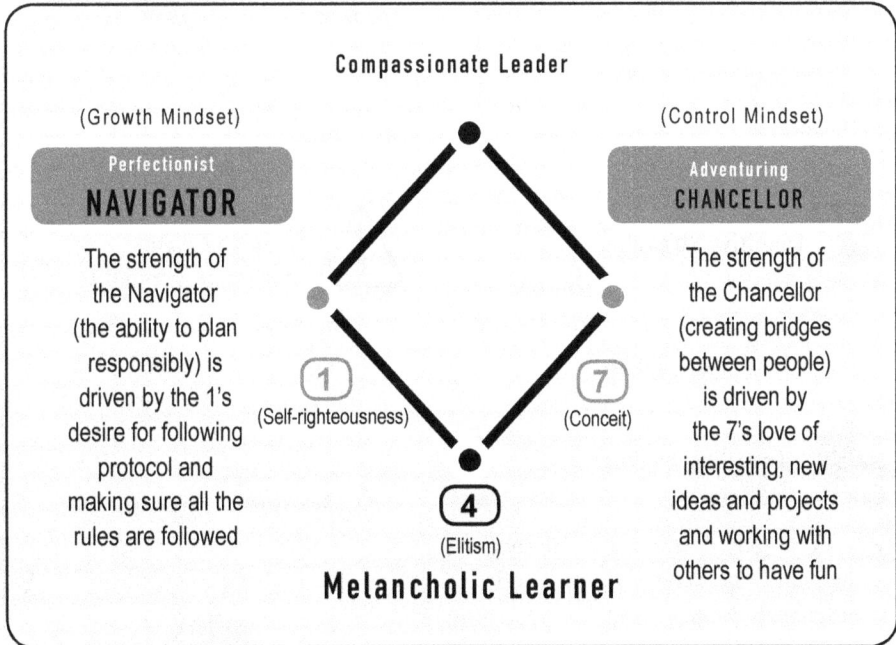

Compassionate Leader

(Growth Mindset)   (Control Mindset)

Perfectionist   Adventuring
NAVIGATOR   **CHANCELLOR**

The strength of the Navigator (the ability to plan responsibly) is driven by the 1's desire for following protocol and making sure all the rules are followed

The strength of the Chancellor (creating bridges between people) is driven by the 7's love of interesting, new ideas and projects and working with others to have fun

1 (Self-righteousness)

7 (Conceit)

4 (Elitism)

Melancholic Learner

Navigator: Power Triad

INNATE CHARACTER

- Stands up for what they know is right
- Displays supportive/protective behaviour for their colleagues
- Creates a sense of security and stability within the team
- Effectively plans work with clear milestones and systems of reporting
- Identifies and manages the risks associated with completing individual or team objectives
- Works at giving other team members confidence

TEAM ROLE (NAVIGATOR)

Navigators can see what is ahead for the team, both internally and externally and can create systems and processes that draw on relevant data to achieve the agreed vision. These systems are then documented in a methodical and comprehensive way. The Navigator has an excellent sense of cause and effect and the ability to sequence activities appropriately.

Cognitive Strengths

- Can balance the future vision with immediate practicalities

Cognitive Weaknesses

- Can get stressed always juggling between vision and implementation

Opportunities for Development

- Needs to learn how to be able to change tack midpoint

Threats to their Leadership Credibility

- Can 'close down' and refuse to budge off the agreed plan, even when change is required

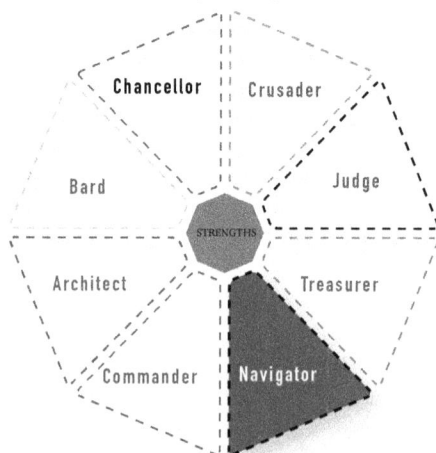

How this Core Belief Profile (CBP) thinks under pressure

When the emotion of pride becomes all consuming then the CBP2 not only avoids their own needs but ceases to be aware that they have any needs at all. The CBP2 is more easily able to recognise the needs of their spouse, family or of the person they are with rather than see their own. This often involves them in transferring their own needs onto other people. For example, if a CBP2 were cold, they may ask someone else, 'Are you cold?' rather than recognising that they themselves are cold. This creates a manipulative tendency where the CBP2 uses the feelings and needs of others to get their own needs fulfilled. Another downside of this tendency is that frequently the help that the CBP2 offers is not the help that is desired or required.

SUGGESTED DEVELOPMENTAL AREAS FOR THIS PROFILE

MANAGE YOUR HABITUAL LIMBIC REACTIONS:

- Turn your compassion onto yourself. Ask yourself, 'What are my real needs? Who really matters to me?' Take time to find out your own feelings, interests and desires.

- Allow people to, sometimes, solve their own problems. Be aware of your tendency to rescue others. Be clear about your roles and responsibilities.

- Appreciate that everyone else is not going to focus on meeting your needs. So have the courage to ask for what you want.

- Ensure that you are performing the content component of your work as well as the interpersonal side.

- Learn to be interdependent rather than dependent. Be realistic in seeing your importance and learn to simply ask for what you want.

- Learn to accept praise without discounting it.

- Learn to deal straight without manipulating.

LOOK OUT FOR THE SIGNS OF DISINTEGRATION

The spiral down for the Navigator is triggered by not effectively playing the role they have been engaged to play. This can fill them with shame and personal disgust. As they spiral down so too does their flexibility. Rigid adherence to plans becomes a clear focus and their management style becomes totally closed to any new suggestions. They could become abrupt, disconnected and autocratic.

Draw on the strengths of your Alter Ego

The Navigator's Alter Ego, the Chancellor, will express itself in humour, a willingness to change tack when new opportunities present themselves and an almost involuntary involvement in the politics of the organisation. The best contribution of the Alter Ego at work, for the Navigator in a leadership position, is the Alter Ego's insistence that their employees are genuinely engaged in understanding, supporting and implementing the strategic direction. The Alter Ego is also responsible for the Navigator's willingness to move jobs and take career advancement opportunities, even if it means moving to another company, city, profession or country.

Navigator Power Diamond of Personality

Whole of Personality

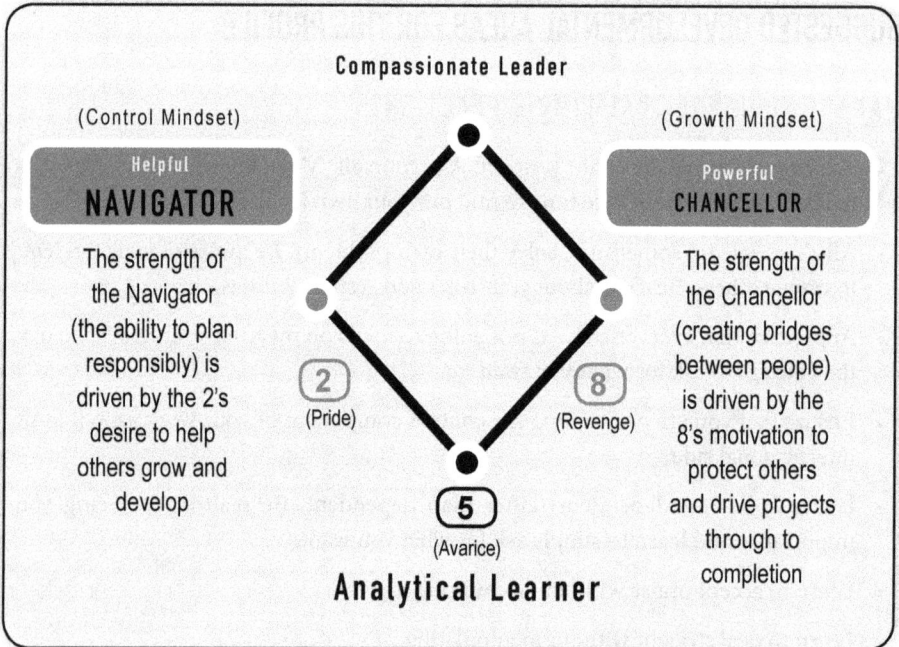

Compassionate Leader

(Control Mindset)

Helpful
NAVIGATOR

(Growth Mindset)

Powerful
CHANCELLOR

The strength of the Navigator (the ability to plan responsibly) is driven by the 2's desire to help others grow and develop

2 (Pride)

8 (Revenge)

5 (Avarice)

Analytical Learner

The strength of the Chancellor (creating bridges between people) is driven by the 8's motivation to protect others and drive projects through to completion

Navigator: Groupies Triad

INNATE CHARACTER

- Stands up for what they know is right
- Displays supportive/protective behaviour for their colleagues
- Creates a sense of security and stability within the team
- Effectively plans work with clear milestones and systems of reporting
- Identifies and manages the risks associated with completing individual or team objectives
- Works at giving other team members confidence

TEAM ROLE (NAVIGATOR)

Navigator's can see what is ahead for the team, both internally and externally and can create systems and processes that draw on relevant data to achieve the agreed vision. These systems are then documented in a methodical and comprehensive way. The Navigator has an excellent sense of cause and effect and the ability to sequence activities appropriately.

Cognitive Strengths

- Can balance the future vision with immediate practicalities

Cognitive Weaknesses

- Can get stressed always juggling between vision and implementation

Opportunities for Development

- Needs to learn how to be able to change tack midpoint

Threats to their Leadership Credibility

- Can 'close down' and refuse to budge off the agreed plan, even when change is required

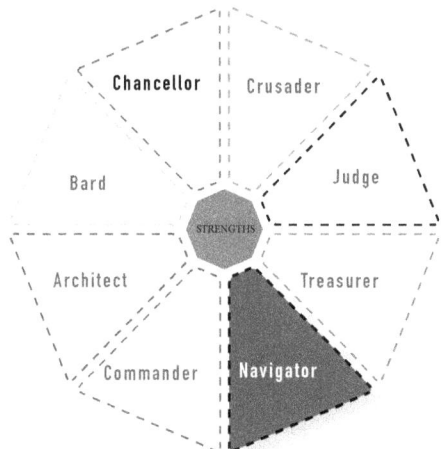

How this Core Belief Profile (CBP) thinks under pressure

The emotions of the CBP6 are manifested through the continuum of phobic to counter-phobic. The flight form of fear, through retreat or through compliance, is the phobic response while the confrontational and antiauthoritarian response is referred to as counter-phobic. While phobic CBP6's may be very present to their fear and seek to avoid it, the counterphobic CBP6 has absolutely no idea that they are fearful because they attack anything that they fear, flying in the face of the most dangerous situations. At their worst the CBP6 spends a lot of time in preparation for possible disasters. They are often thinking ahead to the worst-case scenario and anticipating it. The need for absolute certainty leads to endless planning and procrastination on the part of the CBP6.

SUGGESTED DEVELOPMENTAL AREAS FOR THIS PROFILE

MANAGE YOUR HABITUAL LIMBIC REACTIONS:

- Practise having confidence. When 6's look for ways to trust others, they will find them.

- Some 6's assume that their leader has all the answers and that they have none. They become completely compliant in order to avoid the constant doubting of no change authority. You must find your own inner sense of authority.

- Do not be afraid to play the role of devil's advocate. After all, it is what you do best anyway. You have developed formidable skill at cutting through pretence and exposing what will not work. Show where the problems and pitfalls are. Learn to give compliments; 6's tend to have a problem with gratitude.

- Define your own positive goals and focus on them just as much as on where you can go wrong.

- To avoid constantly laying blame, focus on the problem and not on the person.

LOOK OUT FOR THE SIGNS OF DISINTEGRATION

The spiral down for the Navigator is triggered by not effectively playing the role they have been engaged to play. This can fill them with shame and personal disgust. As they spiral down so too does their flexibility. Rigid adherence to plans becomes a clear focus and their management style becomes totally closed to any new suggestions. They could become abrupt, disconnected and autocratic.

Draw on the strengths of your Alter Ego

The Navigator's Alter Ego, the Chancellor, will express itself in humour, a willingness to change tack when new opportunities present themselves and an almost involuntary involvement in the politics of the organisation. The best contribution of the Alter Ego at work, for the Navigator in a leadership position, is the Alter Ego's insistence that their employees are genuinely engaged in understanding, supporting and implementing the strategic direction. The Alter Ego is also responsible for the Navigator's willingness to move jobs and take career advancement opportunities, even if it means moving to another company, city, profession or country.

Navigator Groupies Diamond of Personality
Whole of Personality

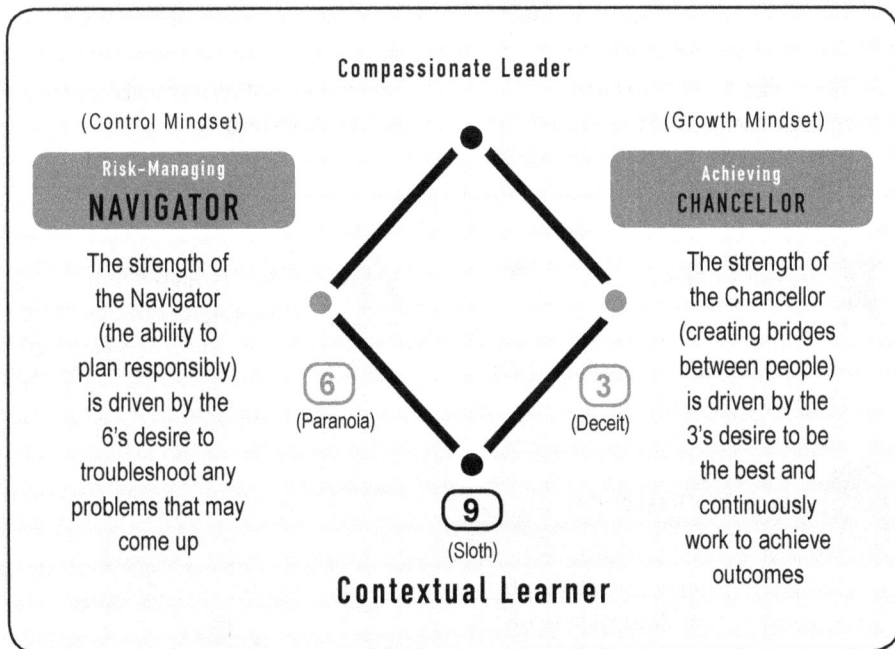

Compassionate Leader

(Control Mindset)

(Growth Mindset)

Risk-Managing
NAVIGATOR

Achieving
CHANCELLOR

The strength of the Navigator (the ability to plan responsibly) is driven by the 6's desire to troubleshoot any problems that may come up

The strength of the Chancellor (creating bridges between people) is driven by the 3's desire to be the best and continuously work to achieve outcomes

6
(Paranoia)

3
(Deceit)

9
(Sloth)

Contextual Learner

Architect: Idealist Triad

INNATE CHARACTER

- Ensures all team members 'walk the talk'
- Aligns the activity of the group with the vision of the organisation
- Ensures systems are practical and understood by the people using them
- Considers the wider organisational impact of key decisions or changes made in their area
- Puts forward suggestions to improve work practices and work flows
- Encourages the team to take a strategic approach and focus on undertaking the right action

TEAM ROLE (ARCHITECT)

The Architect can see when systems are not going to produce the desired outcome or where processes are falling short. They can create new systems, paradigms, frameworks or models that better align the process with both the vision and the practical needs of those who will be implementing the approach. They enjoy prototypes or new project work, are discerning by nature and is gregarious yet fiercely independent. They ensure that the leadership 'walks the talk' and is credible.

Cognitive Strengths

- Can integrate the impractical vision with practical structures

Cognitive Weaknesses

- They are disruptive change agents – even when they don't want to be

Opportunities for Development

- Needs to get in touch with the passion of life

Threats to their Leadership Credibility

- Can become bored and mechanical if there is no crisis

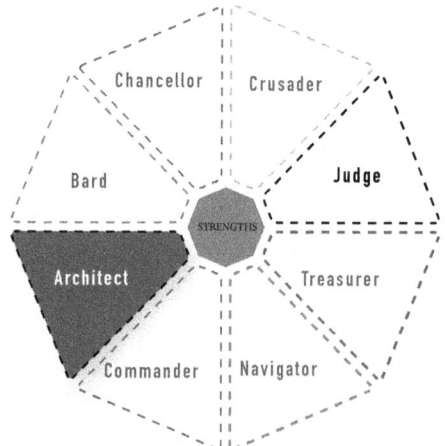

How this Core Belief Profile (CBP) thinks under pressure

At their worst the CBP1 is a hyper-critical, self-righteous individual fixated on adhering to the rules regardless of the situation or circumstance. They can be incapable of giving praise or appreciation for anything or anyone – since nothing ever reaches perfection. At their worst the greatest compliment that a CBP1 can give is, 'There was nothing that I could criticise in the work that you did.'

SUGGESTED DEVELOPMENTAL AREAS FOR THIS PROFILE

MANAGE YOUR HABITUAL LIMBIC REACTIONS:

- Try to model the behaviour that you want to see in others. Do not merely criticise others until they comply with your expectations.
- Appreciate that many of your comments will be taken as criticism, regardless of whether you see them that way.
- Consider the context of any criticism. While it may be appropriate for a specific behaviour, your context may be skewed and may ignore a great deal of relevant information.
- Aspire to your idealism but do not hold yourself and others to attaining it in every area of life.
- Develop realistic expectations for yourself.
- Appreciate and accept that making mistakes is part of the learning process.
- Learn when the given time would be better prioritised on other tasks rather than transforming a workable job to a perfect job.
- Understand that people do not want to be judged. So if you insist on constantly offering criticism you will be shunned and avoided. This will seriously limit your career development.
- Do not adopt the position of moral champion; take a break from the job of policing everyone around you.
- You probably have a tendency to accept and comply blindly with the rules of other people and institutions. You need to develop your own principles and practices based on context.

LOOK OUT FOR THE SIGNS OF DISINTEGRATION

The spiral down for the Architect is triggered by a lack of personal congruity. At the first level they may spiral down to the point that they feel isolated and betrayed and can't figure out why they have been victimised. They may perceive that they have no future, no friends and no courage. In this state, they will reject any sense of personal responsibility and may engage in unconstructive behaviour 'to get through it all'.

Draw on the strengths of your Alter Ego

At work, the Architect's Alter Ego, the Judge, is critical, energetic and driven and this explains the energy and determination that is visible. When angry about an issue, the Architect will be forthright and criticise the behaviour, the system or the situation in a diplomatic way. When fully integrated into the personality, the Alter Ego balances the Architect's strategic focus and detached approach with unlimited passion, clear judgement and unqualified loyalty to those that are close.

Architect Idealist Diamond of Personality

Whole of Personality

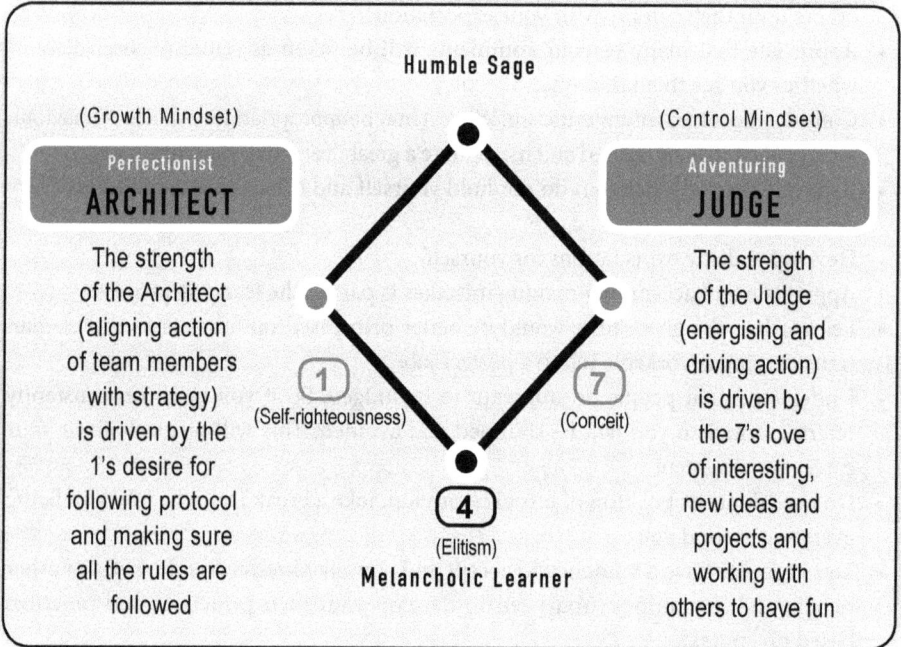

Humble Sage

(Growth Mindset)

Perfectionist
ARCHITECT

(Control Mindset)

Adventuring
JUDGE

The strength of the Architect (aligning action of team members with strategy) is driven by the 1's desire for following protocol and making sure all the rules are followed

The strength of the Judge (energising and driving action) is driven by the 7's love of interesting, new ideas and projects and working with others to have fun

1
(Self-righteousness)

7
(Conceit)

4
(Elitism)
Melancholic Learner

Architect: Power Triad

INNATE CHARACTER

- Ensures all team members 'walk the talk'
- Aligns the activity of the group with the vision of the organisation
- Ensures systems are practical and understood by the people using them
- Considers the wider organisational impact of key decisions or changes made in their area
- Puts forward suggestions to improve work practices and work flows
- Encourages the team to take a strategic approach and focus on undertaking the right action

TEAM ROLE (ARCHITECT)

The Architect can see when systems are not going to produce the desired outcome or where processes are falling short. They can create new systems, paradigms, frameworks or models that better align the process with both the vision and the practical needs of those who will be implementing the approach. They enjoy prototypes or new project work, are discerning by nature and is gregarious yet fiercely independent. They ensure that the leadership 'walks the talk' and is credible.

Cognitive Strengths

- Can integrate the impractical vision with practical structures

Cognitive Weaknesses

- They are disruptive change agents – even when they don't want to be

Opportunities for Development

- Needs to get in touch with the passion of life

Threats to their Leadership Credibility

- Can become bored and mechanical if there is no crisis

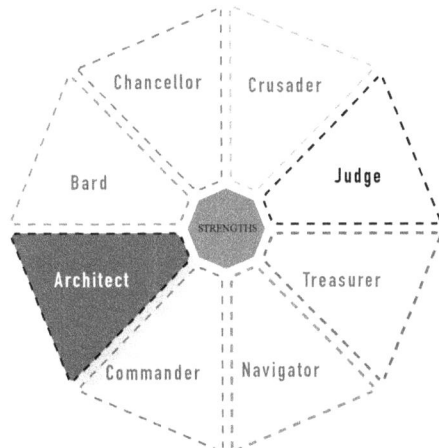

How this Core Belief Profile (CBP) thinks under pressure

When the emotion of pride becomes all consuming then the CBP2 not only avoids their own needs but ceases to be aware that they have any needs at all. The CBP2 is more easily able to recognise the needs of their spouse, family or of the person they are with rather than see their own. This often involves them in transferring their own needs onto other people. For example, if a CBP2 were cold, they may ask someone else, 'Are you cold?' rather than recognising that they themselves are cold. This creates a manipulative tendency where the CBP2 uses the feelings and needs of others to get their own needs fulfilled. Another downside of this tendency is that frequently the help that the CBP2 offers is not the help that is desired or required.

SUGGESTED DEVELOPMENTAL AREAS FOR THIS PROFILE

MANAGE YOUR HABITUAL LIMBIC REACTIONS:

- Turn your compassion onto yourself. Ask yourself, 'What are my real needs? Who really matters to me?' Take time to find out your ow feelings, interests and desires.

- Allow people to, sometimes, solve their own problems. Be aware of your tendency to rescue others. Be clear about your roles and responsibilities.

- Appreciate that everyone else is not going to focus on meeting your needs. So have the courage to ask for what you want.

- Ensure that you are performing the content component of your work as well as the interpersonal side.

- Learn to be interdependent rather than dependent. Be realistic in seeing your importance and learn to simply ask for what you want.

- Learn to accept praise without discounting it.

- Learn to deal straight without manipulating.

LOOK OUT FOR THE SIGNS OF DISINTEGRATION

The spiral down for the Architect is triggered by a lack of personal congruity. At the first level they may spiral down to the point that they feel isolated and betrayed and can't figure out why they have been victimised. They may perceive that they have no future, no friends and no courage. In this state, they will reject any sense of personal responsibility and may engage in unconstructive behaviour 'to get through it all'.

Draw on the strengths of your Alter Ego

At work, the Architect's Alter Ego, the Judge, is critical, energetic and driven and this explains the energy and determination that is visible. When angry about an issue, the Architect will be forthright and criticise the behaviour, the system or the situation in a diplomatic way. When fully integrated into the personality, the Alter Ego balances the Architect's strategic focus and detached approach with unlimited passion, clear judgement and unqualified loyalty to those that are close.

Architect Power Diamond of Personality

Whole of Personality

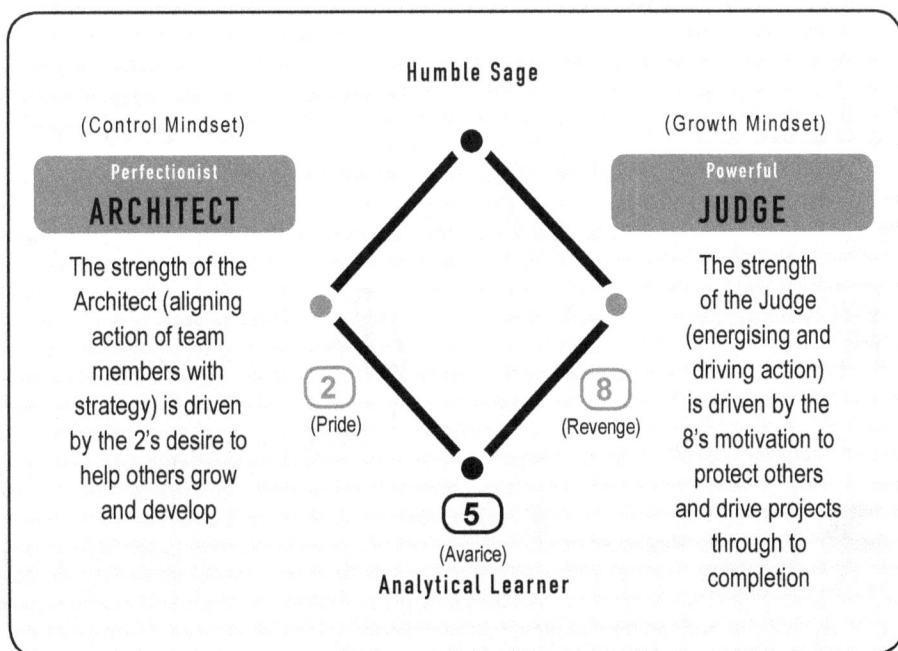

Humble Sage

(Control Mindset)   (Growth Mindset)

Perfectionist   **Powerful**

ARCHITECT   **JUDGE**

The strength of the Architect (aligning action of team members with strategy) is driven by the 2's desire to help others grow and develop

The strength of the Judge (energising and driving action) is driven by the 8's motivation to protect others and drive projects through to completion

2 (Pride)

8 (Revenge)

5 (Avarice)

Analytical Learner

Architect: Groupies Triad

INNATE CHARACTER

- Ensures all team members 'walk the talk'
- Aligns the activity of the group with the vision of the organisation
- Ensures systems are practical and understood by the people using them
- Considers the wider organisational impact of key decisions or changes made in their area
- Puts forward suggestions to improve work practices and work flows
- Encourages the team to take a strategic approach and focus on undertaking the right action

TEAM ROLE (ARCHITECT)

The Architect can see when systems are not going to produce the desired outcome or where processes are falling short. They can create new systems, paradigms, frameworks or models that better align the process with both the vision and the practical needs of those who will be implementing the approach. They enjoy prototypes or new project work, are discerning by nature and is gregarious yet fiercely independent. They ensure that the leadership 'walks the talk' and is credible.

Cognitive Strengths

- Can integrate the impractical vision with practical structures

Cognitive Weaknesses

- They are disruptive change agents – even when they don't want to be

Opportunities for Development

- Needs to get in touch with the passion of life

Threats to their Leadership Credibility

- Can become bored and mechanical if there is no crisis

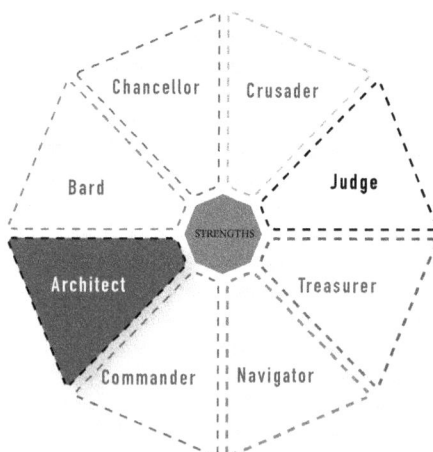

How this Core Belief Profile (CBP) thinks under pressure

The emotions of the CBP6 are manifested through the continuum of phobic to counter-phobic. The flight form of fear, through retreat or through compliance, is the phobic response while the confrontational and antiauthoritarian response is referred to as counter-phobic. While phobic CBP6's may be very present to their fear and seek to avoid it, the counterphobic CBP6 has absolutely no idea that they are fearful because they attack anything that they fear, flying in the face of the most dangerous situations. At their worst the CBP6 spends a lot of time in preparation for possible disasters. They are often thinking ahead to the worst-case scenario and anticipating it. The need for absolute certainty leads to endless planning and procrastination on the part of the CBP6.

SUGGESTED DEVELOPMENTAL AREAS FOR THIS PROFILE

MANAGE YOUR HABITUAL LIMBIC REACTIONS:

- Practise having confidence. When 6's look for ways to trust others, they will find them.

- Some 6's assume that their leader has all the answers and that they have none. They become completely compliant in order to avoid the constant doubting of no change authority. You must find your own inner sense of authority.

- Do not be afraid to play the role of devil's advocate. After all, it is what you do best anyway. You have developed formidable skill at cutting through pretence and exposing what will not work. Show where the problems and pitfalls are. Learn to give compliments; 6's tend to have a problem with gratitude.

- Define your own positive goals and focus on them just as much as on where you can go wrong.

- To avoid constantly laying blame, focus on the problem and not on the person.

LOOK OUT FOR THE SIGNS OF DISINTEGRATION

The spiral down for the Architect is triggered by a lack of personal congruity. At the first level they may spiral down to the point that they feel isolated and betrayed and can't figure out why they have been victimised. They may perceive that they have no future, no friends and no courage. In this state, they will reject any sense of personal responsibility and may engage in unconstructive behaviour 'to get through it all'.

Draw on the strengths of your Alter Ego

At work, the Architect's Alter Ego, the Judge, is critical, energetic and driven and this explains the energy and determination that is visible. When angry about an issue, the Architect will be forthright and criticise the behaviour, the system or the situation in a diplomatic way. When fully integrated into the personality, the Alter Ego balances the Architect's strategic focus and detached approach with unlimited passion, clear judgement and unqualified loyalty to those that are close.

Architect Groupies Diamond of Personality

Whole of Personality

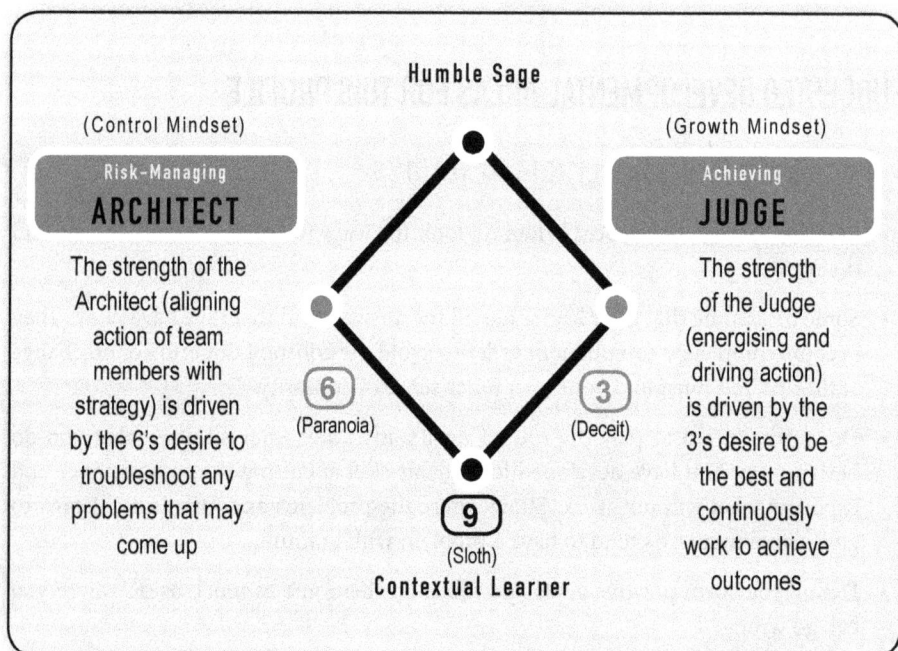

Humble Sage

(Control Mindset)   (Growth Mindset)

Risk-Managing		Achieving
ARCHITECT		**JUDGE**

The strength of the Architect (aligning action of team members with strategy) is driven by the 6's desire to troubleshoot any problems that may come up

6
(Paranoia)

3
(Deceit)

9
(Sloth)

Contextual Learner

The strength of the Judge (energising and driving action) is driven by the 3's desire to be the best and continuously work to achieve outcomes

Judge: Groupies Triad

INNATE CHARACTER

- Looks outside the organisation for innovative ideas that can be applied internally
- Seeks out challenging opportunities to test their skills and abilities
- Manages their time effectively so that all the things for which they are responsible get done
- Celebrates with a sense of satisfaction when a project is completed or a key milestone is reached
- Meets daily challenges with enthusiasm and energy
- Uses questions to clarify team member points of view, team objectives and procedures

TEAM ROLE (JUDGE)

Judges are interested in action and completing tasks. They focus on clarifying exactly what needs to be done, by whom, with what resources and in what time frame. They have an innate sense of urgency and don't walk away from conflict if that is required to reach agreement on tasks and responsibilities. They push the team to make decisions, to allocate resources and agree to timeframes. They energise the team and are the first to roll up their sleeves and get on with the task at hand. They are practical and push to complete the task successfully.

Cognitive Strengths

- Very focused on doing what it takes to achieve the goal

Cognitive Weaknesses

- Can 'burn out' themselves and others

Opportunities for Development

- Needs to keep deadlines and expectations in perspective

Threats to their Leadership Credibility

- Can create needless conflict

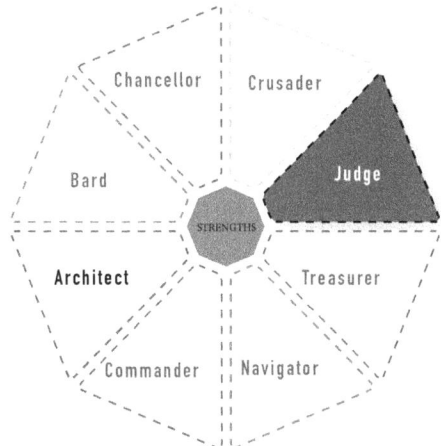

How this Core Belief Profile (CBP) thinks under pressure

The deceit of the CBP3 that is most easily seen is self-deceit. However, it is also the deception of others. Since the CBP3 is constantly changing themselves to be consistent with the most successful image of whatever group or individual they are participating with, they deceive themselves and others that they are actually what it is that they are doing. This deceit can manifest itself as simply putting one's best foot forward by just placing a little spin on the facts to sound good, charm or to self-promote. Deceit is a desire for approval measured by material success.

SUGGESTED DEVELOPMENTAL AREAS FOR THIS PROFILE

MANAGE YOUR HABITUAL LIMBIC REACTIONS:

- Recognise that success is not proof of virtue.

- Recognise that there is a difference between who you are and what you do, and learn to value both independently.

- Note your automatic tendency to take over, whether it is a good idea or not. Allow others to lead and see where they go.

- Take time in your schedule for other people – without an agenda or need for results.

- Develop the ability to be honest about how you feel.

- Develop the capacity to make a personal connection with those around you.

LOOK OUT FOR THE SIGNS OF DISINTEGRATION

As the Judge spirals down they may become intolerant of all other positions and become self-righteous. Their self-righteousness will be based on the rules they absorbed during childhood. They may decide that they are the only ones doing what should be done and that others need to be punished to teach them a lesson. This is done behind the scenes with the Judge pulling the strings and creating chaos, hurt and confusion among his targets. While this is happening, the Judge may genuinely believe they are doing the right thing.

Draw on the strengths of your Alter Ego

The Judge's Alter Ego, the Architect, is dedicated to fast-paced, fast-talking, argumentative action. The Alter Ego looks for the strategic intent of the activity and is motivated by learning new capabilities, that is, the 'how to' of the 'what'. This thirst for new capabilities often draws the Judge to projects that will teach them new skills even if the projects seem strangely unrelated to their current skills, interests or preferences. The Judge's Alter Ego is constantly critiquing behaviour and pointing out inconsistencies. The Alter Ego focuses on truth, honesty and teasing out weaknesses so they can be dealt with strategically. When fully integrated, the Judge's passion, energy and focus on action are balanced by the Alter Ego's strategic outlook and philosophy, drive to learn new capabilities and ability to align all action with the vision and genuine needs and wants of the people involved.

Judge Groupies Diamond of Personality

Whole of Personality

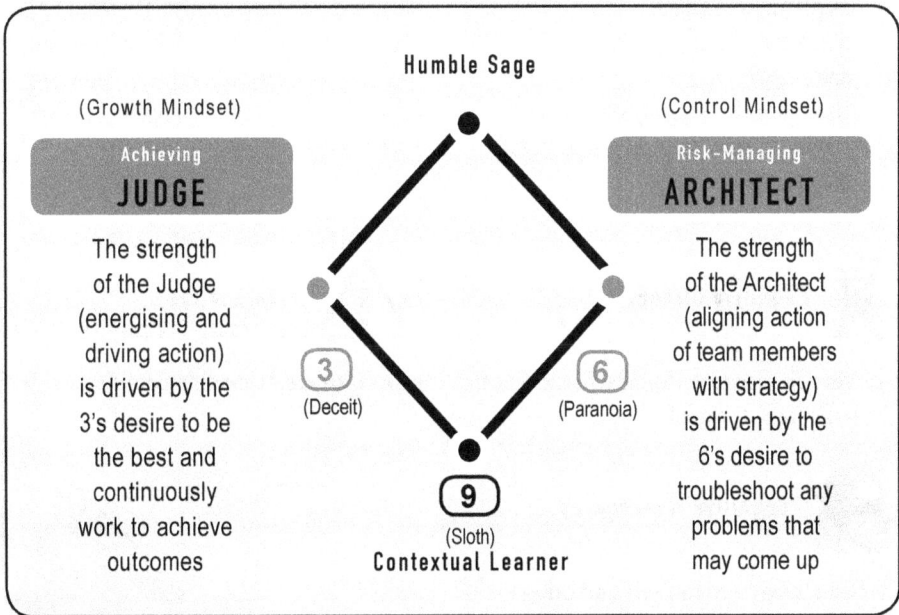

Humble Sage

(Growth Mindset)   (Control Mindset)

Achieving
JUDGE

Risk-Managing
ARCHITECT

The strength of the Judge (energising and driving action) is driven by the 3's desire to be the best and continuously work to achieve outcomes

The strength of the Architect (aligning action of team members with strategy) is driven by the 6's desire to troubleshoot any problems that may come up

3 (Deceit)

6 (Paranoia)

9 (Sloth)

Contextual Learner

Judge: Idealist Triad

INNATE CHARACTER

- Looks outside the organisation for innovative ideas that can be applied internally
- Seeks out challenging opportunities to test their skills and abilities
- Manages their time effectively so that all the things for which they are responsible get done
- Celebrates with a sense of satisfaction when a project is completed or a key milestone is reached
- Meets daily challenges with enthusiasm and energy
- Uses questions to clarify team member points of view, team objectives and procedures

TEAM ROLE (JUDGE)

Judges are interested in action and completing tasks. They focus on clarifying exactly what needs to be done, by whom, with what resources and in what time frame. They have an innate sense of urgency and don't walk away from conflict if that is required to reach agreement on tasks and responsibilities. They push the team to make decisions, to allocate resources and agree to timeframes. They energise the team and are the first to roll up their sleeves and get on with the task at hand. They are practical and push to complete the task successfully.

Cognitive Strengths

- Very focused on doing what it takes to achieve the goal

Cognitive Weaknesses

- Can 'burn out' himself and others

Opportunities for Development

- Needs to keep deadlines and expectations in perspective

Threats to their Leadership Credibility

- Can create needless conflict

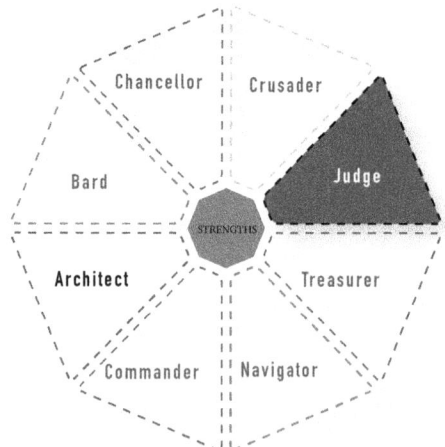

How this Core Belief Profile (CBP) thinks under pressure

In the presence of being trapped or controlled the emotions of the CBP7 will force them to move quickly from one thing to another, sampling but never deepening any particular experience. This is particularly true if the experience could result in emotional pain. CBP7 manifests as gluttony for new, fun and enjoyable experiences. Life is like a smorgasbord and is experienced as a range of experiences rather than a single experience repeated often. At their worst, they will seek absolute freedom without responsibility or commitment.

SUGGESTED DEVELOPMENTAL AREAS FOR THIS PROFILE

MANAGE YOUR HABITUAL LIMBIC REACTIONS:

- Be aware of your tendency to rationalise, to explain away failure and ethical violations without taking responsibility.

- Develop the skill of really listening rather than trying to think of something clever to say later.

- Work! Actually get your work completed rather than thinking about what else you could be doing.

- Practise mental sobriety. Do not just become drunk on ideas.

LOOK OUT FOR THE SIGNS OF DISINTEGRATION

As the Judge spirals down they may become intolerant of all other positions and become self-righteous. Their self-righteousness will be based on the rules they absorbed during childhood. They may decide that they are the only ones doing what should be done and that others need to be punished to teach them a lesson. This is done behind the scenes with the Judge pulling the strings and creating chaos, hurt and confusion among his targets. While this is happening, the Judge may genuinely believe they are doing the right thing.

Draw on the strengths of your Alter Ego

The Judge's Alter Ego, the Architect, is dedicated to fast-paced, fast-talking, argumentative action. The Alter Ego looks for the strategic intent of the activity and is motivated by learning new capabilities, that is, the 'how to' of the 'what'. This thirst for new capabilities often draws the Judge to projects that will teach them new skills even if the projects seem strangely unrelated to their current skills, interests or preferences. The Judge's Alter Ego is constantly critiquing behaviour and pointing out inconsistencies. The Alter Ego focuses on truth, honesty and teasing out weaknesses so they can be dealt with strategically. When fully integrated, the Judge's passion, energy and focus on action are balanced by the Alter Ego's strategic outlook and philosophy, drive to learn new capabilities and ability to align all action with the vision and genuine needs and wants of the people involved.

Judge Idealist Diamond of Personality

Whole of Personality

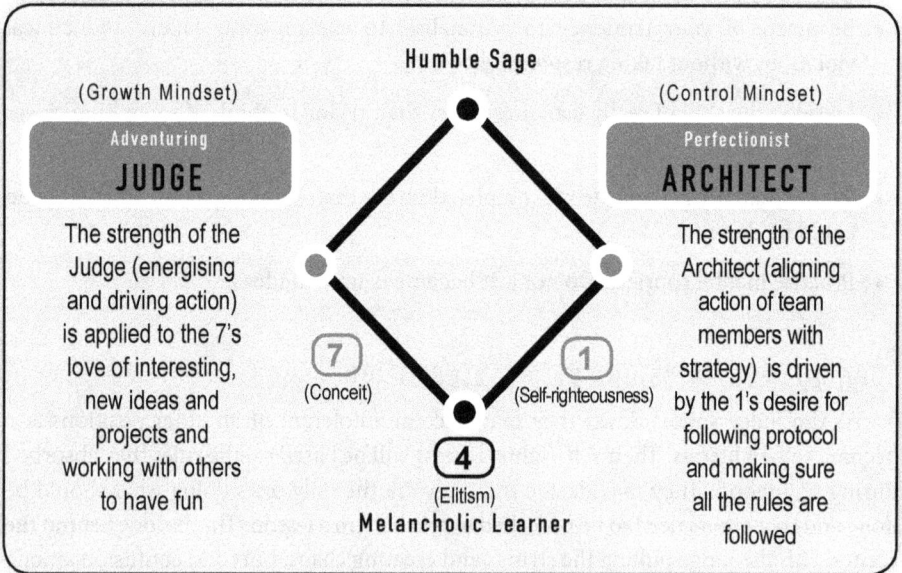

Humble Sage

(Growth Mindset)   (Control Mindset)

Adventuring   Perfectionist
JUDGE   **ARCHITECT**

The strength of the Judge (energising and driving action) is applied to the 7's love of interesting, new ideas and projects and working with others to have fun

The strength of the Architect (aligning action of team members with strategy) is driven by the 1's desire for following protocol and making sure all the rules are followed

7 (Conceit)

1 (Self-righteousness)

4 (Elitism)

Melancholic Learner

Judge: Power Triad

INNATE CHARACTER

- Looks outside the organisation for innovative ideas that can be applied internally
- Seeks out challenging opportunities to test their skills and abilities
- Manages their time effectively so that all the things for which they are responsible get done
- Celebrates with a sense of satisfaction when a project is completed or a key milestone is reached
- Meets daily challenges with enthusiasm and energy
- Uses questions to clarify team member points of view, team objectives and procedures

TEAM ROLE (JUDGE)

Judges are interested in action and completing tasks. They focus on clarifying exactly what needs to be done, by whom, with what resources and in what time frame. They have an innate sense of urgency and don't walk away from conflict if that is required to reach agreement on tasks and responsibilities. They push the team to make decisions, to allocate resources and agree to timeframes. They energise the team and are the first to roll up their sleeves and get on with the task at hand. They are practical and push to complete the task successfully.

Cognitive Strengths

- Very focused on doing what it takes to achieve the goal

Cognitive Weaknesses

- Can 'burn out' himself and others

Opportunities for Development

- Needs to keep deadlines and expectations in perspective

Threats to their Leadership Credibility

- Can create needless conflict

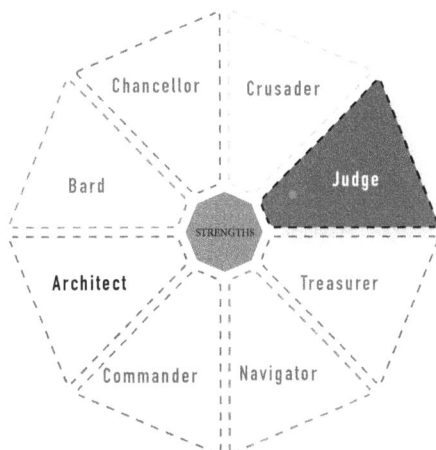

How this Core Belief Profile (CBP) thinks under pressure

At their worst the CBP8 will entertain an enormous lust for life. They will seek intensity in all things as the hallmark of a fulfilling life. If they enjoy something, then there can never be enough. They always want more. Moderation is death when the emotion of the CBP8 is high. Always they want more, better, faster and louder. This sometimes leads to difficulty with people or friends who cannot 'keep up' with their energy. This intensity is used to control others through the creation of physical, material or emotional dependence. Intensity sorts out the strong from the weak. This CBP reports that most people fall into two categories – those that can't help being weak and those that can.

SUGGESTED DEVELOPMENTAL AREAS FOR THIS PROFILE

MANAGE YOUR HABITUAL LIMBIC REACTIONS:

- Feeling as if someone is taking advantage of you is not the same as someone actually taking advantage of you. Check the details before you automatically retaliate.

- Choose your battles. Constantly ask yourself, 'Is this fight worth it?'

- Before you totally attack someone, ask yourself whether you are willing to deal with the consequences.

- For many people, your threats and tirades are not effective, no matter how much you may enjoy putting them on.

- When giving instructions, be very specific about the behaviour that will satisfy your expectations.

- Find ways to use others' talents and give them a sense of ownership and empowerment rather than just being a hired hand.

LOOK OUT FOR THE SIGNS OF DISINTEGRATION

As the Judge spirals down they may become intolerant of all other positions and become self-righteous. Their self-righteousness will be based on the rules they absorbed during childhood. They may decide that they are the only ones doing what should be done and that others need to be punished to teach them a lesson. This is done behind the scenes with the Judge pulling the strings and creating chaos, hurt and confusion among his targets. While this is happening, the Judge may genuinely believe they are doing the right thing.

Draw on the strengths of your Alter Ego

The Judge's Alter Ego, the Architect, is dedicated to fast-paced, fast-talking, argumentative action. The Alter Ego looks for the strategic intent of the activity and is motivated by learning new capabilities, that is, the 'how to' of the 'what'. This thirst for new capabilities often draws the Judge to projects that will teach them new skills even if the projects seem strangely unrelated to their current skills, interests or preferences. The Judge's Alter Ego is constantly critiquing behaviour and pointing out inconsistencies. The Alter Ego focuses on truth, honesty and teasing out weaknesses so they can be dealt with strategically. When fully integrated, the Judge's passion, energy and focus on action are balanced by the Alter Ego's strategic outlook and philosophy, drive to learn new capabilities and ability to align all action with the vision and genuine needs and wants of the people involved.

Judge Power Diamond of Personality

Whole of Personality

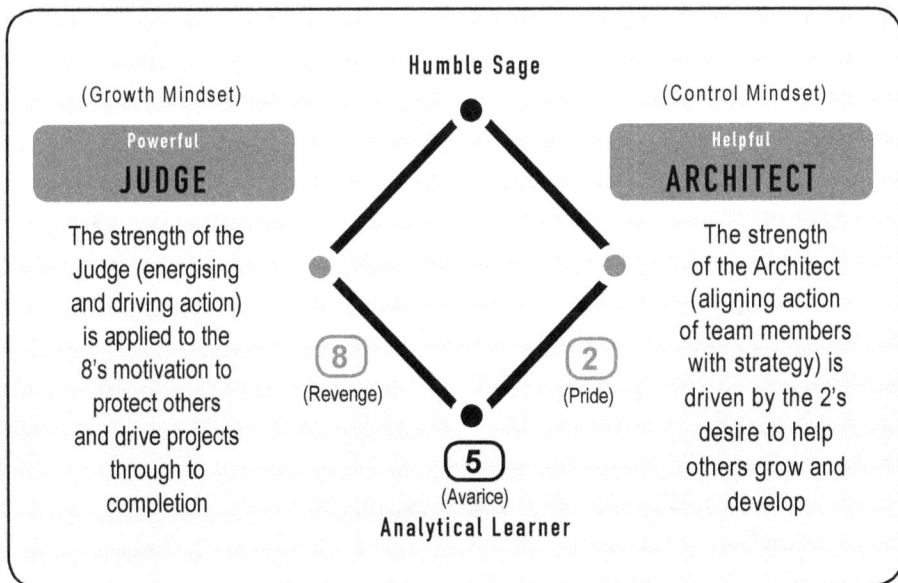

Humble Sage

(Growth Mindset)   (Control Mindset)

Powerful
JUDGE

Helpful
ARCHITECT

The strength of the Judge (energising and driving action) is applied to the 8's motivation to protect others and drive projects through to completion

The strength of the Architect (aligning action of team members with strategy) is driven by the 2's desire to help others grow and develop

8 (Revenge)

2 (Pride)

5 (Avarice)

Analytical Learner

APPENDIX 2

Neuro-Rational Type Test

TEST INSTRUCTIONS

Following are eight paragraphs that give an overview of each of the Neuro-Rational Types. These are not comprehensive descriptions. Instead, they are written to focus on the main features of the type.

1. Read each of the eight paragraphs and select the top two that sound most like you.

2. Make your selection based on the sense of the whole paragraph that most sounds like you, rather than a sentence here or there or aspects of one.

3. Prioritise the paragraphs.

4. If you find it difficult to narrow your selection to two, because aspects of all the types sound like you, consider how others would describe you and use that as a guide.

5. It may also be helpful to make your selection based on how you acted in your early twenties; this is when our Neuro-Rational Type is usually at its most strident and obvious.

6. You may also consider having your significant other look at the paragraphs and make a selection, granted that they observe your behaviour all the time.

THE NEURO-RATIONAL TYPE TEST:

SELECT TWO PARAGRAPHS THAT SOUND MOST LIKE YOU

1. I value straightforwardness, honesty and clarity. I dislike conflict and work hard to complete my responsibilities to the highest standard so that it's difficult to blame me if things go wrong. At work I like to know exactly what is expected of me so that I can complete my role to the best of my ability. I strongly believe in personal integrity – which means that I mean what I say and say what I mean. I don't like people who try to deceive or blur the edges of life – I believe they should just tell it as it is. I am not passionate about all things but some issues around justice really fire me up and I can crusade for what is right and true. I am conservative by nature and live in a house I can afford, drive a sensible car and don't pretend I am somebody I am not. I can't stand pretentious or lazy people who try charming their way through life rather than doing what they are supposed to do. People often say that I look stern or angry even when I'm not. When I do relax, there is another side to me. At social gatherings at the end of a week or project, I don't mind a drink or two and can party and mingle with the best of them. People are often amazed at the difference between the two sides of my personality – my serious side and my party side. By and large, however, I take life pretty seriously. I like to do my best and I resent people who want an easy life and don't do their fair share.

2. People see me as solid, relaxed and reliable. I calm people down when they are emotionally hurting and have an easy way about me. I don't really plan for the future or worry about things as many do. I take each day as it comes and deal with things as they arise. I live in the now. This means that while everyone is too busy to care, I am the one who walks beside people when they are going through a bad patch. I like problem-solving and can keep working at something until I nut it out. At work it's the little things that people ask me to help them with – things that I know nothing about, but seem to work out somehow anyway. My family is very important to me, and so is relaxing and having a laugh with friends. I am practical and prefer to take a hands-on approach to life. Every now and then I wonder what I'm doing with my life and can get a little disappointed with what I have achieved. I also have an internal critic that sits in my head and constantly tells me how I am falling short. I am even-tempered but every now and then people push me too far and if I snap they get to see the wrath of a patient person – which sometimes even amazes me. The only downside with going with the flow is that I find it difficult to set, and discipline myself to follow, my own agendas and priorities.

3. I am friendly, relationship-centred and ambitious. I like others to like me and work hard to accommodate their point of view if I am working with them. When there is conflict between two other people I can often build the bridge to bring two different points of view together. I am optimistic and love meeting new people and almost everyone likes meeting me. I enjoy teamwork and discussing issues. I find reading, paper work and administration difficult although I will do them if I absolutely have to. I seem to see all points of view pretty easily and can sometimes seem to others to be a little indecisive at times if people are at loggerheads and I have to make a call. Good relationships mean a lot to me and I am willing to do what it takes to develop and maintain them.

4. I am a big-picture person. I like to see the vision and work backwards from that. I see the potential in others, in most situations, and often work from this perspective rather than reality. I am sensitive to others and can often see and feel their pain. I am constantly looking to create a better and safer world and put a lot of energy in creating a home and work environment where people feel safe. I can usually tell when people are trying to put on a brave face and somehow seem to be able to see the source of their pain. By nature I look for the best in others and expect them to do the same, although I am constantly amazed at how narrow minded and heartless people seem to be with themselves and others. I like to come up with an exciting or bold plan and then inspire a team to achieve it. I enjoy reading and I find that it settles me down when I am feeling anxious. I love to learn new information and frameworks about success, achievement, and about better understanding myself and others. I am sometimes described by others as having a big personality and it's true that I tend to wear my heart on my sleeve. I love intensity of experience and creating something as close to perfect as possible.

5. I would describe myself as one of life's observers. I like to watch what is happening and make my mind up in my own time. I don't like to be pushed whether at home or at work. I have an excellent memory for details and enjoy collecting information about almost everything. Some people need to talk and make noise for no reason. I like to be quiet and could spend a week by myself if I had interesting books or tasks to complete. If I am by myself with no external stimulus I can get bored. I enjoy creating order out of chaos. I like things to be ordered. They may not always look neat, but I know exactly where everything is and how I can lay my hands on what I need. I like to be self-sufficient, financially and emotionally, and structure my life in line with this. I can cope with chaotic situations better than most, and have the ability to break down any situation or problem into parts and deal with each part one at a time.

6. I like to understand my roles and responsibilities and once I have that understanding I will perform well. This is true at home and at work. When I don't have a role I feel lost and without purpose. I believe in honour and in the importance of the family. My role as parent, son, daughter, husband or wife is very important to me and I take it very seriously. I believe in actively planning my life and the life of those I love. I can see problems ahead and like to work on solving them months, if not years, ahead. I have a life plan that spans years, if not decades, into the future and I have the discipline and conviction to follow the plan. I enjoy using equipment that is purpose-designed and can often get more performance out of a piece of equipment than others can. I have an off-beat sense of humour which often confuses others so I tend to keep it to myself. I like the structure and discipline that comes with being a part of an organisation and don't particularly like those who are more interested in their own glory than the success of the project. I am stable and am able to create stability in teams during periods of intense uncertainty. People who work with me have a sense of certainty.

7. I am spontaneous, quick and energetic. I enjoy getting my teeth into a project and getting it done as quickly as possible. I have a lot more energy than others seem to have and some people say they feel exhausted after they have spent time with me. I enjoy meeting new people and trying new experiences. I believe in the philosophy 'live and let live'. I am intensely loyal to my friends and family and will fight to the death to protect their reputation. I can't stand hypocrites. I don't mind blowing the cover of people who put themselves above the rest of us by asking them difficult questions or turning up the heat in some way. I have a short attention span and get bored very easily so I need to have a few projects on the go at the same time. I don't know why everyone seems to make life so difficult. Life is life. You live it the best you can. I enjoy life overall. What I most enjoy is meeting new people and having new experiences. What is important to me is getting things done quickly, and people that dither around really annoy me – just get on with it! Any action is better than procrastination!

8. I am not easily convinced by bells and whistles. I am amazed at how gullible others seem to be when what is being said is illogical and obviously self-serving. I analyse everything that I see and come to my own conclusions. I'm irritated by loud-mouthed bigots and don't usually waste my energy debating with them unless I feel like an argument, because they can't hear my viewpoint anyway. My home is a pleasant place where my friends and family can relax. I like good food, good wine and good conversation. I have a very good 'bullshit detector' and can see a fraud a mile off. I am practical by nature and like to understand how things will work in practice. At work when new ideas are put forward I am often the one that sees the inconsistency between what is being proposed and the outcomes they are looking for. This irritates people who prefer to live in a make-believe world of ideals and theoretical concepts. I feel betrayed when I have put in the work on a project and somebody else who is more fluent and enthusiastic than I am gets the credit. I am ambitious and like to be acknowledged for my contribution even though I never ask for it. I can think in abstract terms and like discussing philosophical viewpoints. I like to develop systems and practices that ensure the task is completed efficiently and with the minimum of fuss. If I know each team member I am good at placing them in a functional role that best suits their capabilities. Personally I love to learn new capabilities and have quite a number of hands-on skills in a range of different disciplines.

Now, following the instructions, select your top two choices and note the Arthurian characters that are used to describe them.

TEST PARAGRAPH

ONE ⟶ Crusader
TWO ⟶ Commander
THREE ⟶ Chancellor
FOUR ⟶ Bard
FIVE ⟶ Treasurer
SIX ⟶ Navigator
SEVEN ⟶ Judge
EIGHT ⟶ Architect

Make no assumptions at this point about what the name given to each type implies.

Now you are ready to look further into each of the eight types before making your final decision.

Your first choice has a 78 per cent chance of being your Master. There is a 40 per cent chance that your second choice is your Mirror.

APPENDIX 3

Neuro-Rational Type Matrix

Neuro-Rational Type Name	Noble Quality	What This Brings out in Others	Personal Code of Conduct for This Neuro-Rational Type
Crusader (C2 P2 I1)	Integrity	Honesty	• Always keeps sensitive information that has been shared in confidence to themselves • Acts ethically in their dealings with others • Spends time to make sure there is agreement about roles – both theirs and others • Corrects others – clearly, constructively and professionally • Speaks directly to the person they have an issue with without unnecessarily involving other unrelated people • Provides other team members with a sense of purpose
Commander (C1 P1 I2)	Courage	Confidence	• Stands up for what they believe is right • Stands by their actions without fear of reprisals or consequences • Acts justly and fairly in all dealings with colleagues • Solves problems as they arise without fuss and drama • Encourages the team to innovate or adapt if necessary to ensure a quality result • Encourages other team members to be courageous in thought and deed
Chancellor (C1 P2 I2)	Diplomacy	Tolerance	• Acknowledges and considers other opinions in a respectful and non-judgemental way • Considers the opinions of others with an open mind • Ensures all team members have a say in group decisions • Seeks out, listens to and considers opposite viewpoints on any given subject • Offers support to colleagues who may be experiencing difficulties • Encourages others to show their appreciation
Bard (C2 P2 I2)	Inspiration	Hopefulness	• Displays an allegiance to all co-workers (above, below and beside them) • Shows an understanding of how others are feeling • Makes others feel valued and important • Creates a workplace environment where colleagues feel they can try new approaches and take risks • Looks for the unique contribution all colleagues can make to the team • Encourages the team to be honest and open

CRUSADER

COMMANDER

CHANCELLOR

BARD

The Benefit For the Team	Contribution to Team Culture[1]	If not Present in the Team	School of Strategic Thought[1]
Keeps team members accountable	Commitment	No clear vision, purpose or understanding, no honour and no team commitment	**Positioning School** Suggests that only a few key strategies (positions in the economic marketplace) are desirable. Much of Michael Porter's work can be mapped to this school.
Breaks down bureaucracy	Innovation	Everything becomes bogged down at key bottlenecks; there is no courage, no heroes and no decisions	**Learning School** Strategies emerge as people (acting individually or collectively) come to learn about a situation as well as their organisation's capability to deal with it.
Effective teamwork with diversity	Esprit de Corps (the sense of shared purpose and fellowship)	Team members become self-righteous, intolerant and blaming – the team splits into factions	**Power School** This school stresses strategy formation as an overt process of influence, emphasising the use of power and politics to negotiate strategies favourable to a particular interest.
Team members play to their strengths	Empowerment[1]	The physical environment and culture becomes hostile and the team loses hope as the future becomes bleak	**Entrepreneurial School** Strategy formation results from the insights of a single leader and stresses intuition, judgement, wisdom, experience and insight. The 'vision' of the leader supplies the guiding principles of the strategy.

CRUSADER

COMMANDER

CHANCELLOR

BARD

[1] This benefit arises when the individual is at the Blue meme. For more detail, see Chapter 19.

	Shadow Quality	Integration[2]	Disintegration[2]	Exemplar
CRUSADER	Intolerant/ Punitive	Focuses on unconditional love and compassion for self	Descends into competition with, and bullying of, others	• Malcolm Fraser • Estee Lauder • Margaret Thatcher
COMMANDER	Victim/ Dependence	Focuses on being objective	Descends into personal confusion and procrastination	• Bruce Willis • Meg Ryan • Peter Cosgrove
CHANCELLOR	Insecurity/ Manipulation	Focuses on asking the hard questions and seeking the truth	Descends into building castles in the sky (delusion and deceit)	• Bill Clinton • Tony Blair • Barack Obama
BARD	Delusion/ Deception	Focuses on personal integrity and doing the honourable thing	Descends into personal insecurity and manipulation of others	• Walt Disney • Rupert Murdoch • Al Gore

[2] Blue meme integration and disintegration.

Neuro-Rational Type Name	Noble Quality	What This Brings out in Others	Personal Code of Conduct for This Neuro-Rational Type
Treasurer (C1 P1 I1)	Objectivity	Calmness	• Encourages colleagues to develop their technical knowledge and skills • Creates clear audit trails related to activity or key decisions • Learns from mistakes and documents this learning so that other team members can benefit • Shows respect for colleagues' knowledge or expertise • Rationally considers the facts before making key decisions • Models respect for other team members
Navigator (C2 P1 I1)	Responsibility	Security	• Stands up for what they know is right • Displays supportive/protective behaviour for their colleagues • Creates a sense of security and stability within the team • Effectively plans work with clear milestones and systems of reporting • Identifies and manages the risks associated with completing individual or team objectives • Works at giving other team members confidence
Judge (C1 P2 I1)	Drive	Passion	• Looks outside the organisation for innovative ideas that can be applied internally • Seeks out challenging opportunities to test their skills and abilities • Manages their time effectively so that they get all things done for which they are responsible • Celebrates with a sense of satisfaction when a project is completed or a key milestone is reached • Meets daily challenges with enthusiasm and energy • Uses questions to clarify team member points of view, team objectives and procedures
Architect (C2 P1 I2)	Discernment	Competence	• Ensures all team members 'walk the talk' • Aligns the activity of the group with the vision of the organisation • Ensures systems are practical and understood by the people using them • Considers the wider organisational impact of key decisions or changes made in their area • Puts forward suggestions to improve work practices and work flows • Encourages the team to take a strategic approach and focus on undertaking right action

TREASURER

NAVIGATOR

JUDGE

ARCHITECT

	The Benefit For the Team	Contribution to Team Culture[3]	If not Present in the Team	School of Strategic Thought[3]
TREASURER	Rational inquiry	Understanding	No records of meetings or decisions and no audit trail. There is no group learning and ignorance prevails	**Planning School** Formal procedure, formal training, formal analysis, and lots of numbers are the hallmark of this approach. The simple informal steps of the design school become an elaborated sequence of steps. Produce each component part as specified, assemble them according to the blueprint, and strategy will result.
NAVIGATOR	Creates a sense of certainty within the team	Stability	Fear and uncertainty prevail – every man or woman for themselves	**Cognitive School** Strategy formation is a cognitive process that takes place in the mind of the strategist. Strategies emerge as the strategist filters the maps, concepts and schemas shaping their thinking.
JUDGE	Healthy debate which leads to action	High workload	No energy or enthusiasm – everyone is exhausted	**Design School** Proposes a model of strategy making that seems to attain a fit between internal capabilities and external possibilities. Probably the most influential school of thought, and home of the SWOT (Strengths, Weaknesses, Opportunities and Threats) technique.
ARCHITECT	Effective strategic analysis	Systems and practices suitability[3]	The leadership has no credibility and the team focuses on the wrong action	**Environmental School** Presenting itself to the individual as a set of general forces, the environment is the central actor in the strategy making process. The individual must respond to the factors or be 'selected out'.

[3] This benefit arises when the individual is at the Blue meme. For more detail, see Chapter 19.

	Shadow Quality	Integration[4]	Disintegration[4]	Exemplar
TREASURER	Arrogance/ Disassociation	Focuses on personal courage and spontaneity	Descends into being inflexible and controlling others	• Clint Eastwood • Kylie Minogue • Kevin Costner
NAVIGATOR	Inflexible/ Controlling	Focuses on 'walking the talk'	Descends into personal arrogance and detaches from reality	• John Howard • HRH Prince Charles • George W. Bush
JUDGE	Competitive/ Bully	Focuses on empathising with others and building bridges with them	Descends into being intolerant and punitive	• Richard Branson • Bette Midler • Billy Connolly
ARCHITECT	Confusion/ Procrastination	Focuses on taking personal responsibility and having confidence in themselves	Descends into being a victim which leads to co-dependence	• Dalai Lama • Lady Diana Spencer • Albert Einstein

[4] Blue meme integration and disintegration.

APPENDIX 4

Process of Integration and (Dis)integration

NOBLE QUALITY	INTEGRITY / CRUSADER	COURAGE / COMMANDER	DIPLOMACY / CHANCELLOR	INSPIRATION / BARD	OBJECTIVITY / TREASURER	RESPONSIBILITY / NAVIGATOR	DRIVE / JUDGE	DISCERNMENT / ARCHITECT
Applying personal discipline and willpower to achieve the objectives (P.7)	Focuses on asking the hard questions and seeking the truth	Focuses on 'walking the talk'	Focuses on unconditional love and compassion for self	Focuses on empathising with others and building bridges with them	Focuses on taking personal responsibility and having confidence in themselves	Focuses on being objective	Focuses on personal integrity and doing the honourable thing	Focuses on personal courage and spontaneity
Applying creativity to create a better world (C.6)	Focuses on being objective	Focuses on unconditional love and compassion for self	Focuses on 'walking the talk'	Focuses on personal courage and spontaneity	Focuses on personal integrity and doing the honourable thing	Focuses on asking the hard questions and seeking the truth	Focuses on taking personal responsibility and having confidence in themselves	Focuses on empathising with others and building bridges with them
Renegotiating contact between self and the outside world by aligning insight with constructive somatic expression (I.5)	Acting with honour	Focuses on empathising with others and building bridges with them	Focuses on personal courage and spontaneity	Focuses on 'walking the talk'	Focuses on asking the hard questions and seeking the truth	Focuses on personal integrity and doing the honourable thing	Focuses on being objective	Focuses on unconditional love and compassion for self
Turning insight into action (C.4)	Focuses on 'walking the talk'	Focuses on asking the hard questions and seeking the truth	Focuses on being objective	Focuses on taking personal responsibility and having confidence in themselves	Focuses on empathising with others and building bridges with them	Focuses on unconditional love and compassion for self	Focuses on personal courage and spontaneity	Focuses on personal integrity and doing the honourable thing
Integrating the Mirror into the self (P.3)	Focuses on personal courage and spontaneity	Focuses on personal integrity and doing the honourable thing	Focuses on taking personal responsibility and having confidence in themselves	Focuses on being objective	Focuses on unconditional love and compassion for self	Focuses on empathising with others and building bridges with them	Focuses on 'walking the talk'	Focuses on asking the hard questions and seeking the truth
Using creativity to create a more evolved self (C.2)	Focuses on empathising with others and building bridges with them	Acting with honour	Focuses on personal integrity and doing the honourable thing	Focuses on asking the hard questions and seeking the truth	Focuses on 'walking the talk'	Focuses on personal courage and spontaneity	Focuses on unconditional love and compassion for self	Focuses on being objective
Resolving the fundamental wound of the type by increasing awareness (I.1)	Focuses on unconditional love and compassion for self	Focuses on being objective	Focuses on asking the hard questions and seeking the truth	Focuses on personal integrity and doing the honourable thing	Focuses on personal courage and spontaneity	Focuses on 'walking the talk'	Focuses on empathising with others and building bridges with them	Focuses on taking personal responsibility and having confidence in themselves
Individual lives their own code of conduct (TRIGGER)	Focuses on personal integrity and doing the honourable thing	Focuses on personal courage and spontaneity	Building the bridges of understanding	Focuses on unconditional love and compassion for self	Focuses on being objective	Acting with honour	Focuses on asking the hard questions and seeking the truth	Focuses on 'walking the talk'

INTERNAL

TRIGGER

← TOWARDS INTEGRATION ←

TRIGGER	SHADOW QUALITY	CRUSADER — INTOLERANT/PUNITIVE	COMMANDER — VICTIM/DEPENDENCE	CHANCELLOR — INSECURITY/MANIPULATION	BARD — DELUSION/DECEPTION	TREASURER — ARROGANCE/DISASSOCIATION	NAVIGATOR — INFLEXIBLE/CONTROLLING	JUDGE — COMPETITIVE/BULLY	ARCHITECT — CONFUSION/PROCRASTINATION
C - 1	Individual breaks their own strict code of conduct	Loses personal integrity	Becomes a victim which leads to codependence	Becomes personally insecure and manipulates others	Builds castles in the sky (delusion and deceit)	Becomes personally arrogant and detaches from reality	Becomes inflexible and controlling of others	Becomes self-righteous and punitive	Becomes personally confused and procrastinates
P - 2	Personality uses avoidance and becomes delusional	Becomes competitive with and bullying of, others	Becomes personally confused and procrastinates	Builds castles in the sky (delusion and deceit)	Becomes personally insecure and manipulates others	Becomes inflexible and controlling of others	Becomes personally arrogant and detaches from reality	Becomes self-righteous and punitive	Becomes a victim which leads to codependence
	Moves into their Mirror's childlike willpower (introjection)	Becomes personally arrogant and detaches from reality	Builds castles in the sky (delusion and deceit)	Becomes personally confused and procrastinates	Becomes a victim which leads to co-dependence	Becomes self-righteous and punitive	Becomes competitive with, and bullying of, others	Becomes inflexible and controlling of others	Becomes personally insecure and manipulates others
C - 3	Uses deflection to avoid reality	Becomes inflexible and controlling of others	Becomes personally insecure and manipulates others	Becomes a victim which leads to co-dependence	Becomes personally confused and procrastinates	Becomes competitive with, and bullying of, others	Becomes self-righteous and punitive	Becomes personally arrogant and detaches from reality	Builds castles in the sky (delusion and deceit)
I - 4	Boundaries break down	Becomes personally confused and procrastinates	Becomes competitive with, and bullying of, others	Becomes personally arrogant and detaches from reality	Becomes inflexible and controlling others	Becomes personally insecure and manipulates others	Builds castles in the sky (delusion and deceit)	Becomes a victim which leads to co-dependence	Becomes self-righteous and punitive
C - 5	Uses projection	Becomes a victim which leads to co-dependence	Becomes self-righteous and punitive	Becomes inflexible and controlling of others	Becomes personally arrogant and detaches from reality	Builds castles in the sky (delusion and deceit)	Becomes personally insecure and manipulates others	Becomes personally confused and procrastinates	Becomes competitive with, and bullying of, others
P - 6	Internalises action	Becomes personally insecure and manipulates others	Becomes inflexible and controlling of others	Becomes self-righteous and punitive	Becomes personally arrogant and detaches from reality	Becomes personally confused and procrastinates	Becomes a victim which leads to co-dependence	Builds castles in the sky (delusion and deceit)	Becomes personally arrogant and detaches from reality
C - 7	Uses creativity to complete the delusion, distract them from real issues and give perceived substance to idea that the world is angry, dangerous and trying to kill them (disassociation)	Builds castles in the sky (delusion and deceit)	Becomes personally arrogant and detaches from reality	Becomes competitive with, and bullying of, others	Becomes self-righteous and punitive	Becomes a victim which leads to co-dependence	Becomes personally confused and procrastinates	Becomes personally insecure and manipulates others	Becomes inflexible and controlling of others

DISINTEGRATION – SURVIVAL REACTION

TOWARDS INTEGRATION

APPENDIX 5

Exploration of the Mirror

Exploring the Master and Mirror

I first met Maria when she was in her early twenties. Thin, intelligent and charming, she wore the latest fashion with style and grace. She could hold her own in academic discussions and was bright enough to have missed a year of school and attended university a year early. She was balanced, attentive and successful. Or so it seemed.

There was another side of Maria. With a little alcohol or stress, Maria would change from being logical and controlled into being vindictive and aggressive – verbally attacking people, especially those she loved, destroying prized possessions and even physically attacking her partner. When the damage had been done, Maria would flip back to her old self and apologise and try to clean up the mess. It was as if Maria had two completely different personalities. And it was as if each of these personalities were completely independent with opposite positions on virtually everything. Maria was confused. She knew that she had to do something about the situation if she was to keep her husband and her family. Until recently, scientists would have been at a loss to know what was creating this apparent split personality but now new research may be able to give us some answers.

Maria's situation might seem extreme, but the idea of each of us being made up of two autonomous personalities isn't unique to Maria and it isn't new.

The culturally ancient Central American Indians, the Maya Lenca, talk about each of us having two distinct personalities: a Master or Hero personality and a Mirror. Carl Jung's concept of individuation requires us to integrate the rejected side of ourselves, which he describes as our shadow. Many Eastern and Middle Eastern philosophies emphasise the importance of integrating the Yin and the Yang – the two opposite parts of us.

But while the concept is clear, the application of the concept into our daily lives is a little less accessible. In the past ten years excellent research has been conducted in this area, both in identifying the nature of the two personalities and in discovering how they impact on our lives.

Perhaps some of the best research in this area has been conducted by Frederic Schiffer MD, a US-based psychiatrist and researcher. His groundbreaking work on dual-brain psychology published in his book *Of Two Minds* (1998) documents the existence of two distinct personalities in all of us regardless of our mental and emotional health, and the impact on our life of having these two distinct personalities. He details case after case where, like Maria, individuals of different personalities, backgrounds, education levels and emotional maturity go through a process of discovering and beginning the work of integrating the two personalities that reside within them. The stories are both surprising and inspiring. In his own words:

The aim of dual-brain therapy [what NeuroPower would call working with your Mirror] is to mend the archaic, destructive ideas and emotions of the mind on the troubled side [Mirror] to teach it that it is safer and more valuable than it learned during some traumatic experiences, and to help it appropriately grieve and come to terms with its actual losses and disappointments so that it can appreciate its abundant gains... to teach patients how to recognise and listen for the mind in their troubled hemisphere, and then how to speak to it – out loud! I show patients also how to strengthen their more mature minds [Master] and, most importantly, how to improve the relationship between the two.

While the focus of Schiffer's work was on the process of discovering the identity, behaviours and emotions associated with both personalities, *NeuroPower* allows users immediate access and insight into both their Master and Mirror Neuro-Rational Types and outlines the process for healing and integrating them for personal growth, success, balance and creativity.

When I work with large corporations wanting to increase their employees' level of capacity I explain the interaction between the Master and Mirror using a matrix that plots the current level of Master and Mirror satisfaction. This in turn gives us a broad idea of our current level of capacity. All the motivation and will in the world does not help us achieve our personal or corporate objectives if we do not have the personal capacity to achieve them.

THE ROLE OF THE MASTER (WHAT YOU WANT)

The Master controls our self-identity (who we think we are), our language, our image (how we see ourselves) and our wish list (our wants). In the West, we are all employed for the value we bring to the marketplace – that is, the skills, capabilities and attitudes of our Master. The Master is our hero, able to achieve almost any task it is given. If our Master is getting what it wants, it is enthusiastic and talks highly of the situation. Society is generally only interested in our Master.

THE ROLE OF THE MIRROR (WHAT YOU NEED)

Our Mirror, however, expresses itself through our behaviour. If our Mirror is getting what it needs from a situation, we stay; if not, we leave. Our Mirror, regardless of our Master's effort to keep it in the closet, longs for expression and takes any opportunity to make itself heard.

HOW EMPOWERED IS YOUR MASTER? (WHAT YOU WANT)

To clarify what you want start the exercise by focusing on your Master. What is your Master's Genius? Does your current situation enable you to use this Genius? Score out of 10 the degree to which the situation (job, task or relationship) enables your Master to develop your Genius, take risks, and apply its knowledge. (For more information about your Genius, see Principle #2).

HOW SATISFIED IS YOUR MIRROR? (WHAT YOU NEED)

Now score out of 10 the degree to which the situation (job, task or relationship) addresses the specific focus of attention for your Mirror. For example, if you are an Architect, your Judge would be looking for tangible rewards, clear recognition, the ability to make an immediate difference and to have some fun.

When you have a score out of 10 for both your Master (Want) and Mirror (Need) multiply them for a 'best guess' figure, which represents your current capacity in percentage terms.

The intersection of our scores will place us in one quadrant on the capability matrix: trapped incompetents, short-term performers, transient moaners or long-term performers. An example of how this 'best guess' plotting works is detailed overleaf in Diagram A5.1, as is an in-depth explanation of the matrix's four quadrants.

APPLYING THE INSIGHT FROM THE CAPACITY MATRIX AT WORK

Leaders, managers and supervisors find this framework provides them with a very powerful way to increase the capacity of their workforce by attending to their employees' wants (which they can articulate) and their employees' needs (which they cannot articulate because their Mirror cannot speak).

APPLYING THE INSIGHT FROM THE CAPACITY MATRIX IN LIFE

This method of analysis also holds true for friendships, marriages, partnerships, projects and hobbies – any activity requiring your focus. For example, in your marriage you could be a short-term moaner or in a friendship you may be a trapped incompetent.

In my experience, many leaders, managers and high performing individuals in all walks of life report that understanding their Master and Mirror was an important plank to achieving personal performance, satisfaction and stability.

Earlier, I introduced Maria's situation. With an understanding of her Master (in her case an Architect) and her Mirror (in her case a Judge) the stage is set to explore what her Judge is needing but not getting. If the issue is the relationship, the Judge is kept carefully under wraps until the controlling Architect is drunk. Only then can the Judge come out of hiding and express the frustration of not getting the praise, excitement, recognition, intensity and reward it wants. An understanding of the Master and Mirror enabled a focused exploration of these issues, which lay below the conscious mind of the Architect.

Each of us works very hard to carefully craft an image that aligns with our ideal selves. This image is our Master Neuro-Rational Type. This Master tries to control every aspect of the way we represent ourselves to the world. This Master also creates a pressure cooker for our Mirror, who is trapped in our skin and just waiting for the Master to lose control. This internal battle causes many of the inner conflicts we all feel. This internal conflict often spills over into the outside world in spontaneous outbursts or uncontrollable behaviour. We are employed for the skills of our Master; we often get fired for the behaviour of our Mirror. We get married for the better; the worse is often the Mirror.

DIAGRAM A5.1 CAPACITY MATRIX

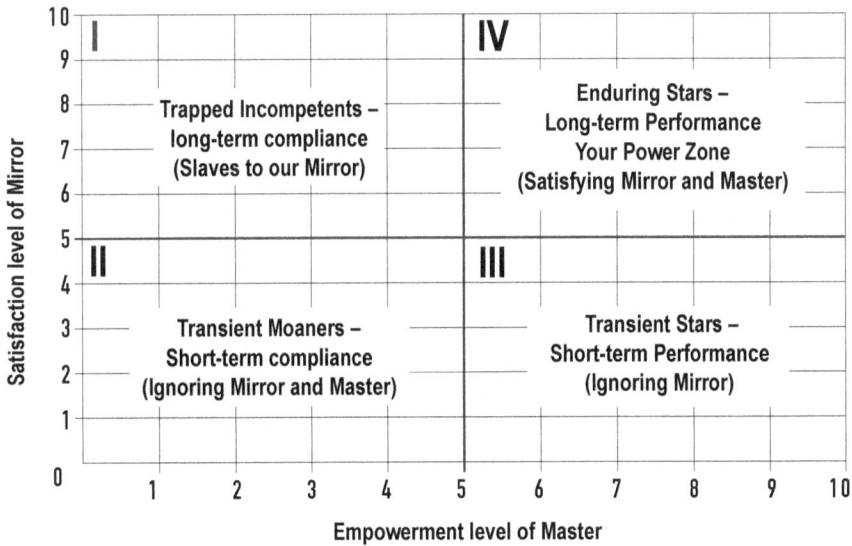

THE FOUR QUADRANTS EXPLAINED

1. Trapped Incompetents (Slaves to our Mirror)

If we are getting what we need but not what we want, we can easily become trapped incompetents. This happens because when we are getting what we need the Mirror will refuse to let us move, even if the Master finds the job dull and unrewarding. The Master will complain about the job and will refuse to study or improve skills that they don't want to improve. The Master will feel trapped. The Mirror will feel content.

2. Transient Stars (Ignoring our Mirror)

If we are getting what we want – but not what we need – our Master will enthusiastically learn new skills and capabilities, read and attend training, and talk highly of the role and organisation. Despite all this good press, however, we will move on because our Mirror simply isn't getting what it needs. When asked why we are moving on, confusion abounds because we can't even understand it ourselves.

3. Transient Moaners (Ignoring our Mirror and Master)

The Transient Moaner is simply an individual who is not getting either what they want or what they need. Both their Master and Mirror are unimpressed. They don't like it on any level; they will feel bored at a Master level and unsatisfied at the Mirror level. They will play politics, try to get fired or simply use the role as a stepping-stone before their real job emerges.

4. Enduring Stars: Your Power Zone (Satisfying our Mirror and Master)

The long-term performer is an individual whose Master is getting the challenge, opportunities and role they want and the Mirror is getting all they need. This is the individual's 'power zone'. From here most people get promoted with increased responsibility, money and praise. These people are the organisation's leaders and shape the organisation's positive culture. In employee terms, they are pure gold.

For example: If my Master is a Bard and my Mirror a Treasurer, I give the following scores out of 10:

Master Bard

Degree to which my Bard is able to create visions and heal: 8/10

Mirror Treasurer

Degree to which my Treasurer has order, security and money: 8/10

$8/10 \times 8/10 = 64/100$ or 64%.

In this situation I am running at about 64 per cent capacity (on average, even the most inspired individual can only maintain an average of about 75 per cent).

To understand personality, it is absolutely critical to understand the role both the Mirror and Master play and to personally and intimately know both characters. This takes good mirroring from friends, family and colleagues and requires the individual to develop the ability to self-observe.

One of the most frustrating and irritating aspects of the Mirror is that while everyone else in the world seems to be able to see your Mirror, at first you often won't be able to see it yourself.

I am sometimes employed to work with dysfunctional boards where Mirrors and Core Belief Profiles (see Chapters 11-18) are dominating proceedings. When I can see that the individuals' Masters are brilliant and mature but the Mirrors are less mature and holding court, I sometimes video the session for later viewing. The look of surprise on the faces of the Masters, when I show them their Mirrors is very amusing. They have no idea that they personally behave the way they do. Their Masters have no visibility of their Mirrors. And without the video they simply will not believe the feedback from associates. Like their Core Belief Profiles, they have to see their Mirror to believe it.

Capacity Management Quadrants

QUADRANT	TELLTALE INDICATORS	CAUSE	LEADERSHIP INSIGHT / ACTION REQUIRED
I Trapped Incompetents (Long-term compliance)	• Low staff turnover • Cynicism / game playing • Process driven • Constant high stress • Low staff morale • Low performance • Tall Poppy Syndrome	• Misalignment of corporate responsibilities and the individual ideal role • Non-empowered staff • Incompatible communication style • Want to leave but are not empowered enough to go	• Realignment of roles and responsibilities of staff • Leadership communication style tailored to the individual to build trust • Culture rejuvenation through more effective communication
II Transient Moaners (Short-term compliance)	• High staff turnover • Low effort • Constantly missed deadlines • Apathy / frustration	• Don't want to stay • Don't like the role • No conscious or unconscious reason to try harder • Want to keep their options open and earn as much as possible with as little effort as possible	• Start by re-aligning the staff's preferred role with the organisational structure • Understand staff unconscious profiles (Mirror profiles) and build a reward system based on 75 per cent of the staff • Introduce new coaching program and cultural emergency first aid

QUADRANT	TELLTALE INDICATORS	CAUSE	LEADERSHIP INSIGHT / ACTION REQUIRED
III Transient Stars (Short-term performers)	• High enthusiasm • High staff turnover • A company of stars • Highly competitive environment • Constant staff complaints about lack of recognition	• While there is compatibility between their role and the culture, the staff fundamentally feel uninvolved • Low unconscious loyalty • An over-inflated sense of achievement	• Overhaul the reward system based on the predominant unconscious profile of the team as a whole (Mirror profile) • Consider the most effective intrinsic and extrinsic reward systems • Introduce a new coaching program and cultural emergency first aid
IV Enduring Stars (Long-term Performance Your Power Zone)	• Low turnover and high discretionary effort • Genuine job satisfaction • Individuals and teams take responsibility for achieving agreed objectives	• Team members feel they are appropriately rewarded doing the right work and playing their preferred role • Team members are committed to putting in high discretionary effort and their conscious and unconscious frameworks align	• Manage the team composition • If the unconscious or conscious profile of 75 per cent of the team changes, so too must the culture and the reward system • Train leaders/ managers organisation-wide in the principle of how to enhance organisational capacity

APPLICATION: So What Can We Do?

The Seven Steps to Effectively Working with your Master and Your Mirror

1. Observe the Mirror in action – How old is your Mirror?

The first step is to recognise, observe and experience the Mirror. If the Mirror is a child it will have a tendency to over-dramatise and catastrophise events and see the worst in everything and everyone. It does this because it expects the old situation to be repeated and to create certainty. This often becomes a self-fulfilling prophecy.

2. Create an outlet for your Mirror and open negotiations

If you are high in I1 (Treasurers, Navigators, Judges and Crusaders), your Mirror will express itself through conversation with a trusted friend, family member or counsellor. If you are high in I2 (Bards, Chancellors, Architects and Commanders), your Mirror will express itself through the written word. (Automatic writing and personal journals are very powerful.) The key is to express the Mirror's point of view and then have the Master seriously assess it and either dismiss it or integrate it into its position. For all Mirrors a powerful technique is to have the Master or counsellor talk directly to the Mirror with explicit instructions about how the Mirror must behave.

3. Strengthen your Master

Your Master is your own internal hero. This hero needs to be strengthened into being a healthy leader who can guide and parent your Mirror. The Master needs to be strong enough to listen to the Mirror's concerns and emotional troubles without being dragged down into them.

To be effective the Master needs to be more grounded, more evolved, more responsible and less impulsive. To achieve this requires that the Master receive support, encouragement and training. Ironically, the Master will be at its strongest only when its adult Mirror joins it. Our true strength is only achieved when the Master has worked with the Mirror and the two function as a team.

4. Challenge the Mirror's Assumptions

The Mirror is absolutely convinced that whatever trauma it has received will be repeated. When this doesn't happen the Mirror becomes even more anxious, knowing that the inevitable has simply been delayed and probably amplified (an accumulation of dammed-up disaster is building). The Master must carefully and systematically assess if the Mirror has a good point or not. When healthy, the Mirror is a powerful and insightful ally that helps us make powerful and insightful decisions. The job of the Master is to determine if the Mirror is talking truth or gibberish.

5. Talk to your Mirror

To convince your Mirror to change is no different than persuading someone else to change – your Master, counsellor or therapist will need to use the same techniques. But successful persuasion is based more on the credibility of the persuader than the strength of the argument. The Master must be patient, polite, gentle and caring. The Master must be able to convince the Mirror that it cares, it understands and it can cope.

6. Manage the relationship between the two characters

Your Mirror and your Master have a special relationship, which, like all relationships, follows some principles (this internal relationship is often reproduced externally with partners, family and friends).

   a. *Firstly, they influence each other.* If we cannot see that, it is because we have not developed the ability to observe the Mirror in action. When we come out of discussions, for example, wondering why we said some things that we don't even believe, the Mirror has shown itself. We need to develop very keen insight into the Mirror and ways for it to be valued and to express itself so that it doesn't need to show up in uncontrollable outbursts.

   b. *Secondly, we need to look at the nature of the Master/Mirror relationship and determine where it sits on the continua of co-operation-antagonism, dominance-submission, parent-child and success-failure.* What you want is a loving and trusting relationship between the two. This might initially start as parent (Master) and child (Mirror), but move towards a collegial relationship of mutual understanding and respect.

c. Thirdly, the nature of the relationship will be influenced by the relative power of the Master and the Mirror. It is the job of the Master to ensure that it keeps ultimate control regardless of the payoffs. The Master is the hero not the victim of the paranoid Mirror.

7. Manage your Life so that the Master Gets what it Wants and the Mirror what it Needs

Your Master wants challenges, risk-taking to expand its comfort zone, new ideas, education, courses and 'great, big, hairy, audacious goals'. This needs to be balanced with your Mirror, which needs to be nurtured, persuaded into any change and reassured at every step of the way. The task of the individual is to balance the activities of life so that both characters are catered for, rather than wildly swinging from satisfying one to satisfying the other with one always unhappy and offside and ready to ambush the other.

Ultimately we want a constructive adult relationship based on mutual respect and harmony that can integrate the two opposing wisdoms in such a way that we get Courage with Integrity, Diplomacy with Responsibility, Inspiration with Objectivity and Enthusiasm with Discernment.

APPENDIX 6

Intelligence Compatibility Matrix

Intelligence Compatibility Matrix

Legend:
• = Least Compatible Combination
⠿ = Most Compatible Combination

Column groups: Recessive (C2, I1, I2, P2, C1, P1) · Most Dominant (C2, I1, I2, P2, C1, P1) · Dominant (C2, I1, I2, P2, C1, P1)

Row labels: Recessive C1, Dominant C1, Most Dominant C1, Recessive C2, Dominant C2, Most Dominant C2, Recessive P1, Dominant P1, Most Dominant P1, Recessive P2, Dominant P2, Most Dominant P2, Recessive I1, Dominant I1, Most Dominant I1, Recessive I2, Dominant I2, Most Dominant I2

APPENDIX 7

The Path of Integration
for each Neuro-Rational Type

The Path of Integration for the Crusader

LEVEL	1. AWARENESS		2. CLARITY		3. ACTION		4. ASSESSMENT	
	Step 1	Step 2	Step 3	Step 4	Step 5	Step 6	Step 7	Step 8
1. BEIGE	Survival	Survival	Survival	Survival	Survival	Survival	Survival	Survival
2. PURPLE	Modest	Charming	Reverent	Contemplative	Faithful	Self-Reliant	Loyal	Ethical
3. RED	Confronting	Negotiating	Self-Controlled	Independent	Protecting	Disciplined	Enthusiastic	Seeks Justice
4. BLUE	Inspirational	Diplomatic	Courageous	Discerning	Responsible	Objective	Driven	Seeks Integrity
5. ORANGE	Visionary	Strives for Esprit de Corps	Ingenious	Capable	Role Excellence	Specialist	Entrepreneurial	Strives For Excellence
6. GREEN	Liberating	Kind	Enabling	Unifying	Principled	Masters Systems	Motivational	Magnanimous
7. YELLOW	Empowering	Genuine	Harmonious	Strategic	Conquering	Expert	Enlivening	Benevolent

The Path of Integration for the Bard

LEVEL	1. AWARENESS		2. CLARITY		3. ACTION		4. ASSESSMENT	
	Step 1	Step 2	Step 3	Step 4	Step 5	Step 6	Step 7	Step 8
1. BEIGE	Survival	Survival	Survival	Survival	Survival	Survival	Survival	Survival
2. PURPLE	Ethical	Loyal	Self-Reliant	Faithful	Contemplative	Reverent	Charming	Modest
3. RED	Seeks Justice	Enthusiastic	Disciplined	Protecting	Independent	Self-Controlled	Negotiating	Confronting
4. BLUE	Seeks Integrity	Driven	Objective	Responsible	Discerning	Courageous	Diplomatic	Inspirational
5. ORANGE	Strives For Excellence	Entrepreneurial	Specialist	Role Excellence	Capable	Ingenious	Strives for Esprit de Corps	Visionary
6. GREEN	Magnanimous	Motivational	Masters Systems	Principled	Unifying	Enabling	Kind	Liberating
7. YELLOW	Benevolent	Enlivening	Expert	Conquering	Strategic	Harmonious	Genuine	Empowering

The Path of Integration for the Chancellor

LEVEL	1. AWARENESS		2. CLARITY		3. ACTION		4. ASSESSMENT	
	Step 1	Step 2	Step 3	Step 4	Step 5	Step 6	Step 7	Step 8
1. BEIGE	Survival	Survival	Survival	Survival	Survival	Survival	Survival	Survival
2. PURPLE	Loyal	Ethical	Faithful	Self-Reliant	Reverent	Contemplative	Modest	Charming
3. RED	Enthusiastic	Seeks Justice	Protecting	Disciplined	Self-Controlled	Independent	Confronting	Negotiating
4. BLUE	Driven	Seeks Integrity	Responsible	Objective	Courageous	Discerning	Inspirational	Diplomatic
5. ORANGE	Entrepreneurial	Strives For Excellence	Role Excellence	Specialist	Ingenious	Capable	Visionary	Strives For Esprit de Corps
6. GREEN	Motivational	Magnanimous	Principled	Masters	Enabling	Unifying	Liberating	Kind
7. YELLOW	Enlivening	Benevolent	Conquering	Expert	Harmonious	Strategic	Empowering	Genuine

The Path of Integration for the Commander

LEVEL	1. AWARENESS		2. CLARITY		3. ACTION		4. ASSESSMENT	
	Step 1	Step 2	Step 3	Step 4	Step 5	Step 6	Step 7	Step 8
1. BEIGE	Survival	Survival	Survival	Survival	Survival	Survival	Survival	Survival
2. PURPLE	Self-Reliant	Faithful	Ethical	Loyal	Charming	Modest	Contemplative	Reverent
3. RED	Disciplined	Protecting	Seeks Justice	Enthusiastic	Negotiating	Confronting	Independent	Self-Controlled
4. BLUE	Objective	Responsible	Seeks Integrity	Driven	Diplomatic	Inspirational	Discerning	Courageous
5. ORANGE	Specialist	Role Excellence	Strives For Excellence	Entrepreneurial	Strives for Esprit de Corps	Visionary	Capable	Ingenious
6. GREEN	Masters	Principled	Magnanimous	Motivational	Kind	Liberating	Unifying	Enabling
7. YELLOW	Expert	Conquering	Benevolent	Enlivening	Genuine	Empowering	Strategic	Harmonious

The Path of Integration for the Architect

LEVEL	1. AWARENESS		2. CLARITY		3. ACTION		4. ASSESSMENT	
	Step 1	Step 2	Step 3	Step 4	Step 5	Step 6	Step 7	Step 8
1. BEIGE	Survival	Survival	Survival	Survival	Survival	Survival	Survival	Survival
2. PURPLE	Faithful	Self-Reliant	Loyal	Ethical	Modest	Charming	Reverent	Contemplative
3. RED	Protecting	Disciplined	Enthusiastic	Seeks Justice	Confronting	Negotiating	Self-Controlled	Independent
4. BLUE	Responsible	Objective	Driven	Seeks Integrity	Inspirational	Diplomatic	Courageous	Discerning
5. ORANGE	Role Excellence	Specialist	Entrepreneurial	Strives for Excellence	Visionary	Strives for Esprit de Corps	Ingenious	Capable
6. GREEN	Principled	Masters Systems	Motivational	Magnanimous	Liberating	Kind	Enabling	Unifying
7. YELLOW	Conquering	Expert	Enlivening	Benevolent	Empowering	Genuine	Harmonious	Strategic

The Path of Integration for the Navigator

LEVEL	1. AWARENESS			2. CLARITY			3. ACTION			4. ASSESSMENT
	Step 1	Step 2	Step 3	Step 4	Step 5	Step 6	Step 7	Step 8
1. BEIGE	Survival	Survival	Survival	Survival	Survival	Survival	Survival	Survival
2. PURPLE	Contemplative	Reverent	Charming	Modest	Ethical	Loyal	Self-Reliant	Faithful
3. RED	Independent	Self-Controlled	Negotiating	Confronting	Seeks Justice	Enthusiastic	Disciplined	Protecting
4. BLUE	Discerning	Courageous	Diplomatic	Inspirational	Seeks Integrity	Driven	Objective	Responsible
5. ORANGE	Capable	Ingenious	Strives for Esprit de Corps	Visionary	Strives For Excellence	Entrepreneurial	Specialist	Role Excellence
6. GREEN	Unifying	Enabling	Kind	Liberating	Magnanimous	Motivational	Masters Systems	Principled
7. YELLOW	Strategic	Harmonious	Genuine	Empowering	Benevolent	Enlivening	Expert	Conquering

The Path of Integration for the Treasurer

LEVEL	1. AWARENESS			2. CLARITY	3. ACTION		4. ASSESSMENT	
	Step 1	Step 2	Step 3	Step 4	Step 5	Step 6	Step 7	Step 8
1. BEIGE	Survival	Survival	Survival	Survival	Survival	Survival	Survival	Survival
2. PURPLE	Reverent	Contemplative	Modest	Charming	Loyal	Ethical	Faithful	Self-Reliant
3. RED	Self-Controlled	Independent	Confronting	Negotiating	Enthusiastic	Seeks Justice	Protecting	Disciplined
4. BLUE	Courageous	Discerning	Inspirational	Diplomatic	Driven	Seeks Integrity	Responsible	Objective
5. ORANGE	Ingenious	Capable	Visionary	Strives For Esprit de Corps	Entrepreneurial	Strives for Excellence	Role Excellence	Specialist
6. GREEN	Enabling	Unifying	Liberating	Kind	Motivational	Magnanimous	Principled	Masters Systems
7. YELLOW	Harmonious	Strategic	Empowering	Genuine	Enlivening	Benevolent	Conquering	Expert

The Path of Integration for the Architect

LEVEL	1. AWARENESS			2. CLARITY	3. ACTION		4. ASSESSMENT	
	Step 1	Step 2	Step 3	Step 4	Step 5	Step 6	Step 7	Step 8
1. BEIGE	Survival	Survival	Survival	Survival	Survival	Survival	Survival	Survival
2. PURPLE	Charming	Modest	Contemplative	Reverent	Self-Reliant	Faithful	Ethical	Loyal
3. RED	Negotiating	Confronting	Independent	Self-Controlled	Disciplined	Protecting	Seeks Justice	Enthusiastic
4. BLUE	Diplomatic	Inspirational	Discerning	Courageous	Objective	Responsible	Seeks Integrity	Driven
5. ORANGE	Strives For Esprit de Corps	Visionary	Capable	Ingenious	Specialist	Role Excellence	Strives For Excellence	Entrepreneurial
6. GREEN	Kind	Liberating	Unifying	Enabling	Masters Systems	Principled	Magnanimous	Motivational
7. YELLOW	Genuine	Empowering	Strategic	Harmonious	Expert	Conquering	Benevolent	Enlivening

APPENDIX 8

NeuroPower and its Synergy with Maya Lenca Philosophy of Personality, Wellness and Illness

BY LEONEL ANTONIO CHÉVEZ, 2006

NeuroPower is a body of knowledge or 'Grand Theory' as defined by Skinner (1985), with Grounded Theory as its methodology. *NeuroPower* was developed by Peter Burow over the last fifteen years and is increasingly used as a propriety tool in the business, wellness and professional development fields. *NeuroPower* incorporates major psychological theories that are cohesively interlocked with philosophical approaches that give substance and practical applicability to the system as a whole. As a theory, it is heavily based on observation and ongoing research for its refinement. This process guarantees that the model grows and incorporates current scientific and philosophical thinking that mirrors the evolution of human thought.

NeuroPower is integrative in nature; that is, it incorporates key frameworks, theories, philosophies and spiritual concepts from key cultures around the globe. Among these philosophies is the indigenous world view of the Maya Lenca tradition (Chevez, 1989; Stanislawski, n/d). The Maya Lenca is one of several Maya tribes with a small number of living members. Their philosophy proposes a systemic view on the wellness and illness equation. In the Maya Lenca land (eastern El Salvador), a Maya Medicine System (MMS) has been practised for millennia and has been documented recently by Alvarez (1990). The survival of some aspects of MMS was a result of the El Salvadoran civil war (1980–1992); a civil conflict characterised by intensive fighting, internal displacement of the population and a virtual collapse of government health services provided in small villages (WHO, 2002; Arnson, 1993; Johnston, 1995; Byrne, 1996; Boland, 2001). Under siege and isolated, many indigenous communities reverted to their ancient methodologies of health promotion, prevention and treatment.

This paper explores the assumptions on wellness and illness as posited by *NeuroPower* and the Maya Medicine System and examines the relative synergy and merits that both approaches have when applied to human health and wellbeing.

The first aspect to be explored is the perspective of the Maya Medicine System (MMS) regarding human personality, health and wellbeing. This indigenous medical approach suggests that in humanity, there is a well organised and definable set of human characters (personalities), with a gradient from the lowest possible state of being to the highest and noblest form of existence (Chévez, 1989). This philosophical concept is elegantly explained in the '*Cantares del Pinol*', a collection of recitals and philosophical enunciations from the elders of the Lenca land. In this document, it is suggested that the universe is stratified in three main levels. In addition, it is proposed that humans act as fuses between these three levels. These levels and sub-dimensions are described in the following chart.

MMS describes the three domains in the following ways:

The Upper World	The Middle World	The Under World
Divided into thirteen levels of consciousness not affected by the laws of Newtonian physics. Seven of these are accessible to humans. These are higher order thinking mental planes. To access these levels the individual must evolve into one of the eight (Bacabs) or 'bearers of the universe'. These can be referred to as archetypes.	The physical and earthly plane, affected by the laws of Newtonian physics. This is the plane where humans are required to co-create. They are bestowed with six endo-dynamic energies (Coyopits) that give rise to human personality. Failure to access these solar forces leads to the human personality disintegrating into an unhealthy and primitive state (Xibalba).	Divided into nine levels; is the reservoir of a large proportion of mental and physical ailments. This is called Xibalba and is the place of fear. Disintegrated humans enter the state of Xibalba where key conditions are experienced. Among these are: fear, rage, envy, jealousy, shame, delusion, self-harm, criminal behaviour, and many more.

The notion of a three-tiered universe in which human existence takes place is a firm belief among traditional Mesoamerican indigenous sages. This philosophy goes beyond the predominantly Western thought of linear existence where reality and existence is split in two factors such as good and bad, light and darkness, good and evil. Furthermore, this proposition disagrees with the notion of aiming at living in the 'here and now' as the ultimate and noblest goal in life. The MMS proposes that humans act as conduits that stream the universal forces across the three universal levels, equalising the universe as whole. This implies that as humans we are co-creators and not just passive creatures without any effect on our reality. The three tiers proposed by MMS are also reflected in the *NeuroPower* theory. *NeuroPower* describes these three domains in the following ways:

The Upper World	The Middle World	The Under World
NeuroPower proposes that these are levels of consciousness. The first eight of these levels can be understood through concepts such as the theory of Spiral Dynamics by Cowan and Beck, 1996 (based on the research by Dr Clare Graves, 1974) and integral theory by Ken Wilber, 2000. (Burow, 2005, pp. 153-196; 485-565)	NeuroPower describes six thinking functions that when combined in specific groups of three, produce an adult Neuro-Rational Type with the capacity to co-create and access noble qualities. The remaining three thinking functions that are not part of the Neuro-Rational Type create the individual's Mirror profile. (Burow, 2005, pp. 23-150)	NeuroPower describes the process of personality disintegration which collapses down to nine predictable amygdala responses (Neuro-Limbic Types) that restrict the individual's understanding of the world through applying Core Beliefs. It is labelled as the low road and is the seat of many disorders contained in the DSM-IV (Diagnostic and Statistical Manual of Mental Disorders, Fourth Edition). (Burow, 2005, pp. 455-484)

Burow, PL (2005) *NeuroPower*

NeuroPower theory echoes the pioneering thinking that suggests that human consciousness is not fixed and that as humans we are born free willed, so that we can live life fully, accessing all levels of consciousness and evolving as a race.

For example, in 1974 Dr Caleb Rosado published an article in *The Futurist*. The title was 'Human Nature Prepares for a Momentous Leap'. His article dealt with the key points at the core of Spiral Dynamics which are summarised as follows:

1. Human nature is not static, nor is it finite. Human nature changes as the conditions of existence change, thus forging new systems. Yet, the older systems stay with us.

2. When a new system or level is activated, we change our psychology and rules for living to adapt to those new conditions.

3. We live in a potentially open system of values with an infinite number of modes of living available to us. There is no final state to which we must all aspire. [Here is where Graves differed from Maslow and most other psychologists. Maslow, before his death, told Graves that he (Graves) was correct and he (Maslow) was wrong in thinking of human development as a closed state.]

4. An individual, a company, or an entire society can respond positively only to those managerial principles, motivational appeals, educational formulas, and legal or ethical codes that are appropriate to the current level of human existence.

5. A spiral vortex best depicts this emergence of human systems as they evolve through levels of increasing complexity. Each upward turn of the spiral marks the awakening of a more elaborated version on top of what already exists. The human spiral, then, consists of a coiled string of value systems, world views, and mindsets, each the product of its times and conditions. In other words, new times produce new minds.

From: Value Based Management. http://www.valuebasedmanagement.net/ methods_ graves_spiral_dynamics.html

The above excerpt agrees with the *NeuroPower* and MMS theories that see humans as an open system that evolves as it accesses greater complexity of consciousness. It is not surprising that when studying different periods of humanity, most cultures around the world present similarities that have emerged as a result of evolving into humanhood.

THE CORPORATE MIND AND THE INDIGENOUS PHILOSOPHY?

As mentioned before, *NeuroPower* is the end product of Peter Burow's decades of work as a leadership, communication and strategy consultant within Australia's leading corporate and government sectors. This corporate expertise and experience gave him the resources needed for pursuing his personal quest into studying the encoded insight in the ancient stories and philosophical arguments within several ancient cultures and how these insights dovetail with modern rational psychological and bio-medical concepts. From the Celtic traditions, the Buddhist traditions and the Maya Lenca traditions, among others, Burow concluded that these cultures have an inherent assumption that posits that human thinking and behaviour are major determinants of health and illness; and most importantly, that thinking and behaviour changes as the human personality integrates or disintegrates (Burow, 2005).

Having tested his initial concepts within the Australian corporate sector, in the late eighties, Burow's exploration of ancient philosophies, myths and folklore led him to undertake further in-depth research into specific elements of the Maya Lenca theory of Coyopits (six endo-dynamic energies). The indigenous view is that from the twenty energies or solar emanations of their 'Tzolkin' (gestational calendar), six are innately accessed by every human being. The access or lack thereof, gives rise to human personalities, which are visibly distinct and classifiable. Burow's theory (*NeuroPower*) was that individuals have access to six key Intelligences; the combination of these six Intelligences gives rise to eight personality profiles that enable humanity to operate in a healthy, rational and creative manner (Burow, 2005). When examined more closely, the Maya Lenca describe the energies using specific animals that best convey the characteristics of each energy; that is, armadillo, rabbit, jaguar, turtle, monkey and eagle. Burow uses modern concepts of neurobiology and developmental psychology and has codified these six Intelligences as P1, C1, P2, I2, I1, C2 (Burow, 2006). Once these components are harmonised, the essence of the two (*NeuroPower* and MMS) are interchangeable.

Both *NeuroPower* and MMS frameworks also have clear alignment when the six energies or Intelligences are combined, to create the higher order Neuro-Rational Type where creativity, health and progress take place.

The second aspect of alignment between *NeuroPower* and MMS revolves around the Maya Lenca philosophy that proposes that the human being 'Antawinikil' (the human self), is a composite of two distinct, independent, free willed persons in one dual system (each of these two parts relies on three Intelligences). The existence of the 'human self' as a dual unit is repeatedly represented in the Maya philosophy such as in the stories of the hero twins and their trials in the underworld written in the *Popol Vuh*, the sacred book of the Maya, and in several other stories from the Maya region. Searching for corroboration and to examine the depth of these concepts, Burow travelled to eastern El Salvador where ninety-year-old elder woman and Maya Medicine Doctor (MMD) Francisca B.G.R contributed to his work by sharing key concepts that she preserves from her Maya tradition. Burow argues that her contribution brought vital clues to the grand theory of a dual human unit.

Francisca suggested to Burow that the human self has access to a dynamic energy system that enables the individual to have one of eight personalities that are endowed with the six intelligences. These eight Neuro-Rational Types are represented in Maya philosophy by the four sky bearers (the four Bacabs and their consorts). In order to confirm this hypothesis, Burow explored, documented and applied drugless MMS techniques that enabled him to reveal and talk to each side of the personality. This technique is what he calls the Master Mirror Integration Process (MMIP). It is an ancient technique that has been practised by the natives for thousands of years as part of their medical system. More recently, it was also used successfully with war-traumatised individuals treated by the indigenous doctors in the isolated communities.

Once again, pre-existing data from Burow's research on the existence of two distinct personalities within the self, correlates harmoniously with the MMS assumption of the Master profile and the Mirror profile within the self.

The last aspect to be considered is the MMS theory regarding the psychopathologies or illnesses stemming from personality. *NeuroPower* describes this as the disintegrated self. The indigenous Maya Lenca elder states that while there are eight co-creative 'healthy' personalities, there are nine that serve as indicators of ill health.

In the following extract from Spence's version of the Popol Vuh (1908, pp. 29-31) there is a short account of how the hero twins faced trials in the houses of the underworld. This account is based on the Maya Quiché tradition. The Maya Lenca version, however, focuses more specifically on the physical and mental experiences of the twins while being tested by the nine lords of the night. The story incorporates several levels of meaning. At a basic level it tells us of the nine different trials; it emphasises the constant state of fear and state of survival, as well as the polarisation of good and bad. These nine trials are what are commonly called 'causality consciousness'.

> Thus they [the twins] did not salute the mannikins on their arrival at the Xibalban court, nor did they sit upon the red-hot stone. They even passed scatheless through the first ordeal of the House of Gloom. The Xibalbans were furious, and their wrath was by no means allayed when they found themselves beaten at the game of ball to which they had challenged the brothers [twins]. Then Hun-Came and Vukub-Came ordered the twins to bring them four bouquets of flowers, asking the guards of the royal gardens to watch most carefully, and committed Hun-Ahpu and Xbalanque to the 'House of Lances' the second ordeal where the lancers were

directed to kill them. The brothers, however, had at their beck and call a swarm of ants, which entered the royal gardens on the first errand, and they succeeded in bribing the lancers. The Xibalbans, white with fury, ordered that the owls, the guardians of the gardens, should have their lips split, and otherwise showed their anger at their third defeat.

Then came another ordeal in the 'House of Cold'. Here the heroes escaped death by freezing by being warmed with burning pine-cones. In the fourth and fifth ordeals they were equally lucky, for they passed a night each in the 'House of Tigers' and the 'House of Fire' without injury. But at the sixth ordeal misfortune overtook them in the 'House of Bats', Hun-Ahpu's head being cut off by Camazotz, 'Ruler of Bats', who suddenly appeared from above.

The beheading of Hun-Ahpu does not, however, appear to have terminated fatally, but owing to the unintelligible nature of the text at this juncture, it is impossible to ascertain in what manner he was cured of such a lethal wound. This episode is followed by an assemblage of all the animals, and another contest at ball-playing, after which the brothers emerged uninjured from all the ordeals of the Xibalbans.

But in order to further astound their 'hosts', Hun-Ahpu and Xbalanque confided to two sorcerers named Xulu and Pacaw that the Xibalbans had failed because the animals were not on their side, and directing them what to do with their bones, they stretched themselves upon a funeral pile and died together. Their bones were beaten to powder and thrown into the river, where they sank, and were transformed into young men. On the fifth day they reappeared like men-fishes, and on the sixth in the form of ragged old men, dancing, burning and restoring houses, killing and restoring each other to life, with other wonders. The princes of Xibalba, hearing of their skill, requested them to exhibit their magical powers, which they did by burning the royal palace and restoring it, killing and resuscitating the king's dog, and cutting a man in pieces, and bringing him to life again. The monarchs of Xibalba, anxious to experience the novel sensation of a temporary death, requested to be slain and resuscitated. They were speedily killed, but the brothers refrained from resuscitating their arch-enemies.

Announcing their real names, the brothers proceeded to punish the princes of Xibalba. The game of ball was forbidden them, they were to perform menial tasks, and only the beasts of the forest were they to hold in vassalage. They appear after this to achieve a species of doubtful distinction as plutonic deities or demons. They are described as warlike, ugly as owls, inspiring evil and discord.

Their faces were painted black and white to show their faithless nature.

The Maya Lenca version of the trials of the underworld varies from the Maya Quiché version in two ways. Firstly, the Maya Lenca recognises nine chambers (Xibalba), and each one of these is ruled by one lord of the night (Bolontiku). Secondly, the Maya Lenca version is more medically centred as observed in the following excerpt from the elder Francisca's account.

'And then the twins descended into Xibalba. There, they faced the nine lords of the night, each one with its own trial that tormented the mind and the body of the twins. There, in the nine chambers of the underworld, there in the place of fear is where pain and despair flourishes and consumes the flesh, the mind and the soul; there in the depth of Xibalba is where the nine fearful calamities of human kind spring' (Francisca Guevara Romero, MMD).

The existence of the nine phantasmagoric characters (Bolontiku) has been explored in various contexts by Mayanists and researchers who have corroborated and oftentimes found the encoded presence of these characters within the counts of days and other iconographic works in Mesoamerican art (Aveni, 1980; Schele, 1991, 1993; Frumker, 1993, 1998; Thomson, 1929, 1942, 1971).

As explained before, the Lenca views regarding these nine characters are less sacred; the Lenca see them merely as nine states of psycho-somatic illnesses. The indigenous medicine practitioner argues that the Xibalba System - XS (the Maya Lenca nine-ill profiles), is a deficiency centred tool to locate and classify psychological illness in individuals who have disintegrated personalities, which in turn translates into mental and physical health problems.

'One cannot say that experiencing cancer has any good for the individual. The same can be said if a person happens to remain in any of the nine states; they are illness, they are described as nine hells in our philosophy.' (Francisca Guevara Romero, MMD).

Burow's interpretation using modern biology, physiology and neurobiological concepts is that the Maya Medicine System is referring to the states of dis-ease and unhelpful behaviours experienced by humans when operating from the fear response triggered by the amygdala when under perceived threat (Burow, 2005). After exploring the philosophical basis of this proposition, Burow went on to research how the nine states of unhealthy self are clustered, giving rise to his work on *Core Beliefs*. In this work, he presents a comprehensive explanation regarding the Neuro-Limbic Types (NLTs) stemming from the fear response which is a time when the higher brain is disengaged and therefore behaviour becomes irrational and reactive rather than rational and proactive. His contribution to the in-depth study of key aspects of the Maya Medicine system saw him awarded a Diploma in Maya Medicine issued by the indigenous council of the Lencas. The award was presented by one of the last Maya medicine practitioners who supported Burow's ideas and empirical research.

By incorporating this insight as a subsystem within *NeuroPower*, Burow has provided a clear and logical mapping of human possibility, for full, potential transformation to the higher self, the experience of all types and the trials ahead when taking the low road. The theory of *NeuroPower* as presented by Burow is quantum friendly and does not subscribe to deterministic views of fate, influenced by unknown forces on the human destiny. *NeuroPower* provides the instruction manual for the 'software' that each one of us possesses within the 'self'. It is an attempt to explain the infinite potential within us; the aspect of humanity that due to suppression, repression, trauma, persecution, censure and many other causes, has been demoted to the depth of oblivion. *NeuroPower* reacquaints and guides us on how to access and use our minds so that we can tap into the wider matrix to bring about co-creative processes in our lives. It attempts to do this by means of processes that transform our bio-psychosocial existence into nobility.

NeuroPower is an integrative platform and is an integrally informed system. Similarly to MMS, *NeuroPower* suggests that right and wrong are subjectively perceived, and that these two aspects are essential parts that make the complete whole. Being whole is being free. In this state of wholeness, the individual has true free will to bring the highest or the lowest part of the self into the world. *NeuroPower* provides the navigation chart, road signs and landmarks to alert and inform us not only about our personality, but most importantly, it tells us where we are in the journey of our life of fulfilment.

In conclusion, this paper has explored *NeuroPower* and the Maya Medicine System (MMS) as viewed by the Lencas of El Salvador. It has compared the points of similarities in relation to the formation and definition of human personality, personal integration, disintegration and human health.

It is concluded that *NeuroPower* makes a significant contribution to understanding humanity by contextualising ancient concepts in a rational and contemporary language and comprehensive framework, applicable to health and human development. Burow's work has been credited with the utmost respect and recognition from the Maya Lenca elders, colleagues, and leaders in the corporate world. *NeuroPower* is an essential resource for anyone studying philosophy, developmental psychology, health, human behaviour, human resources management, and human consciousness.

REFERENCES

Alvarez, E.A. (1990). Community Study on Maya Medicine Doctors. ENLACE, Unp.

Arnson, Cynthia (1993). El Salvador, Accountability and Human Rights: The Report of the UN Commission on the Truth for El Salvador. America's Watch, NY.

Aveni, A. (1980). Skywatchers of Ancient Mexico, University of Texas Press.

Beck, D. E. & Cowan, C.C. (1996). Spiral Dynamics. Blackwell Pub.

Boland, R. (2001). Culture and Customs of El Salvador. Westport, Conn.: Greenwood Press.

Byrne, H. (1996). El Salvador's Civil War: A Study of Revolution. Boulder, Colo.: Lynne Rienner Publishers.

Burow, P. L. (2005). NeuroPower, Life editions.

Burow, P. L. (2005). Core Beliefs, Burow and Associates P/L.

Burow, P.L. (2005). Personality and Performance, Burow and Associates P/L.

Chevez, L. A. (1989). Cantares del Pinol, ENLACE, Unp.

Frumker, B. (1993). 'Wuk Ah, The Fourth Lord of the Night', Texas Notes on Precolumbian Art, Writing and Culture, No. 51, March.

Frumker, B. (1999). 'Nights Errant: A Look at Wayward Lords of the Night', Research Reports on Ancient Maya Writing 43, Center for Maya Research, Washington DC.

Guevara, R. F. B. (1989). Interviews series on Maya Medicine, Unp.

Goetz, D. and Grisworld, M. (1954). POPOL VUH: from Adrián Recino's translation from Quiché into Spanish.

Johnstone, I. (1995). Rights and Reconciliation: UN Strategies in El Salvador. Boulder, Colo.: Lynne Reinner Publishers.

Keoke, E.D. and Porterfield, K. M. (2001). Encyclopedia of American Indian Contributions to the World: 15,000 years of inventions and innovations. Facts of File.

Spence, L. (1908). The Popol Vuh: The Mythic and Heroic Sagas of the Kichés of Central America. Published by David Nutt, at the Sign of the Phoenix, Long Acre, London.

Schele, L. (1991). Workbook for the 1991 Workshop on Maya Hieroglyphic Writing, with Commentary on the Inscriptions of Bird-Jaguar of Yaxchilan, Art Department, University of Texas.

Schele, L. (1992). Nikolai Grube and Federico Fahsen, 'The Lunar Series in Classic Maya Inscriptions: New Observation and Interpretations', Texas Notes on Precolumbian Art, Writing and Culture, No. 29, October 1992.

Skinner, Q. (Ed) (1985). The Return of Grand Theory in the Human Sciences. Kindle.

Thompson, J. E. (1929). 'Maya Chronology: Glyph G of the Lunar Series', American Anthropologist n. s., 31, 1929: pp. 22-31.

Thompson, J. E S. (1942). 'Observations of Glyph G of the Lunar Series', Notes on Middle American Archaeology and Ethnology, No. 7, July 25, 1942.

Thompson, J. S. (1950). Maya Hieroglyphic Writing: An Introduction, Third edition, University of Oklahoma Press, 1971 (first edition 1950).

Value Based Management. Net retrieved from: http://www.valuebasedmanagement.net/methods_graves_spiral_dynamics.html on 12/09/06.

WHO (2002). Health in the Americas, 2002 edition. Washington, D.C.: Pan American Health

Organization, Pan American Sanitary Bureau, Regional Office of the World Health Organization.

Wilber, K. (2000). A Theory of Everything: Gateway.

Please source this document as follows:

Chevez, L. A. (2006). The Human Operating System, *NeuroPower* and its Synergy with Maya Lenca Philosophy of Personality, Wellness and Illness.

APPENDIX 9

The Celtic Cross

THE TRANSFORMATION CYCLE AS SHOWN SYMBOLICALLY BY THE CELTIC CROSS

Symbols can be profound expressions of human nature that simultaneously speak to our intellect, our hearts and spirit. They can represent human communication simultaneously at its most primitive and its most evolved. It is primitive in that it is one of the earliest means of communicating. It is evolved in that symbols take on meaning and power over time and through usage until they encapsulate complex concepts and meanings at a deeply unconscious level.

Since all human communication involves the reduction of subjective interpretations of perceived reality, symbolism is both the purest and the crudest means of communication. For example, you could refer to a specific form of canine, say a Chihuahua, which brings to mind specific images. Alternatively, you could refer to the generic 'dog' in which case a wider variety of imagery would be evoked. The Platonic concept of a 'World of Forms' suggests that there exists an archetypal 'dog' from which all other dogs are merely shadowy representations. Symbols, therefore, can represent concepts and processes in a whole form without the reductionist conceptualisation necessary in verbal communication. The Celtic cross is one of the oldest, most powerful and most pervasive symbols and is used to this day, as a tombstone, to enable us to touch a deeper part of ourselves and to interpret the complex emotions associated with death.

Diagram A9.1 Transformation Cycle

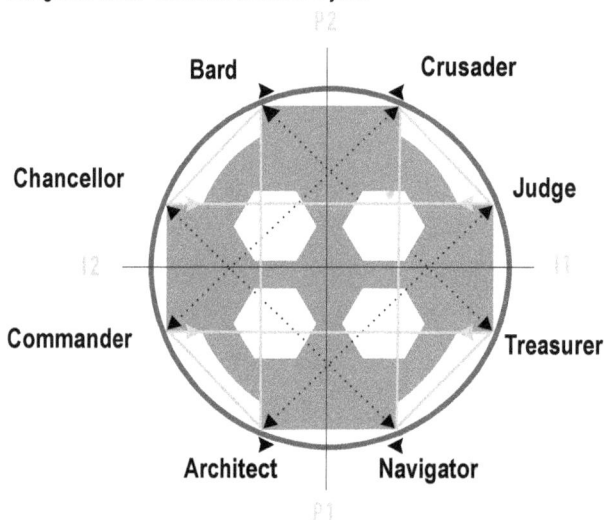

The Swiss psychologist Dr Carl Gustav Jung interpreted symbolism and mythology as expressions of our collective unconscious which is the seat of those instinctive

Diagram A9.2
Transformation Cycle Points

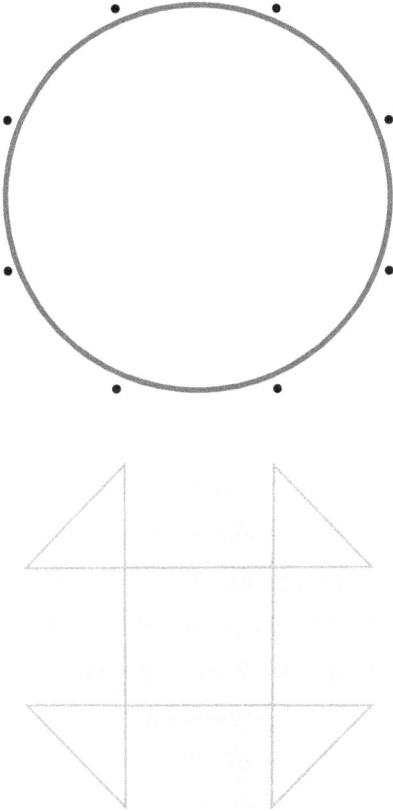

patterns of thought and behaviour that millennia of human experience have shaped into what we now recognise as emotions and values. Furthermore, myths are symbolic journeys and their complex characters represent our ego on a mission to incorporate its strengths and weaknesses through personal integration.

I believe the Celtic cross represents our collective journey towards integration, which is the heart and soul of Celtic psychology told through the hero's quest (Rowan, 2003). What is the hero's quest in Celtic mythology? It is the hard road of change and integration. The hero faces opponents from this world and the other in a battle to make the world a better place for himself and his people, and to bring about justice. The hero has only one way to succeed in this journey, and that is to grow and fulfil the noble aspects of his being. For this reason the Celtic cross is an ideal symbol for this work.

The Celtic cross is made up of two simple geometric shapes, a circle and a cross. The circle is the Celtic symbol of femininity while the cross is the Celtic symbol of masculinity.

The circle is equally broken into eight points (see Diagram A9.2). At a literal level of interpretation, these eight points symbolise the sequential nature of the corporate transformation process. This talks to us about the power of the seasons and the constant unfolding of life in a structured, predictable and yet constantly fresh way.

Of the eight Celtic personalities, the four types with male creativity, the Crusader, the Bard, the Architect and the Navigator, follow the points on the circle's circumference as their personal path of transformation. This may be because the Master profile has already integrated C2, which was considered by the Celts to be a male expression of creativity. Transformation requires the integration of female creativity which is achieved by moving either clockwise or anti-clockwise around the circle.

If, however, the Master profile has already integrated C1, Commander, Chancellor, Treasurer or Judge, which was considered by the Celts to be a female expression of creativity, transformation requires the integration of male creativity which is achieved by moving through the points of the cross.[1] Follow the arrows on Diagram A9.1.

The cross also represents the *Four Faces of Truth* and the true nature of polarities (see Diagram A9.1).

In terms of the integration process, our life quest is to integrate all aspects of truth into one comprehensive viewpoint. This requires the quester to grow and to become a full and complete being, with an understanding of the true nature of themselves and the world.

In practical terms, the Celtic cross is a symbolic way to see your path of integration and, if you follow the line in reverse, your path of disintegration.

Some find that they can still their mind by focusing on the cross and meditating on their specific path forward. We use the Celtic cross within NeuroPower as a timeless symbol of integration and transformation at both the corporate and personal levels. The four hexagons in the middle represent the four NeuroPower Leaders. The dotted lines link each type's Master and Mirror.

---

1   The inventor of psychoanalysis, Dr Sigmund Freud, saw symbolism as the expression of frustrated and repressed sexual desires. As such, any symbol that can be penetrated represents female sex organs, while any symbol that is erect or can be erected represents a male's genitals. This corresponds with the cross being a symbol of masculinity, and the circle of femininity. And there are many other important concepts embedded within the Celtic cross.

The cross is sometimes shown to represent the union of heaven, earth and the underworld. It also represents male generative power. In Celtic tradition, the four points often are shown to represent the four elements of earth, fire, air and water. In the Eastern Orthodox Church, Christ's halo (a symbol of divine radiance) is often represented having a cross within it. The cross has also been portrayed as holding the four Hebraic letters of the Tetragrammaton, which is thought to originate in God's statement to Moses in Exodus, 'I am that I am.'

The four points of the cross can represent the four beasts that circle the throne of God, mentioned in Ezekiel, Isaiah and Revelations. These beasts also represent different aspects of the work of Jesus Christ here on earth. The lion is royal rule, the man is humanness, the ox is servitude, and the eagle divinity.

The seven steps in the integration process represent the biblical number of perfection. That is, the seven days of creation, the seven deadly sins, etc.

The circle is a symbol of the female generative principle. It appears in pagan cultures as a symbol for the sun god. It also represents eternity, which is symbolic of female reproduction. The circle can also be seen as an eye that carries many geometrically significant factors. It can sometimes be described as an eye that takes the outside world into the inner and it can also project the inner world onto the outer.

APPENDIX 10

One of the Greatest Stories Ever Told

THE STORY OF KING ARTHUR AND CAMELOT

Our story begins about 1500 years ago when Merlin, the greatest Wizard of all time, foresaw the coming of a great king. Merlin believed this new king could save Britain from Christian rule, unite the kingdoms of the country to create a land of peace and power, create a period of learning, of tolerance and understanding between religions and beliefs, and could serve the cause of his gods.

At the time King Uther Pendragon suffered a burning passion to be with a beautiful woman called Igraine. But Igraine was already married to the Duke of North Wales, Duke Urien.

Merlin helped Uther to woo Igraine, and subsequently to lie with her on the night of Urien's death. As payment, Merlin wrought a promise from Uther that the son born of this union would be raised by Merlin himself.

ARTHUR IS BORN AND TAKEN FROM HIS PARENTS

Igraine was in fact Merlin's daughter by Vivianne. When it came to the heartbreak of relinquishing her first son to her father (she had several daughters to Urien), she attempted to hide her son away.

ARTHUR WAS ENTRUSTED TO THE CARE OF ECTOR AND HIS WIFE

Merlin prevailed and carried Arthur off (at only four weeks old) to be fostered by Ector ap Ednywain and his wife Anna at Caer Gei. He insisted Arthur be hidden both to protect him from ill-wishers and to rear him with the knowledge of the old ways. This would have been near impossible at court.

MERLIN TRAINS ARTHUR IN THE 'OLD WAYS'

Merlin made regular but fleeting visits during Arthur's childhood, returning every year just after Beltane[1] and Samhain. When Arthur turned eight, Merlin became Arthur's tutor. Arthur thought he was meeting Merlin in secret because he was not entitled to tutoring, and certainly not by a man of Merlin's stature.

ECTOR KNEW ABOUT ARTHUR'S LESSONS WITH MERLIN

Ector was fully aware of the lessons, and ensured the chosen classroom, oak wood grove,was undisturbed during the tutorials.

The Relationship between Arthur and Ector

Ector never pretended that Arthur was his own son. Arthur was reared believing that he was an orphan who had been taken in as a favour to a knight (not far from the truth).

Merlin's Background

Merlin, a wise and powerful Druid, was confidant to Uther and many say he was confidant to kings prior to Uther (it is whispered he has foretold the future for many hundreds of years, but Merlin denies this saying only that Avalon moves to a different time than the parallel world in which worshippers of other religions move).

It is also rumoured that Merlin came from a line descended directly from Atlantis, his father being the renowned bard Taliesen. Others say Merlin is Taliesen himself. Merlin was also known as Emrys, others say Emrys was Taliesen's father, and this is partly why Merlin seems to be so timeless.

As a Bard of repute, Merlin disguised himself as a wandering musician when searching out the truth of matters. He often appeared at the King's side with a lute in hand and occasionally conceded to play haunting, captivating songs for the enjoyment of all.

---

1   Beltane and Samhain are part of the Druidic Festivals of the Sun. Beltane is the first festival of the summer, celebrated on May 1st, and Samhain is celebrated with the arrival of the first frost on November 1st.

Cai and Arthur Receive Military Training

Merlin also encouraged Ector to send the young men to Benwick for military training in readiness for Arthur's king-making.

Cai's Character

The peasants living on his father's estate found Cai (Ector's son) to be fair, consistent, reliable and a stickler for following their yearly contribution requirements. He was lenient enough, however, to allow them to present cases of hardship if they offered other methods of contributing to the income of the estate. He was always fair, and he always wanted all the facts in front of him before making a decision.

Although he liked to keep largely to himself, or in the quiet company of Arthur, Cai thoroughly enjoyed the seasonal hunts his father hosted. In his sixteenth year, he speared a deer in its prime about six years old while the others were caught in bramble trying to outwit a wild pig.

Arthur was hot on his heels and claimed he alerted Cai to the deer, and no one noticed Cai slipping him the second cup of blood from the deer's heart when they cut it open, as a thank you.

ARTHUR BECOMES CAI'S MANSERVANT

At eight, Arthur was assigned to Cai as his manservant; Cai was ten. The two boys were virtually inseparable, and Cai was both good-natured and sensible. He also liked things to be organised and approached life in a logical, most detached way. When he saw that Arthur had a gift for fighting and riding, Cai used these gifts to his own advantage by having Arthur learn how to do many of his duties for him.

This benefited both boys, as Arthur learned many skills a manservant would normally take a lifetime to learn, and Cai learned how to manage people and gained the personal discipline to make the best use of his time.

By the time Cai was a teenager, he was required to manage large amounts of his father's holdings. He quickly learned the best way to ride the land, ascertain where any trouble spots were and relate these details to his father.

Cai and Arthur were sent abroad to Benwick when Cai turned eighteen, for a three-year duty. They were assigned to Ban's cavalry, where they both learned much about Arabian horses and fighting from horseback. Arthur was mainly invisible to the other knights, except for Lancelot, Ban's elder son, who was noted for his exceptional fighting skills.

Lancelot befriended Cai, partly as a way to learn more about Arthur, but also because Cai was so dependable and level-headed in battle.

As a crown prince, Lancelot was broadly educated and taught battle strategy from an early age. He was encouraged to take on his father's vision for a strong, independent Benwick, at peace and strongly defended from invaders. He embellished this vision, and planned to overthrow a number of smaller neighbouring lands (and, possibly, some of the larger ones as well) to ensure Benwick's safety and prosperity.

Lancelot was drawn to Cai and Arthur, partly by curiosity as to what he might learn from them, and partly by the obvious friendship these two enjoyed. Lancelot had never experienced this kind of friendship himself. He enjoyed being included in this circle of friends, although naturally he expected that one day these two would come to his aid, not he to theirs.

ARTHUR BECOMES KING

When King Uther was dying, Merlin approached him and in the sight of all the Lords, made him acknowledge his son Arthur as the new king. Uther died soon afterwards. He was buried by the side of his brother Aurelius Ambrosius within the Giant's Dance now known as Stonehenge.

Merlin had ensured that Arthur had the political support of the nobility but he still needed to win over the ordinary folk.

To do this he had a great sword fashioned and used his magic to embed it in a large stone shaped like an altar. To get the point across, he put a message on the sword which read 'Whoso pulleth out this sword of this stone, is rightwise king born of all

Lancelot was Born to Rule

Lancelot was the Crown Prince of Ban and had been trained to inherit his father's kingdom his whole reason for being was to lead and protect his country. His younger brother, Galahad, was good natured and, while competitive with his older brother, held no dreams of disenfranchising him and ruling in his stead; he was happy to be the Prince. Lancelot, however, bore his inheritance like a badge, taking it very seriously, constantly reminding those around him of his responsibilities and his future, almost to the point of martyrdom. Almost ....

the land.' Of course, all the men of the land, from the greatest to the least tried in vain to pull the sword from the altar – all except one young manservant called Arthur. When he succeeded, everyone was amazed and cries went across the land, 'We have Arthur unto our King, we will put him in no more delay, for we all see that it is God's will that he should be our King and who that holdeth against it we will slay him.'

When Arthur was safely installed and recognised as King, one of his first tasks was to appoint his senior advisers and members of his inner court.

> **NOTE: These eight appointments are the eight key archetypal personalities.**

KING ARTHUR APPOINTS CAI AS TREASURER

His first appointment was Cai, who was awarded the role of Seneschal, Steward or Treasurer of the kingdom. Arthur was sure Cai would do a brilliant job at creating order and at keeping tabs on every cent as he had done at his father's estate, Caer Gei. Arthur respected Cai's cool head under pressure and his ability to keep tabs on complex financial affairs in a systematic and fair way.

When Arthur was crowned, Cai was initially shocked, angry, and a little jealous. However, he recovered within days to become Arthur's most ardent supporter, and thrust himself into the role of assisting him to deal with the accusations, intrigues and attempts to minimise his claim to the throne.

The roles had been reversed. Once Cai had come to terms with this, he accepted Arthur's inheritance and was determined to help him put things in order quickly and efficiently.

Sir Cai, Arthur's foster brother and seneschal of his court, bears an azure shield on which are the two silver keys of his office.

He was also pragmatic enough to realise that as Arthur's right hand man, he would have a lot more power than as inheritor of Caer Gei.

Arthur's vision for a united Britain, and indeed the conquest of northern Europe, became his own, and Cai helped Arthur, using the skills he was most adept at, managing Arthur's estates, horses, and most importantly, his treasury.

Many saw Cai as powerful as Arthur in many areas. However, he rarely exercised that power except in Arthur's absence, when necessary.

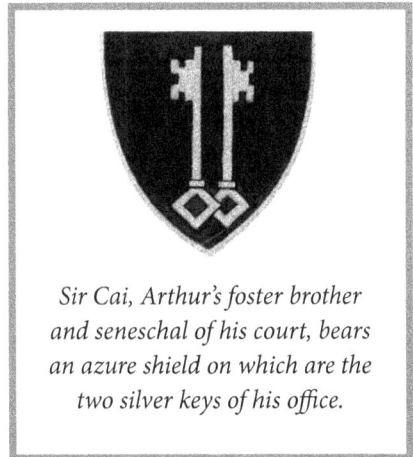

Occasionally, he allowed himself to indulge in fantasies, where he imagined what life would have been like with Arthur as his manservant and he as Lord of Caer Gei. He also imagined what it would be like when Britain would be at peace, enjoying wealth and supremacy over other nations.

Following his nineteenth birthday, Cai married Ralla, daughter of one of the neighbouring chieftains of his father's estates. Ralla was beautiful, expressive, creative and sensitive. The combined estate was quite large, and Ralla tended to base herself there rather than at court, running the estate and rearing their five children — three girls and two boys.

MERLIN STAYS AS ARTHUR'S PRINCIPAL ADVISER AND BARD

The new King kept Merlin the Druid and master of the Old Ways as his principal adviser. Arthur leaned heavily on Merlin for his wisdom and counsel, despite Merlin's obvious ultimate devotion to the 'Otherworld' rather than to Arthur himself. He did this because Merlin had made it clear that his plans rested on Arthur becoming and remaining King.

Arthur was constantly amazed at Merlin's ability to anticipate what would happen and at his ability to shape his future. Merlin always knew what to do in any situation and could make things happen almost by magic. He was also very gifted at reading the motives of people and at identifying the hurt that they nursed that was preventing them from reaching their full potential.

To ensure that Arthur's military commander was completely loyal to Arthur as King, Merlin encouraged the young King to replace Uther's commander, Owain, with the Numidian Commander, Sagramore.

ARTHUR APPOINTS SAGRAMORE AS HIS COMMANDER

Sagramore was a black Numidian soldier who had travelled home with Arthur and Cai from Benwick when Merlin recalled him. Sagramore was a playboy, a storyteller, a rascal, and a fierce fighter. Arthur respected his ability to solve almost

Merlin's Influence

Widely acknowledged as Arthur's 'maker', Merlin is known as the Kingmaker, Lord of Avalon and the High Priest Druid. He was confidant and counsellor to King Arthur and represented the final word on matters relating to the priests and priestesses of Avalon.

Sagramore the Numidean Commander

Sagramore had originally fought for King Ban as a mercenary, and then decided to throw his lot in with Brittany. Only a few years older than Arthur and Cai, he warmed to these two – particularly Arthur with whom he felt a kindred spirit. Arthur was an orphan, with no idea who his parents were, was considered lowborn, yet inspired respect from his fellows for his skills and the mutual friendship between himself and Cai. Although Sagramore knew his own parentage, he had been disowned by his father who wanted another wife when his mother died, and had decided to make his own history in another country.

Sagramore was an inspired warrior, and quickly rose through Ban's ranks to become a unit commander. A large portion of his rapid rise to power was the direct result of one of his irregular but terrifying explosions of rage.

Sagramore tended to harbour grievances, not responding at all until he was goaded or he found a reasonable excuse to 'explode' on the poor unfortunates in his way. These did not happen often, but often enough to earn him a reputation as someone you didn't want to cross.

On one particular occasion, when he had received notice that his father had died, leaving nothing to him of his family's considerable wealth, Sagramore led his men into battle and fought like a man possessed, taking his rage, hurt and injustice out on the enemy. He literally mowed his opponents down like weeds, killing scores of men.

Despite his rare outbursts, Sagramore was known to be careful of his warriors' health and wellbeing, and cautious in war strategy. He preferred to take war strategy direction from King Ban, and then ensure the success of every battle through his quick thinking and practical, quick action. He relished surprises in battle and could decisively change tack in time to win the day.

Sagramore's soldiers became very loyal to him, and would seek him out almost as a father figure to solve conflict and even personal problems. He was often asked to represent the warriors' concerns to King Ban and then negotiate an agreeable solution for any conflicting parties. His overriding concern, however, was to ensure his team remained happy working for him so they would fight well in battle.

any problem. Arthur also liked how available Sagramore was to his friends and the people throughout the kingdom. He was there when others were in need and many considered him a friend indeed.

Sagramore was tall, thin and grimly laconic, although he could be persuaded to tell a story in his terribly broken British, and could keep halls of fighting men enthralled for hours with tales from other lands. With his few confidants, he was very vocal.

He was a worshipper of the Roman god Mithras, a bull-based deity. Initiation into the cult was through rigorous testing, where survival depended purely on mindless obedience, even when it seemed ridiculous to do so. Mithras was much loved by warriors for this reason. Once initiated, worshippers were permitted to see the tests in broad daylight, and it became obvious they were all very harmless if the instructions were obeyed. Otherwise, dreadful harm would result with participants receiving either burns or broken limbs.

Lancelot was Exiled from Ban for Ten Years

The year that Arthur was recalled to Britain to fulfil his inheritance as Pendragon, Lancelot came into frequent conflict with his father. Lancelot was frustrated that Benwick seemed always to be defending its borders instead of widening them, and he urged his father to take the offensive. King Ban was convinced that invading and conquering lands would only drain the treasury for little good other than short-lived glory and refused to give any credence to his son's increasingly voiced counsel.

Finally, desperate to prove himself right (and his father wrong), Lancelot took a fighting unit of knights and invaded the borders of a land that was enjoying a one-time treaty with Benwick. His unit was merciless, following his orders to completely hold the territory. He returned from his foray jubilant, intent on demonstrating to his father how easy it had been and convinced the new land would be rapidly absorbed into Benwick.

King Ban met Lancelot at the border of Benwick in a black rage. He publicly disowned Lancelot for disregarding a treaty, for defying his orders and for the 'murder' of men and women under the protection of the treaty. He forbade Lancelot to return to Benwick for ten years; in such time he hoped his son would learn diplomacy and compassion.

Galahad was catapulted into Edling, which role he assumed readily. However, he reminded all who served him that Lancelot could one day return. Lancelot wasted no time in joining Arthur's court, becoming as loyal to Arthur as Cai.

Sagramore's skin colour aided his fighting ability in Britain, as most men had never even heard of a black man, let alone seen one. Many believed he was the agent of the devil come to kill them – or Merlin's creation – and nothing save sorcery could stop him.

The Saxons were particularly in awe of him and later when Arthur achieved treaties with Aelle and his sons, they sought his company to try to determine just what sort of creature Sagramore was.

LANCELOT LEAVES BAN TO JOIN ARTHUR AS HIS CRUSADER

Arthur appointed Sir Lancelot (whom Arthur had met when he and Cai had travelled to Brittany when Cai was being trained to be a liege lord and warrior knight), as his lead knight. Arthur, Cai and Lancelot were close friends. Around the campfire, Lancelot would talk for hours of his dreams for Benwick and many of these images helped form Arthur's vision of Camelot.

ARTHUR APPOINTS BERIN AS HIS JUDGE

Arthur appointed Berin from Amesbury as his Magistrate to the court of Camelot.

Berin constantly amazed Arthur with his energy. No matter what the task, no matter what time of day or night, Berin would plunge himself headlong into the task with contagious enthusiasm. With Berin at the table, sparks would fly, words would be exchanged and action would follow. He loved talking, arguing and getting things done. He could single-handedly rekindle the enthusiasm of everyone within earshot on any endeavour.

During Arthur's first year of reign, Berin had his twenty-fifth birthday, and was the youngest appointed magistrate in Britain. He was given the city of Amesbury (his birthplace) to preside over.

In contrast to Arthur, who was only eighteen, Berin felt rather seasoned, and when he was occasionally called upon by the King's court to give judgement, he did so fairly, and to the letter of the law, to demonstrate to the King that he could dispense the law without thought of politics.

Amesbury was only a two-hour horse ride from Camelot, and Berin found Arthur called upon his services more and more as his rule continued. However, Arthur recognised that Berin was more committed to the law than to justice so, in his dealings with Berin, Arthur showed him that in his passion to ensure that the law was carried out, he would sometimes flaunt the proper process.

While Berin's strong Christian principles prevented him from compromising his position, he always seemed to find ways around the system to suit his purposes. His usual method was to present the facts in a manner more conducive to a particular verdict than otherwise might have been the case.

Berin's Career

Berin of Amesbury had known from a very young age that he would become a priest within the Christian church. His parents were both Christians, attending church regularly, and he found the sanctity and absolute rightness of the church very comforting and reassuring. His father was a modestly successful merchant, who balanced his entrepreneurial skills with prayer on Sunday.

As the second son, Berin was not required to marry. In fact, had he done so it would have created tension between him and his older brother, Daffyd, who stood to inherit his parents' estate which, although minor, was still capable of providing a comfortable life for one family member. Once his brother was safely married, Berin felt free to dedicate his life to the priesthood and once he had completed his novice training, he was called before the senior monk who recommended that he go into training as a legal counsellor.

The monk had seen that Berin had an excellent memory, with the ability to regale even his superiors with facts and figures with which they were unfamiliar, yet he had little sympathy for any of his fellow novices or indeed 'God's flock'. Berin saw immediately the truth in his superior's words; he knew that his arguments often offended, and in many instances during his theological training, he had been more concerned with winning the argument than reaching a higher understanding of his soul.

He also realised that his love of comfort, indeed luxury, would be sorely tested in his new life of austerity. He had already realised he would need to rise to the ranks of supervising monk rapidly and, in order to do this, numerous more qualified monks would need to decline the position – which he felt was highly unlikely. There was, however, a great shortage of legal counsels in the kingdom, and one with monastic training would surely be well sought after.

After a number of years understudying the local magistrate in Amesbury, Berin was appointed to a township in North Wales known for its fierce loyalty to the local chiefs, who often bickered over borders, dues, even blood feuds going back several generations. This was a true testing ground, one where, if he performed, he could find himself well regarded throughout Britain, as many of the chiefs would report well of him to the king himself.

Berin discovered the best way to 'tame' the chiefs and their clans was to entertain and mingle unceasingly, showing by his enthusiasm that he was committed to giving the best verdict based on as much information as he could gather. The Welsh found him attractive – he reacted to their aggression with aggression, which they respected, and he had a sense of humour which he used willingly; in short, they enjoyed his company.

Despite his commitment to the process, he was still dogged by the focus on 'rightness' that drew him to the church, and he had not yet learned the talent to soften his verdicts with explanations or even words of empathy or sympathy. This naturally led to conflict with a number of chiefs, who passionately disliked Berin.

Arthur silently condoned this, knowing that systems for systems' sake can be more binding than necessary, as only a warrior can understand. He also understood that Berin, although brusque and at times aggressive, was essentially his agent for good.

Berin accepted Arthur's right to rule unequivocally. He also led by example, often completing the paperwork for cases himself, and preferring to confer with subjects before hearings to ensure he had all the facts. His underlings learned that he prized practical solutions, and was willing to let his helpers think outside the square if it offered a solution.

When Arthur required his magistrates to begin conferring on a truly national system of law – certainly one of Arthur's most ambitious projects which, unfortunately, was not as inspiring as his Quest Berin undertook an enormous workload to ensure Arthur's vision became a reality. He doubled his team of novices and drove them hard to meet his requirements.

Once he had set the tasks, Berin was renowned for his inflexibility on moving either the deadline or the agreed outcome, and this also encouraged creative solutions.

The resulting ill will from a number of other magistrates, who were not as committed to Arthur's new laws, affected him little. He complained about the trouble that he was having with other magistrates to whoever would listen, but most disregarded his grumbling, knowing how much he actually enjoyed the task set before him.

He drew strength from the rewards he found at Arthur's court and when Arthur bestowed on him a special honour as Magistrate of Camelot, he revelled in his achievement. He also found himself always wanting to acquire new capabilities. Any endeavour that enabled Berin to increase his hands-on personal effectiveness he found absolutely irresistible.

ARTHUR APPOINTS BEDWIN AS HIS BISHOP AND CHANCELLOR

Bedwin's career was a fascinating story of extraordinary political acumen and personal ambition. Bedwin's father had been an influential Druid based in Dumnonia and it was in the surroundings of power and knowledge that Bedwin developed into an ambitious Druid novice who decided the way of Avalon would be lost in the 'new order' of Christianity.

In the main, he had been reared by his mother, Morvanny, who was not a priestess. She was permitted to visit Bedwin's father regularly and was widely regarded as his consort, yet she was not privy to the learnings of the priestesses of Avalon and in fact showed little interest. As Bedwin began to be aware of power and hierarchy, he became annoyed with his mother's apparent lack of concern for his future standing and asked to become a novice.

Bedwin undertook two years of the eight-year noventia before becoming disenchanted with the gentle pace of Druidism. About this time, a garrison of Uther's soldiers had reinforced a stronghold near Bedwin's village and, fascinated by the energy exuding from the men and their entourage, he often spent his days and evenings at the fort.

When the Christian priest of the garrison began preaching to Bedwin, as one he rightly hoped to convert from paganism to Christianity, Bedwin listened with interest to the very different message of sinning and atonement. At first sceptical, Bedwin came to appreciate the political message and power of the Christian theology and decided his future would be more assured as a Christian priest – or perhaps, one day, a bishop.

Well educated by the Druids, Bedwin proved an excellent student and very quickly surpassed the local priest in his knowledge of the Scriptures and his ability to interpret them to suit any particular occasion or need. The local priest began to rely on Bedwin to write his sermons and, within a short eighteen months, Bedwin was in effect running the garrison's church and leading the troops in worship.

Attendance at Bedwin's sermons was popular, often with standing room only in the small wooden hall built for the purpose.

When Uther attended the garrison and one of Bedwin's sermons, he identified a

Bedwin Took a Risk because he Believed in Arthur

When Arthur took the throne five years after Bedwin's appointment by King Uther as High Priest, Bedwin offered a very persuasive argument that he needed to stay in Arthur's court to offer continuity of Christian service as one of Uther's trusted servants but naturally, to convince Arthur of his standing, he would need a higher posting. Bedwin was summarily made a bishop at the age of twenty-six. Although many of the others would have liked to be the King's counsellor, many of the contenders lacked the courage to take up the role because Arthur was an unknown quantity and it was a high risk to be associated with him.

Bedwin had seen Arthur in war while visiting Ban a few years earlier. Although he was as surprised as everyone else at his heritage, he did not for one moment doubt that Arthur could be King of England and even Pendragon. He also recognised Arthur's requirement for loyalty from his subjects and knew if he was one of Arthur's original court, he would be guaranteed a position as long as Arthur reigned and Bedwin could offer advice.

talent he wished for in his own entourage and instantly appointed him as assistant to his own priest, who was ailing in health. Although this upset the established Christian hierarchy, Uther was sufficiently confident in his own mind to disregard the advice to appoint a more experienced candidate who had already been selected by the Christian priests as the next counsellor to the King.

Bedwin quickly realised that climbing the Christian hierachy depended on obtaining the approval of the other bishops and the Christian council.

He swung all his political skills into ingratiating himself with these men, and learned much about what motivates others during this time.

Surviving this post for two years, Bedwin proved Uther had chosen a resourceful and determined servant. When Uther's own priest died of pneumonia, Uther did not hesitate to appoint Bedwin in his stead. Bedwin's own abilities as a courtier were proven when the Christian hierarchy accepted Bedwin's appointment without complaint and some small congratulations were offered.

It was only six months later that Bedwin was offered the post of High Priest, despite not having served any length of time in a monastery. At the time, many of the established Christian powerbrokers did not like the idea of a novice priest outranking them by virtue of his closeness to the King.

Bedwin's intuition and his own sense of achievement alerted him to the fact that if he could placate these powerbrokers and contrive to complete some learning, he could potentially rise to the standing of Bishop in a far shorter time than he had hoped. He approached the local monastery to begin a highly irregular course of study, undertaking two or three hours a day and returning to Uther's court for the balance, and to eat and sleep.

He kept this up for nearly six months, until he felt the other bishops knew of it and he had skimmed nearly all the interesting references in the monastery's library. Only then did he discontinue his double life. In return for the local monastery's understanding of his position, he offered them a significant bursary to enable them to 'discover' a juniper bush such as the one Joseph of Arimathea had first brought to England (in fact, was it not the very one…?).

Even though Bedwin saw himself as flexible in all things, Arthur noticed that Bedwin always worked best when there was a very clear vision and plan to get there.

Bedwin was an astonishing politician and strategist. His natural talent was being able to persuade virtually anyone of anything.

Under Bedwin's leadership, the Christian church flourished. Bedwin derided and discounted the teachings of the Druids and the 'old ways' in his sermons, although he was careful to word it so that he did not show any great understanding of the druidic lore so as to not offend the Druids. His goal was to convert as many of the 'flock' as he could for Arthur's kingdom.

Many in the Christian hierarchy questioned his motives when he began to set up monasteries across Dumnonia, believing his loyalty had actually changed from serving God to serving the King. They had cause for this suspicion.

Bedwin had set himself the enormous task of opening a monastery every fifty miles to ensure the people were educated in Christian ways and therefore were loyal to the King.

Bedwin's typical modus operandi was to identify a site and set a building completion date, then move on to the next site, leaving a trail of consternation as the deadline for the completed building drew nearer with no obvious signs of work begun.

Derwynt Combined People, Vision and Process

Derwynt grew up around the dust and clatter of cutting stone, and the quiet of evenings spent carefully drawing up building plans and measuring fixtures. Although stone masonry did not reach its heyday until nearly six centuries later when flying buttresses made their appearance, stone was an integral part of the more permanent features of major towns and cities.

Many of these were a legacy from the Romans, as were the paved roads and waterways; however, each major centre had a reputable mason who repaired dwellings. The more talented could also design and organise construction of new buildings. Derwynt's father, Balin, was one such and recognition of his skills spread across Dumnonia, north through Gwent and even into Powys.

From his father, Derwynt learned to see a building before it was constructed and the best way of constructing it there were natural laws that needed to be applied to stone masonry if a building was to last more than ten years. A talent he developed when apprenticing to his father was to identify the skills of people working for Balin and suggest the best areas for them to work. This talent enabled him to succeed his father in the masonry guild as Master Mason when Balin died, and many were convinced Derwynt was in fact even more gifted than his father.

As he learned to oversee the construction of larger projects, Derwynt continuously questioned the accepted way as taught by his father, particularly as he saw how differently individuals tackled the same jobs. Improving on the 'natural laws' enabled Derwynt to build larger, taller and more aesthetically pleasing buildings than ever considered possible.

Bedwin would appear at the site a mere six months before completion was due, conscript all the local masons and wood workers to work around the clock (with Sundays off, of course) and miraculously complete the building in time. He felt that building any other way was too slow and wasted too much thought when it could be done in one-fifth of the time it took anyone else. This typified his entire character.

ARTHUR APPOINTS DERWYNT AS THE ARCHITECT TO BUILD CAMELOT

As his most senior stone mason or architect he appointed Derwynt, the eldest son of Balin, the Master Mason of the Honourable Guild of Masons and of Ynys Wydryn (Glastonbury and Somerset).

Arthur particularly respected Derwynt's logical mind and his ability to see what wasn't right in any situation. It was Derwynt who would see the inconsistency in new policy or could clearly identify why a new church or public building would or wouldn't work. Derwynt's words were not always what people wanted to hear but if they were acted on they would solve countless problems before they happened. Derwynt had the unique ability to build castles on the ground that others built in the sky. He turned fiction into bricks and mortar.

Under Derwynt's vision, the buildings he designed took on a quality previously unknown by British builders, with relief structure and patterns in stone. In the interiors of his buildings, some breathtaking mosaics were also created under his direction.

THE BUILDING OF CAMELOT

When Arthur came to build his fort at Camelot, he sought out Derwynt on the advice of Bedwin (who planned to use Derwynt to- construct his own monasteries), and Berin, who admired Derwynt's work and hoped one day to judge in a court hall built by him.

Derwynt accepted the project eagerly he knew he could design and build a castle of magnificent proportions given enough funding, which in Britain at that time was rare.

Labourers came from all surrounding lands to earn what they hoped would be a tenure for life castles took years to build, in some instances, decades. They were to be disappointed in this hope. Derwynt had devised time plans and construction methods to see the castle complete in just three years.

The urgency was placed on him by the King and Merlin, who knew Britain was sorely threatened and needed a stronghold not just for battle purposes but also as inspiration to the recently united nation.

The disappointment of the labourers bubbled over into resentment in a number of

Camelot was Derwynt's Signature Building

Finally, after many years of work and much later in Arthur's reign, the completion of the castle was Derwynt's magnum opus. With it, he was appointed Grand Mason of the Mason Lodge at the age of forty. He inspired other masons to build similar buildings around the country, particularly in the far north and in isolated regions requiring reinforcements. The cost and time frame (usually fifteen years or so) prohibited many from leaving the drawing board until the middle ages, when the French brought to England their Master Masons, and their money.

instances, and Derwynt found he needed to use his understanding and interpretive skills as never before.

By talking about the greatness of the castle, and the wonderment others would see when it was complete and in such a short time, too all those who had worked on the building would be sure of work for life, wherever they went. He personally would provide letters for each and every one describing their contribution.

The reduced time frame relied on larger teams of workers, longer hours and even extra shifts into the nights. This reduced the effect of winter in the first year, as the foundations were placed before the first frosts and this meant that building could continue, for the most part, through the numbing cold. This reduced the time needed by two years, for every year of construction.

Additionally, Derwynt used innovative methods of stone masonry to cut and move the blocks, halving the time needed once again.

A few still continued with their discontent, and Derwynt decided they were fools and not to be tolerated. Rather than dismiss them, he found other construction sites nearby that were suffering because of the drain on labourers the castle had created, and suggested they would profit greatly by offering their much needed service there.

He rarely expressed anger; when frustrated, he would seek a quiet spot and list the priorities requiring attention, and then seek out those he needed to help him. Any conflict within his workforce was dealt with unemotionally, using logical arguments which most felt unable to refute.

Convinced of the surety of the natural laws taught by his father, Derwynt would, however, aggressively state the way a job was to be done, in a tone that brokered no argument. Because he had so skilfully placed people in jobs they felt suitable for, the workers would generally overlook this aggression as passion and get on with the job, the way Derwynt wanted it done.

The clarity of vision he held for the castle when complete enabled Derwynt to keep the construction on track, even when obstacles seemed unsurpassable.

Keenly aware of the need to reassure Arthur and Merlin, Derwynt developed a pattern of regularly reporting to the King's Court. This was a service hitherto not usually offered by masons who were considered to be on-site managers rather than project managers.

Derwynt was possibly one of the masons who paved the way for architects and project developers in later centuries to be placed in the upper echelons of society. Of course, he was largely unaware of the customs he was ignoring; he just wanted to get the job done efficiently and well, and keep true to his vision.

ARTHUR DREW ON THE KNOWLEDGE OF INGER THE SAXON NAVIGATOR TO REBUILD HIS FLEET

Inger was originally seconded to Camelot to train the Briton troops and to oversee the building of galleys that could help alert the Britons to future attempts at an invasion. Arthur had them upgrade his role to help him rebuild his ships so that they were faster, lighter and more seaworthy.

Arthur grew to depend on Inger's trustworthiness, his straightforward approach, his self-discipline, his ability to keep to an agreed plan and his strength of character.

Initially, arrival in Britain had held an unwelcome surprise for Inger. He had been instructed to reconnoitre the southern land of Dumnonia, and he chose the straits between Hibernia and the northern tip of the huge peninsula that formed the grain field of Britain, the food storehouse for the new nation.

With five long ships, he had entered what seemed a backwater bay with a small village on one side, in the hopes of a quick plunder and to set sail again in a few hours. Unfortunately, the current of that particular bay made navigation impossible at the turn of the tide. As his ships floundered, five empty fishing boats approached his ships, only to burst into flames as they neared. Four of his long boats were lost, with most of the men on board. He managed to turn and sail out, to head for the other side of Britain in what the British called Lloegyr (lost lands) to report on the cunning of the native peoples.

A few weeks later he discovered the fishing boat ploy had been a tactic of none other than King Arthur himself, who had been touring those lands seeking support for his new order, his construction and horse breeding projects. Rather than hating this man who had killed nearly 300 of his countrymen, Inger admired the British King from that moment on.

A few years later, the Saxon leader, Aelle, wrought a treaty with Arthur to keep the Lloegyr in return for leaving the native British alone and fighting other Germans who were arriving daily to take their share of the green island.

Inger's Background

Inger came with Aelle to the shores of Britain to find a better life, in a more forgiving country. His own lands were overcrowded, and were regularly invaded by those from further west. The promise of the green shores of the island of Britain lured strongly.

He thought to find a wife there, and to fish and perhaps fight to protect his new land after Aelle had conquered the old natives, who were reported to have no high king, no unity and no purpose.

Purpose! Inger could talk of purpose simply to find and culture enough food to last the winter would be a luxury. He had grown up in an overpopulated area of Germany, and at fifteen had joined Aelle's army mainly to ensure he was at least fed every day, and also to bring predictability and regularity to his life.

He was fond of his parents, especially his mother Ulla, and the decision to leave for Britain was not taken without consideration of her feelings. But he was hopeful he would prosper enough to send word for them to come to the isle and share his hut with his new family.

His rise through Aelle's army to Captain was achieved through hard work rather than blinding talent. He was dutiful, loyal, responsible and predictable all qualities sought after in a fighting unit. He admired the captains of the galleys that set sail for foreign lands and returned with rich plunder, sometimes beautiful women and always tales of wealthy lands to the east.

He learned to navigate by the stars from his mother's father, who had learned the craft from an olive-skinned visitor from southern lands, and found this tool invaluable in reaching other shores and returning quickly, often days ahead of the other vessels in the fleet.

The system he saw in the stars reassured him that all life followed a pattern and that anything was achievable if he simply stuck at it long enough. He thus found it difficult to be aware of underlying meanings, political games or manipulation. This delayed his promotion for a few years, while Aelle learned to recognise the strengths of Inger without self-promotion.

When he was appointed Shipmaster, Inger's men knew to expect tolerance from him in most aspects of life at sea and on shore, apart from failing in basic duties. If ropes were not coiled in the right direction, if sails were not mended promptly or oars not replaced, Inger was merciless in punishment.

Arthur requested Aelle lend a shipmaster to the British army, to train them in sea lore and potentially oversee the building of galleys which would, if not equal the power of the Saxons, at least alert the British of Saxon arrivals.

Inger was appointed to this duty, and he went willingly, hoping to learn from Arthur's brilliance in strategy and commandment. He modified the woefully out-classed British boats to enable them to move faster through high seas, and introduced the art of star navigation to a few handpicked leaders. When his secondment was complete, Inger found himself torn between the loyalty of his own nationality, and the refinement and reasoning of the British. In the end, his predicament was solved by Arthur requesting Aelle second Inger permanently to his British army. Aelle agreed.

One of the reasons Inger had felt conflicting loyalties was that he had fallen in love with a Saxon-born maid to Cai's wife, Ralla. Ralla had claimed Helna from slavery after one of Sagramore's victories, taught her English and was even starting on the basics of counting and writing. Inger and Helna met when Ralla visited Camelot for a rare court appearance, and Inger's heart was captured.

As the ship fleet grew and Inger's men began to use their skills in warning the land army of approaching danger, even winning the occasional skirmish, Inger was admitted into the King's circle of advisers and inner court members. He bravely asked Cai for the hand of Ralla's maid, half expecting a rebuff. Although sad to lose such a promising student, Ralla was happy for Helna to set up her own house and still provide services to her household as housemaid rather than personal attendant.

GUINEVERE WINS ARTHUR'S HEART

Unfortunately for the Druids, Merlin was unable to control Arthur's head or heart when it came to matters of love and lust. Despite his urging to marry Ceinwyn who was faithful to the old ways and daughter of petty king Gorfyddyd, King of Powys, Arthur chose Guinevere, the daughter of a chieftain of Roman descent, Leodegrance, who had recently converted to Christianity.

Guinevere was as beautiful as Ceinwyn and more ambitious. Through her wiles, she captivated Arthur in one weekend during a hunting visit and elicited a promise of marriage, where Ceinwyn had failed in months of courting.

Cai privately did not approve of Guinevere, for she was far too Christian for his preferences and not schooled in the mysteries- she could not even ride well enough to participate in a hunt! However, she was Arthur's chosen woman, and so he offered her his unwavering loyalty.

Merlin attempted to discredit Guinevere by emphasising her Christianity and linking her romantically with Lancelot. However, his usual adeptness at intrigue failed with Guinevere Arthur was completely devoted to her and blind to her faults. In the end, of course , Merlin's exaggerations became self-fulfilling prophecies.

THE BIRTH OF MORDRED

Determined to ensure his vision remained pure, Merlin contrived for one of Arthur's half-sisters by Igraine, named Morgaine, who was in training for the role of High Priestess, to lie with Arthur at Beltane. This was a pagan religious ritual in which Arthur, at that time, still partook. Morgaine bore a son to Arthur after this event, some say the only son – certainly there were no children to Guinevere.

The son was named Mordred, and he was raised in Avalon until Morgaine married Lot of Lothian, who then adopted him out of respect for Merlin, Morgaine and the priestesses of Avalon.

Merlin had prophesied that great danger should come to Arthur and his kingdom through this child, so when the King heard of the birth, he requested Morgaine conceal the child and raise him secretly.

GUINEVERE THE CHRISTIAN

As a devout Christian, Guinevere constantly lobbied to have Christianity installed as the official religion. While this infuriated Merlin and many of the devout Druids, it delighted Bedwin who could see that the shift in power could bring the warring tribes of Britain together and could provide the platform for huge personal influence and glory.

When Guinevere met Bedwin she was delighted to meet a man with so much passion and focus for the church and so much loyalty to the King.

Guinevere encouraged Bedwin's efforts in every way she could. Arthur at first tolerated and then actively supported them, believing the monasteries could promote learning and enlightened peace.

Merlin loathed them, believing they were spreading like a disease across his beloved country and straining his relationship with Arthur even more.

Merlin and Bedwin often verbally crossed swords, sometimes heatedly, in Arthur's court. As the years passed, however, they both developed a grudging admiration– for the other, recognising in each other all the qualities they both respected ability to strategise, to see the weaknesses and strengths in others, to capture an audience, to use knowledge to further their cause.

SAGRAMORE FALLS IN LOVE

Meanwhile, Sagramore fell in love with a Saxon chief's daughter after spending a month guarding a tribe of warriors his men had captured during a raid. Her father had been killed in a previous battle, and Sagramore's men caught up with them while they were retreating to the coastline. Her name was Aileann (Eileen), and she was beautiful by modern day standards – blonde-haired, blue-eyed, fair-skinned and tall.

Many British men found her too pale, preferring brunettes and redheads, but none could deny her attractiveness.

She was fierce in nature and fearless when dealing with Sagramore and their love grew to be passionate. They were striking as a couple, and everyone at Arthur's court liked to be seen with them at social gatherings. Aileann initially accompanied Sagramore on some of his battles, but fell pregnant and then, to her dismay, he insisted she stay at court.

Being Saxon, she did not have a good grasp of the British tongue and few of the women attempted to befriend her. She did become a fast friend of one of Guinevere's ladies-in-waiting, who eventually married Balin, Derwynt's father and Arthur's chief building supervisor.

Guinevere quickly developed the opinion that Sagramore had far too much influence over Arthur and was therefore eager to make Aileann uncomfortable in his presence. Guinevere also did not like Sagramore's worship of Mithras and his encouragement of his warriors to join the cult.

Arthur noticed Aileann's predicament, and granted Sagramore his own lands in the Summer Country or Dumnonia (south England), which was a popular dispatch point to Benwick, and considered to be Merlin's stronghold. Aileann made an attractive home there, and also managed to accompany Sagramore on numerous battles throughout Arthur's twelve-year reign.

Aileann offered curt, but unbiased advice on many occasions, and helped maintain Sagramore's reputation for his ability to keep order without offending anyone.

Sagramore also determined fairly early on in Arthur's reign that Lancelot could be a threat to a peaceful kingdom, pointing out that Lancelot, as Ban's elder son, was used to getting his own way. When necessary, he would gently remind Arthur of Lancelot's heritage when making decisions about who should perform what duties in battle or on quest.

For some reason, Galahad (Lancelot's brother) was never placed under the same scrutiny by Sagramore, and ultimately he did indeed remain faithful to Arthur, disowning his own brother when his affair with Guinevere was revealed.

GUINEVERE AND LANCELOT

On the day of Arthur's wedding to Guinevere, Arthur sent Lancelot to collect his bride. On this journey, Merlin's prophecy came to pass, and Lancelot and Guinevere fell passionately in love.

For Lancelot, love of Guinevere came instantly, with no doubt or hesitation. He knew his heart could only be Guinevere's from the instant she spoke to him and looked into his eyes. In one way it was part of his character to need to have an unfulfilled desire. In another it was because he knew Guinevere was the strong, determined and often ruthless Queen whom he could have had by his side in Benwick. She was also breathtakingly beautiful.

Guinevere's affection for Lancelot was also instantly returned, initially for the thrill of forbidden fruit and then eventually because she truly believed, too, that under different circumstances she might have ruled at Lancelot's side.

Lancelot was taller than Arthur and, where Arthur was ruggedly attractive, Lancelot was refined, courtly and handsome. Eventually, this love would radically change their lives and the lives of everyone at Camelot forever.

GUINEVERE'S INFLUENCE GROWS

As Guinevere's influence at court grew, Merlin and Arthur's relationship grew strained. In battle, however, Arthur relied totally on the Druids for guidance, despite Guinevere's beseechment to consult her priests. Even at court, Merlin still held sway in matters of dispute and future planning as many of the petty kings still followed the old ways.

Merlin would periodically disappear from court to meet his obligations as High Priest, clarify his vision and partake of his Druidic rituals which strengthened his purpose and resolve. This left Arthur to listen to the voices of others, usually Guinevere's men.

Guinevere quickly developed relationships with those in Arthur's inner circle, although she maintained a cool distance from Sagramore and his wife Aileann, avoiding speaking directly to either of them at court or in social situations.

GUINEVERE IS CAPTURED BY KING MELWAS AND SAVED BY LANCELOT

When Arthur was away fighting, Guinevere was captured by a petty king, King Melwas. Without a moment's hesitation Lancelot rescued her, sustaining grievous wounds in the fight. Secretly, although Lancelot had no concerns about protecting his Queen, he felt Arthur had failed her in his absence during her greatest need.

When Arthur returned, Lancelot requested to fight Melwas to the death, fully expecting Arthur to forbid him and to fight Melwas himself. When Arthur allowed him the duel (believing this was the fulfilment of unfinished business) Lancelot pronounced himself the Queen's Champion, a role that had not been filled for many generations.

This gave to Lancelot and Guinevere an enduring legitimacy for regular consort, although always in full sight of the intimates of the court.

Both were determined that Arthur would never have cause to suspect their stolen love. Lancelot eagerly undertook the battles within Britain, then in warring countries and then sought the Grail on the ten-year Quest. Being absent from court in this way played a major part in the role he saw for himself in bringing peace and prosperity to Britain.

He enjoyed being at court, often passionately arguing to invade a particular land, or take a particular course to retrieve the Grail. Although his time at court was sometimes tainted by constantly seeking glimpses of Guinevere, it was also thrilling when she glanced at him over a glass of wine, or brushed his hand in passing.

Many maidens at court vied for his attention, and at one stage he even betrothed himself. It was an effort to stave off the unwanted attentions as well as the rumours that he may not like women (although he certainly took his fill when on Quest, often secretly partaking of less than wholesome activities, which he justified to himself as a way to forget Guinevere for a moment).

The time he and his bride-to-be spent together became her most relished memory, as the knight offered her his hand and they enjoyed an affectionate courtship. She had one of the most envied positions at court. She brought forth Lancelot's first born son, yet was not affected when Lancelot brought shame upon himself and Guinevere in later years.

Lancelot never married the unfortunate maiden, even after she became pregnant. He then contrived a situation for one of his knights to be caught wooing her so he could righteously accuse her of a wandering affection.

LANCELOT AND GUINEVERE ARE CAUGHT TOGETHER

But stolen love cannot exist forever it – must either run its course or be fulfilled. Some believe that without Mordred's meddling, Lancelot would have returned to Benwick to resume his inheritance and left his passion for Guinevere in Britain. However, Mordred and his brothers, Agravain and Gareth, contrived for Lancelot to receive a message from the Queen to attend her in her chambers during one of Arthur's campaigns.

They arranged to lay in wait for Lancelot to visit the Queen's bedchamber. Sir Bors,

Arthur's trusted adviser, and Sir Tristram, one of the original Knights of the Round Table, tried to prevent Lancelot from visiting her but he was insistent.

When Agravain and Gareth smashed open the door, Lancelot killed them and then fled. Mordred reported this to the King, who wept because he foresaw the trial of Guinevere and Lancelot and the possible end of the Round Table.

There is much speculation as to whether Lancelot and Guinevere ever fulfilled their passion for each other before the brothers burst in on them that fateful evening. However, there was little left for Lancelot to do but fight them to the death and escape with Guinevere to forestall the trial that would surely be held for their treason.

While fleeing, Guinevere realised Lancelot would never be allowed to rule Benwick with this on his hands, and that she would be doomed to live with him in a fort somewhere far from her beloved Lloegyr in the east midlands. She convinced Lancelot to return her to Arthur, hoping Arthur might forgive her.

Arthur was disposed to forgive, not believing Guinevere and Lancelot had actually committed the physical act. However, Arthur found the overwhelming counsel from his court was to put her to trial and found that even he was not strong enough to go against these wishes.

When the trial of Guinevere was held, Berin was not surprised and dispensed the verdict of guilty quickly and concisely, knowing Arthur would find some way of preventing her death. She was sentenced to live in a monastery for the remaining term of her life.

The only way Arthur could soften the banishment was to present her to a monastery in her home land Lloegyr, close to family and her few childhood friends.

Lancelot fled to France. Arthur gathered a great host of warriors to attack him there and a great battle ensued, with many losses on both sides. Eventually, Lancelot submitted and Arthur required him to give up his knighthood and, like Guinevere, become a recluse in a monastery.

BISHOP BEDWIN DIES BEFORE THE END OF ARTHUR'S REIGN

Towards the end of Arthur's reign, Bishop Bedwin was in his late thirties not old, but in those times considered to be mature. Bedwin showed a tolerance for both the Roman and pagan religions he had not displayed in his earlier years, which angered the other Christian bishops who could not now displace Bedwin from his position of total trust and reliance with the King. Bedwin attributed his growing tolerance to his friendship with Merlin and also the wisdom of years showing him that most philosophies and faiths had merit if they are believed and lived.

He also began to understand that most people had innate good in them– it just required someone to offer them the opportunity to show it, whether that was in the service of God or King or simply living an honest and full life. Although he had not covered Dumnonia in monasteries (he called a halt to the program after the 15th, believing this was probably enough for the souls of the people without depleting the treasury too much), he had achieved a great deal and realised that his purpose had as much worth as any other man. And equally, any other man's purpose probably had as much worth as his own.

Grateful for his youthful energy and ambition, which had enabled him to achieve so much (so he could reflect without regret), Bedwin grew to relish his discussions with Merlin and other old adversaries more than his love of the Church and even his ambition.

Bishop Bedwin died unexpectedly after an unseasonable cold snap in early summer. It was possibly simply a severe cold which caught him unawares, although the appointment of the fanatical Priest Sansum in his place raised questions among Bedwin's confidants as to the true nature of his ailment…

He was remembered by all those who worshipped under him as a purposeful, energetic priest who loved his God and his King passionately, with the ability to bring out the best in people. He was mourned by Merlin and others as a tolerant and knowledgeable peer.

THE LAST YEARS OF ARTHUR'S REIGN

During the last years of Arthur's reign, **Derwynt the Royal Architect** oversaw the construction of several large buildings and applied much of what he learned when working with Arthur.

At Arthur's court he had learned about politics and had seen some truly good and some truly evil events. He realised that there were both good and bad in the world, not just processes in which things happened.

One of his greatest joys was standing on the battlements of the castle during the parade to celebrate the completion of the building, knowing that he had created something of intrinsically good value, no matter what would go on within the walls later.

To him it was as if a white light was descending with the sun's rays, shining on him and uplifting him to unspeakable joy and happiness (as well as relief!) focusing on the beautiful structure he had created.

ARTHUR'S CAMPAIGN FOR EMPEROR

On his fourteenth birthday, Mordred, Arthur's bastard son, was brought to see the

King by his mother, Morgan Le Fay. This was the first time Arthur had met Mordred, who was his only child since Guinevere had never given birth. Arthur accepted Mordred as his son and heir.

Arthur then embarked on a campaign to free Britain from the shackles of Rome, which had attempted to impose a levy for her protection. He sailed to Brittany and formed an alliance with King Ban and won the day. During this period of battle, one of Brittany's lesser kings, King Hoel, found that his niece, Helen, had been seized by a monstrous giant.

King Arthur, Cai, Gawain (Arthur's nephew) and Bedivere were too late in their bid to rescue her, but Arthur managed to kill the giant in a single combat. Galahad (Ban's son now grown) requested to join King Arthur's knights, and Arthur appointed him in Lancelot's stead. Filled with success, Arthur then set his sights on Rome to make himself Emperor.

Merlin's consort, Vivianne, left this earth to join her forebears in the Otherworld. Then it happened that Merlin fell in a dotage on one of the novices of the Lake, Nimue, and he let her have no rest, always being with her. He warned King Arthur that he would not be long above earth, but despite his craft he would be put alive into the earth. Merlin further warned him to keep his sword and scabbard safely, for it would be stolen from him.

He then left the King, and travelled with Nimue over the sea to the land of Benwick, in Brittany, where King Ban and Elaine his wife ruled.

Meantime, it happened as Merlin foresaw – Arthur's sister Morgan le Fay stole the sword of Excalibur and its sheath. She gave these to Sir Accolon with which to fight the King himself. When the King was armed for this battle, a maiden came from Morgan le Fay, bringing to Arthur a sword like Excalibur and sheath like Excalibur's. These were brittle counterfeits.

The Lady of the Lake, Nimue, came to the ensuing battle to save the King, for she knew Morgan le Fay wished ill of him. King Arthur's sword broke in his hand, and only after an heroic fight did he get his own sword back and defeat Sir Accolon. Then Accolon confessed the treason of Morgan le Fay and the King granted mercy to him.

THE QUEST FOR THE HOLY GRAIL

After this, the Lady of the Lake became the friend and guardian of King Arthur, in the stead of Merlin the enchanter. She then told Arthur of the need to recover the Grail (brought to the shores of Britain by Joseph of Arimathea, along with the sword – already in Arthur's possession and the spear that pierced Jesus Christ's side), so that Arthur could truly bring peace to the nation. So began the quests for the Grail by the Knights of the Round Table.

MERLIN IS CAPTURED BY NIMUE

The novice priestess, Nimue, who preferred to play politics rather than be confined to the rituals of Avalon, quickly learned most of Merlin's wisdoms after she trapped him in a cave and then adapted his vision to suit her own. Although she loved Merlin passionately, she felt he had not been decisive enough in his administration of his plan.

Her confinement of Merlin to a cave was by the Druid's own consent, believing his time had come to pass the High Priest role to his successor, Gudovan.

She appointed herself as Arthur's protector and counsellor. Guinevere was horrified.

Hearing Merlin had been entrapped and that Arthur was now being advised by Nimue, who had forsaken Avalon for Camelot, Morgaine began to plot the downfall of Arthur. She believed he had forsaken the old ways, and bade Mordred set the crown on his own head during one of Arthur's absences after Guinevere's trial.

THE END FOR KING ARTHUR AND THE GOLDEN AGE OF CAMELOT

At fifteen, Mordred was only just beginning to understand the true nature of power, and Merlin could not free himself in time to halt the tide set in motion. Nimue was not as powerful as she had thought, and was unable to free Merlin quickly enough, so stood by helplessly as Arthur fought Mordred to save his kingdom.

MORDRED DOES BATTLE WITH ARTHUR

In Arthur's absence, Mordred, who had been left in charge of the kingdom, set the crown upon his own head and took Guinevere for his wife. Arthur hastened back and faced him in battle several times. Mordred was fatally wounded, and Arthur was carried to the island of Avalon in an attempt to heal his wounds. This was in vain, however, and Arthur died soon after.

He left his kingdom in the care of Constantine of Cornwall, whose first act was to seek out Mordred's sons and murder them at the sanctuary altar. Many of Arthur's men left the southern lands to serve the new king of Lothian, husband of Ygerna, to protect lands still free from the Saxon thrall. From Ygerna issued a line of kings reputed to uphold the Quest for the Grail for humankind.

Sagramore fought to the bitter end beside his King. He knew life in any other army besides Arthur's would seem second rate. His twelve years of service had been well repaid and, although he had a wife and children and land, he was totally committed to Arthur's plan of a united England. Without Arthur, however, he could not see the plan coming to fulfilment.

Some say he might have retired, or even started his own mercenary army, as fighting was what he did best, if he could have escaped in that last battle. Others say he chose not to. Whatever the reason, Sagramore was forced to stay with Arthur as the King's dwindling forces were essentially routed by Mordred's men.

Sagramore was remembered by a considerable number of warriors, court advisers and their families with something approaching fondness. He had developed over the years into a very stable, even-handed commander who was known to be fair but firm.

He had retained his quick wit and wry humour, and even controlled his rare rages by taking some wretched horse on a mad gallop that lasted until the horse collapsed (he would usually stay out all night while the horse recovered enough to walk and then assign a servant to bring it home) never taking his rage out on humankind.

Sagramore's wife, Aileann, survived Arthur by more than thirty years, and even in old age (as sixty-something was in those days) was considered a beautiful woman. This was mainly credited to her bearing and fierceness, which was never quite contained in the peaceful lands of the Summer Country.

Her three sons and two daughters led varied lives, the eldest son leading a battalion of warriors for one of Arthur's successors (there was never another Pendragon, only Kings), Eochaid Buide, King of Scots, his cousin by his mother's sister, Ygerna. This battalion commander, Salidean, was the only child to inherit Sagramore's night-black skin, the others bearing either olive skin, not unlike the Picts, or pure white like their mother.

At the end of Arthur's reign, and the crowning of Constantine of Cornwall, **Cai** retired at age thirty-three to run his estates and enjoy life with his wife and family. He built one of the largest libraries in the land during this time.

Although Cai still dreamed of a conquered Europe, Constantine was too unpredictable in his favours and not a cautious enough thinker for Cai to feel comfortable at court. One of his sons was killed in service to King Constantine. The other returned home to help Cai run his estate.

When Cai died, his friends and colleagues described him as a pillar of strength, a fair leader and a great wit. He left an efficient and systemised estate with a large library, and collections of everything from armour to art.

Derwynt died soon after Arthur's reign ended. His great passion had been building; there had been little time for women. Many of his buildings lasted for centuries. Some were built over, and some were torn down and the materials used again on the same site, remaining at the heart of the building for up to a millennium.

Berin had built his life on maintaining the status quo through the law, and after Arthur's reign ended, he found it challenging to become a vessel for change, preferring to maintain his court and uphold the law.

His concession to change was a pilgrimage every three years to Tours and twice to

Jerusalem. During these pilgrimages, he discovered even more ideas to open his mind to new or other ways of achieving justice, and some of these ideas he brought home with him to adapt to his own legal courts.

He happily continued in the role of magistrate well into his seventies, through numerous successors to Arthur, fondly remembering his role at Camelot and lamenting the passage of a golden era.

He was remembered by his associates, nephews and nieces as a lively history book, full of detail, ready with an argument – even fun – never quite losing that aggressive edge that kept his court subjects in check even when they were calling for blood.

His legacy was a standard legal system, which he himself defied more and more as he grew older and, some say, wiser.

After the incident with Guinevere, **Lancelot** lived out the remainder of his days in seclusion, growing bitter through his regrets and anger at the deception arranged by his fellow knights when he and Guinevere may have made a life together. However, he did come to understand his passion for the cause and his beliefs, and how other men may have seen him.

The news of Arthur's death didn't surprise Lancelot, but signalled the end of an era that he longed to revisit and relive in a different way.

As he grew older, Lancelot learned to take pleasure from the arts and became quite skilled at painting and sculpture, in which he was permitted to indulge at the monastery as the monks came to understand this man who had fallen so far from grace. Most of his art depicted the pure beauty of the world and the human frailty of emotions it did not attempt to justify his mistakes.

When he eventually passed away at age sixty-five, his gift to the world through his art, was the message that it is enough to 'simply be'.

As **Inger** grew older and settled into British life, he had to overcome his remorse for forsaking his own country, even to the point of killing men like he had been who came in search of a new beginning.

Inger's reliance on the stars grew as he began to test the astrology that his father had taught him, predicting weather and other events based on patterns he knew and, gradually, on feelings he experienced.

Personal experiences such as having children, coping with the long sickness that befell Helna after their first child and the torment of deciding whether to have another child, all led Inger to conclude that life was one huge pattern, so intricate and detailed like the stars that someone or something had to have created it. Man had not been solely responsible for the tragedies, the victories and the beauty of the world.

Time in Avalon

Some Arthurian versions talk of the fact that Avalon ran at a different pace and had circular rather than linear time. This meant that the passage between Avalon and the mainland, through the mists of Avalon, was not a passage only of geography but of time as well. While this bridge was strong during Arthur's reign, it deteriorated afterwards making it virtually impossible to pass between Avalon and the mainland in real time.

Inger lived a long and satisfying life, outliving most of his confreres, and learned to enjoy the magic of experiences as they were happening.

He learned empathy and understanding, rather than tolerance and forbearance. He learned the magic of spontaneity, the value of flexibility and the importance of passion.

After Arthur's reign, Nimue returned to Merlin's cave to begin plans for a new order, and Morgaine retreated to Avalon with Arthur's body where the time differences continued to grow stronger until it was nearly impossible to cross between one and the other.

It is said that Nimue released Merlin, who is to this day wandering the woodlands and hills, working through nature and the basic goodness in society, to bring the influence of the old gods into special moments in people's lives, to cherish and remember, and tell their children.

THE ARTHURIAN CHARACTERS AND THEIR CORRESPONDING ICS

Now that you have read the story of King Arthur and have been introduced to the eight key Celtic archetypes or personalities, we can summarise the list of Arthurian Characters used in NeuroPower. Sir Lancelot the Crusader, Sagramore the Commander, Bedwin the Chancellor, Merlin the Bard, Cai the Treasurer, Inger the Navigator, Berin the Judge, and finally Derwynt the Architect. These can be listed with their corresponding ICs as follows:

1.	C2P2I1	The Crusader	5.	C2P1I2	The Architect
2.	C2P2I2	The Bard	6.	C2P1I1	The Navigator
3.	C1P2I2	The Chancellor	7.	C1P1I1	The Treasurer
4.	C1P1I2	The Commander	8.	C1P2I1	The Judge

APPENDIX 11

The NeuroPower Assumptions

The NeuroPower Assumptions are truisms that NeuroPower practitioners live by when working with NeuroPower.

1. Neuroplasticity is real. Neurons that fire together wire together – our conscious thoughts shape our neural pathways within our brain which is far more plastic (malleable) than we once realised.
2. Our habits reflect our neural pathways.
3. Our Core Beliefs give context through priming while our cerebral cortex gives content through a process of selective attention.
4. Nobility can be hardwired into personality.
5. We all build our understanding of life through our narrative.
6. Our perception of reality is partial.
7. Every 'survival-based' action that you take that is not aligned with a higher attractor field will be met by an equal and opposite force.
8. Everyone acts with pure intentions.
9. Now is made up of the past, the present and the future.
10. People are more than their profile.
11. Everyone wants to grow and develop and be fully human (physis).
12. We breathe life into whatever we place our attention on.
13. Reality and the questions of existence change with each level of consciousness (meme).
14. The way we direct our energy has a huge influence on the people we are with.
15. People are doing their very best with the insight and resources they have at the time.

16. We are more human as we raise our consciousness, use our Genius, and embrace our more noble qualities.

17. Our Master profile affects our self-identity, focus and communications (wants) and our Mirror profile affects our behaviour (needs).

18. It's not who you are but where you are on your Quest.

19. Certainty is often inversely proportional to awareness.

20. People are not broken: they work perfectly well.

21. Every person is unique.

22. We grow through movement – not through being frozen.

23. People have all the resources they need – they just need to access, strengthen and apply them.

24. NeuroPower practitioners must walk the talk and apply the framework in their own life before they use it with others.

25. We all have a Genius which is reflected in our Neuro-Rational Type.

26. We all have a Neuro-Limbic Type that has a highly partial view of life and it is linked to our emotional script.

27. Our Neuro-Limbic Type gives us our energy and social motivation while our Neuro-Rational Type provides us with the higher thinking and complex problem-solving we need in life.

28. Human nobility acts as a powerful attractor field and can dissolve problems and create new realities.

29. Our memory is created in the present by recalling the emotion associated with an event and then creating images that complete the picture.

30. NeuroPower conversion refers to an individual's movement from their Neuro-Limbic Type to their Neuro-Rational Type.

31. NeuroPower transformation occurs in groups and refers to the corporate process that enables individuals to move from their Neuro-Limbic Type to their Neuro-Rational Type.

32. We understand our Neuro-Rational Type's 'brand' of nobility, but we have to learn all the others from the other Neuro-Rational Types.

33. Self-awareness, conscious living and converting the tension caused by problems into nobility is hard work but it is worth it.

APPENDIX 12

Applying the NeuroPower Insight to Make you a Better Leader

P1: Applying the insight to make you a better leader

1. PROVIDE ROLE CLARITY ABOUT HOW THE PERSON 'FITS' IN THE TEAM

As a leader you need to provide clarity about how the person 'fits' in the team. You need to do this for three reasons:

Firstly, once the person feels their role is valued by the group, it reduces up to 50% of their stress and the stress hormones charging around their body. This in turn increases the amount of energy available for goal pursuit, communication and getting things done.

Secondly, if the individual does not feel valued by the group over a prolonged period, it leads to conflict, it triggers the P1 emergency response, (an amygdala reaction or 'crunch') which sends the 'give up' and 'freeze' signal to the body. This creates individuals who are compliant but not engaged. In this state they will do as little as possible to keep out of trouble but not enough to creatively and proactively build the business.

Finally, every individual needs role clarity and to be playing a valuable role in the team - if it is not provided by the leader it will be provided informally by the individual instead. In this case it will rarely be strategically aligned to best achieve the business objectives of the team – instead it will reflect the role the group needs or enjoys having the individual play at the time – roles such as the tension breaker, the socialiser, the negative guy, the nay sayer etc.

Instead, develop clear roles with KPI measurement that links back to the business crusade you are on. It's more important that team members are clear on the importance of their role and the impact it has on the group's performance than having them create a 'designer' role that answers their personal aspirations. These aspirations can be part of the 25% of the individual's role that is discretionary (their "like to do wells") that they can focus on only if they have done their 75% "must do wells".

2. DEVELOP A CODE OF CONDUCT

This is important because the P1 system turns new behaviour into habit if it is repeated often enough. That's why baseline behaviours that are central to the organisation's employee value proposition like employee safety, conflict resolution and escalation processes need to be distilled down into their core 75% behavioural elements and encoded in a 'code of conduct'. This takes the implicit assumptions about how people in the team will act and embeds them in an explicit document that can be followed until the P1 automatic movement systems can take over and it becomes a habit.

3. ENSURE AGREEMENTS ARE KEPT AND THE CODE OF CONDUCT IS ENFORCED – IT ENHANCES TEAM MEMBER SATISFACTION

This is important because the team members will receive a positive endorphin hit only if they feel they are valued members of the team. All teams, by definition, are exclusive, meaning team members exclude those who are not part of the team. Contrary to popular belief, enforcing the code of conduct in a fair, consistent and agreed way reinforces the group norms and values and fosters team cohesion and bonding and significantly contributes to team member satisfaction.

4. BE CONSISTENT

This is one of the most important parts of building trust between yourself and the people you are leading. The more you can attend to the little things like – being on time, being fair, being polite, and saying the same things in front of the individual both when they are there and when they are not there, the more the P1 social centre relaxes and releases mental energy and space for the more important problems to be solved and opportunities to be chased.

5. WHEN YOU HAVE NOT DONE THIS WELL

You'll know when you have not done this well because three distinct kinds of people rise to the top as emergent leaders and exhibit disproportionately high influence over the group.

The first (NLT6) focuses the group on risks, slows decision making and uses bureaucracy to reduce their risk of failure.

The second (NLT2) focuses on anticipating and meeting the needs of the most powerful members of the team – running around 'keeping them happy'.

The third (NLT1) becomes obsessed with following the rules and ensuring everyone at all levels adheres to them regardless of their relevance, the administrative nightmare it can cause or the level of conflict that can ensue.

C1: Applying the insight to make you a better leader

1. MANAGEMENT THAT ENGENDERS CREATIVITY:

As a leader you need to foster a discovery approach that engenders creativity and innovation. You need to do this in four ways (Rosa; Journal of Business Research, 2008).

Firstly, manage organisations so that their knowledge base is more diverse than would occur normally. Creativity emerges from the recombination of existing knowledge. That's why organisations that excel in creativity and innovation like 3M and General Electric expose their employees to a wide range of information, training and learning that is outside their strict role/responsibility requirement. This diversity of knowledge can also be fostered through hiring consultants or team members with diverse professional/cultural/capability/socio-economic backgrounds. This is a technique used by IDEO and other product innovation consultants (Hargadon and Sutton, 1997; Kelly, 2001) (Rosa; Journal of Business Research, 2008).

Secondly encourage a collaborative approach and a thirst for novel approaches. Organisations tend to wait until problems present themselves and only then address them in ways that have worked in the past. This means that problems tend to be solved by the same people in the same roles in the same way. Companies that excel in innovation like Electronic Arts, Whirlpool, Google and QSL foster conversation and dialogue to get the problem out of the trenches and into wider discussion which involves people that are not usually involved in the formulation of the solution. (Rosa; Journal of Business Research 2008) Collaborative genius can only occur when ideas are developed by the group in a social, fun and interactive way rather than a competitive way. Fun triggers the neurobiology around C1, competition triggers the neurobiology around P2.

Thirdly, encourage the quick testing of ideas. Sometimes called rapid prototyping, this quick testing of ideas takes the idea from theory into practice and enables the team to see, touch and feel the idea. This engages the limbic and motor systems of insight and gives the project access to much wider and deeper insight than that found solely in the cortex (Rosa and Malter, 2002; van der Lugt, 2002).

Finally, reward behaviour that supports these principles and punish resistance. (Rosa; Journal of Business Research, 2008) The first three suggestions are risky. This fosters compliance rather than innovation unless there are very clear ground rules about the importance of innovation that are embedded through thoughtfully created performance guidelines that use operant conditioning to embed the desired behaviour and tangibly demonstrate that management and leadership are walking the talk.

2. ENCOURAGE FREEDOM OF EXPRESSION

This is important to remember because the innovative part of the brain is based on extraversion. Suppressed expression suppresses good ideas. What people say and what they do are often unrelated so if managers are able to see them as different it helps create an environment where people are not afraid to speak their mind in groups or to each other in conversation. Conversation helps makes sense of abstract, novel or untried approaches through an approach encapsulated in Weik's (1979) basic sense-making recipe – "How can I know what I know until I see what I say?" This takes spontaneous and random thoughts and translates them into integrated concepts with emotional and cognitive content (Rosa; Journal of Business Research 2008).

3. WHEN YOU HAVE NOT DONE THIS WELL

You'll know when you have not done this well because one distinct kind of person takes the role as emergent leader and exhibits disproportionately high influence over the group.

The (NLT7) focuses on having fun and keeping things light and easy – running around organising parties and wanting every moment to yield new and interesting discussion, ideas and thoughts.

P2: Applying the insight to make you a better leader

1. PROVIDE CLARITY ABOUT HOW THE INDIVIDUAL CAN BE REWARDED

As a leader you need to provide clarity about how the person will be rewarded for strategically aligned performance – what's in it for them? You need to do this for three reasons:

Firstly, work through how the team can be rewarded for achieving strategic lead and lag indicators. This is about team achievement and effort and teamwork. Everyone needs to be rewarded equally with a percentage bonus for each member of the team for the team's overall effort. This is important because it focuses attention on succeeding as a team rather than at the expense of the team, which is the natural function of the motivated and competitive brain.

Secondly, focus any competition with outside groups rather than with each other. Find a way to benchmark the team's effort with external competitors, last year's effort, other similar parts of the business that are in different geographies, etc. The brain rewards success chemically but it is based on a bell curve – winning isn't exciting to the P2 function unless you've beaten someone.

Finally, while the first two points relate to exogenous (outer) goals the effective leader always looks at ways they can reward discretionary effort by creating time or opportunity for the individual to pursue their own endogenous (internal) goals. This can be time off, coursework, the opportunity to meet somebody – anything really that aligns with the individual's sense of self and is something that motivates and interests them.

2. RECOGNITION AND FINANCIAL REWARD ARE THE SAME – SO TREAT THEM AS SUCH

This is important to remember because once the baseline income has been achieved the same parts of the brain respond to recognition and social standing and financial reward. Focus on finding better and better ways of saying thank you for discretionary effort. (For example, annual awards, hall of fame, photographs in the foyer, special trips away for a select group). Build your repertoire of ways to recognise.

3. GOAL SETTING HAS FOUR PARTS AND DIFFERENT TEAM MEMBERS WILL HAVE BRAINS THAT VARY IN THEIR ABILITY TO DO ALL FOUR

The four phases of achievement – (understanding the goal being chased, feeling excited about it, keeping attention on the goal along the way and monitoring our progress along the way) use four different parts of the brain. Most of us don't have equal parts of all four. Effective leaders have the group work together so that all four are covered and the goal is finally achieved.

4. DON'T MOVE THE GOAL POSTS

As we know, it's not a good idea to get between a dog and its food. In the same way, it's not a good idea to start moving the goal posts. This is because when the brain senses that victory is in hand and the game changes it uses ANGER to get things back on track. This is particularly true if the individual has linked their EGO (P2) to the successful outcome and they believe that you are about to take it away. This creates an amygdala reaction (a Crunch) that results in frustration that, if externalised, leads to explosive outbursts of anger which can frighten and spook all the other team members, and if internalised, leads to passive aggressive resistance.

5. WHEN YOU HAVE NOT DONE THIS WELL

You'll know when you have not done this well because three distinct kinds of people rise to the top as emergent leaders and exhibit disproportionately high influence over the group.

The first (NLT3) focuses on looking good (even at the expense of others) and focuses the group on activity at any cost – 'just do something!'

The second (NLT7) focuses on having fun and keeping things light and easy – running around organising Christmas parties and wanting every moment to yield new and interesting discussion, ideas and thoughts

The third (NLT8) becomes obsessed with running roughshod over everyone and getting what they want regardless of the cost.

12: Applying the insight to make you a better leader

1. BE EMPATHETIC AND ATTUNED TO YOUR COLLEAGUES

- Understand what motivates other people, even those from different backgrounds.
- Be sensitive to others' needs
- Listen attentively and think about how others feel
- 'Tune in' to others' moods

2. BE ORGANISATIONALLY AWARE AND UNDERSTAND YOUR CIRCLE OF INFLUENCE

- Appreciate the culture and values of the group or organisation
- Understand the organisation's social networks and know their unspoken norms
- Persuade others by engaging them in discussion and appealing to their self-interests
- Garner support from and offer support to key people

3. DEVELOP OTHERS IN THE ORGANISATION AND BE INSPIRATIONAL

- Coach and mentor others with compassion and personally invest time and energy in mentoring other people
- Provide feedback that people find helpful for their professional development
- Articulate a compelling vision, build group pride, and foster a positive emotional tone
- Lead by bringing out the best in people

4. ENCOURAGE AND FOSTER TEAMWORK

- Solicit input from everyone on the team
- Support all team members and encourage cooperation

11: Applying the insight to make you a better leader

1. PROVIDE CLARITY ABOUT HOW THE INDIVIDUAL CAN LEARN

As a leader you need to provide clarity about how the person can learn everything they need to get the job done. You need to do this in three ways:

Firstly, create a learning organisation – a place where people can learn from each other and are always interested in how they can do something better, faster and more effectively. At the core of this is the idea of sharing information. If the P1 and P2 work hasn't been done well, individuals hold onto information because they believe it can give them an advantage. If it has been done well, individuals freely exchange information so that everyone learns from everyone else.

Secondly, focus on making company information EASY to access. The whole love of learning is based on dopermanic systems in the brain that provide energy for a short-term fix of fascination. In other words, if it is too hard to get information from your systems, by the time people get the information they have lost interest.

Finally, create informal networks that specialise in information about something specific. These groups can then be blogged or asked on-line about issues and data can be supplied almost instantly. This makes learning fast and fun.

2. PRACTICAL INFORMATION DRIVES INTEREST

Encourage on-line resources to be phrased in a way that practically addresses an issue or up-skilling someone for a specific task. Most employees will search for information that will make their job easier or help them to success. If the information is framed in this way it increases uptake and interest significantly.

3. STRATEGY SHOULD BE DRIVEN BY LEAD AND LAG INDICATORS NOT JUST A GOOD IDEA

One key purpose of collecting information is to stress-test your strategy. This is about refining the lead and lag indicators that lay at its foundation and building a competitive strategy through understanding these better than your competition. This thinking and learning needs to be undertaken at all levels of the enterprise.

4. WHEN YOU HAVE NOT DONE THIS WELL

You'll know when you have not done this well because three distinct kinds of people rise to the top as emergent leaders and exhibit disproportionately high influence over the group (see *Core Beliefs* by Burow, 2007)

The first (NLT4) focuses on drawing attention to what is missing and a sense that we succeed because 'we are special' and so the world's insight and learning don't apply to us.

The second (NLT5) focuses on hoarding information in silos and not sharing.

The third (NLT9) become overwhelmed and refuse to make a decision unless they have all the information because they want to get it absolutely right - even if that means holding up decisions.

APPENDIX 13

The Neuroscience of the
Six Intelligences

R E L I S H

| Relatedness | Expression | Leading the Pack | Interpersonal Connection | Seeing the Facts | Hope for the Future |

SUMMARY OF THE KEY NEUROBIOLOGICAL SYSTEMS OF P1 (RELATEDNESS)

THE EVOLUTIONARY SOCIAL BRAIN FUNCTION OF P1

The P1 system enables survival through:

- Membership of a community (kinship) through compliance with a specific social role and understood social rules, socially known as moral behaviour (Ciaramelli et al, 2007)

- Movement of behaviour from a conscious action to a habitual response, freeing up mental energy for novel situations requiring creative thought (Saling & Phillips, 2007)

- Control of behaviour in terms of thoughts and physical reactions (Lieberman & Eisenberger, 2004)

- Sequencing events and behaviours (Ratey, 2002)

- The sense that we are the author and controller of our actions (Frith, 2002)

THE P1 SOMATIC ASPECT

Key neurobiological components in the P1 system:

1. The anterior cingulate cortex (ACC), a highly heterogenous substructure of the brain located between the superior surface of the corpus callosum and the cortex, contains several sub-regions implicated in the control of attention, particularly in tasks involving a conflict between learned automatic behaviour and task requirements (Frackowiak, 2004). Increased activity in the dorsal ACC has also been strongly associated with social distress resulting from social ostracism or exclusion (Eisenberger & Lieberman, 2004).

2. The primary motor cortex (M1), in association with the pre-motor area, is involved in the planning and execution of muscle movement (e.g. movement of the legs, abdomen, shoulder, arm, fingers, tongue etc). The M1 initiates movements "...from pressing an elevator button to performing a gymnastic exercise or tying a shoe it provides the organisation of smooth, timed and rhythmic movements among the many brain structures and the spinal chord" (Ratey, 2002, pp. 163-164).

3. Descending signals from the primary motor cortex are subject to modification by the cerebellum. The cerebellum, a distinct, cauliflower-shaped structure

at the back of the brain where the spinal chord merges with the brain stem, integrates feedback from the body's sensory systems following a movement and adjusts output signals from the primary motor cortex (Jueptner & Weiller, 1998). Damage to the cerebellum often results in poor coordination, clumsiness or ataxia (Greenfield, 2000). The cerebellum has also recently been implicated in the normal functioning of social behaviour (Ratey, 2002), and is equally important in mediating learned automatic responses to physical stimuli. For example, lesions to the cerebellum prevent the acquirement of classically conditioned responses (such as an eyeblink response created by pairing an auditory cue with a tap on the forehead; Bracha et al., 1997).

4. The basal ganglia, a diverse group of structures that sit below the cortex (including, amongst others, the striatum), are important for the execution of sustained movement; progressive degeneration of the basal ganglia is a hallmark feature of movement disorders including Parkinson's Disease and Huntington's Chorea (Greenfield, 2000). The basal ganglia are also involved in the selection of behaviours from a previously learned repertoire, introducing flexibility into learned automatic processes (Saling & Philips, 2007). While well-learned motor processes can be executed without activity in the pre-frontal cortex ('cognition'), subsequent adjustments to these actions will recruit the basal ganglia again (Saling & Philips, 2007).

5. The anterior insula (required for interoception/physical self-awareness; Craig, 2002) in concert with the orbito-frontal cortex (involved in reward and punishment processing; Amodio & Frith, 2006) help us make associations based on experiences of objects, that guide future decisions and may promote our survival (Ratey, 2002).

P1 SOMATIC MARKERS[1]: CHOOSING ACTION TO PROMOTE BELONGING

Somatic markers give the individual access to information about the likely best way forward based on past experience, by using current physiological body states to cue information from previous experiences involving similar states. "When circuits in posterior sensory cortices and in temporal and parietal regions process a situation that belongs to a given conceptual category, the pre-frontal circuits that hold records pertinent to that category become active. Next comes activation of regions that trigger

---

1 Damasio's somatic marker theory has recently been the subject of much debate. While it hasn't been discredited, it will be interesting to see where these ongoing directions take us.

appropriate emotional signals such as the ventromedial pre-frontal cortices, courtesy of an acquired [that is, learned] link between that category of event and past emotional-feeling responses" (Damasio, 2003, p. 147). This 'feeling'-based activation of behaviour shortens the window of time required to choose a response that has previously proved successful in similar situations.

For P1, somatic markers prompt decision-making focused on safety.

P1 EMOTION/FEELING ASPECT

> *Because of the ascending interactions with higher brain areas, there is no emotion without a thought, and many thoughts can evoke emotions. Because of the lower interactions, there is no emotion without a physiological or behavioural consequence, and many of the resulting bodily changes can also regulate the tone of emotional systems in a feedback manner.*

> (Panksepp, 1998, p. 27)

In addition to areas that directly receive sensory input, parts of the brain are dedicated to representational maps of the body's condition, giving rise to our senses of proprioception and interoception (the awareness of 'how you feel'). What we experience as emotions are strongly related to the physiological state of our bodies, as represented in these areas and interpreted by the frontal lobe. These maps are located in parts of the somatosensory cortex (specifically the insular cortex and secondary somatosensory cortex/SII), the hypothalamus and nuclei in the brain stem tegmentum (Damasio, 2003) and, in particular, the anterior insular and cingulate cortices (Craig, 2009). "Almost all recent imaging studies of emotion report joint activation of the AIC [anterior insular cortex] and the ACC [anterior cingulate cortex] in subjects experiencing emotional feelings, including [P1 emotions]... disgust, aversion, inequity, social exclusion, trust" (Craig, 2009, p. 60).

Damasio (2003) reports that positive feelings (i.e. 'happiness') give rise to significant increases in activity of the pre-frontal cortex, while negative feelings ('sadness') give rise to marked deactivation in pre-frontal cortices, consistent with a loss of cognitive fluency in those who are distressed. In the P1 emotional circuit, this includes positive feelings of acceptance and safety, and negative feelings of rejection and ostracism.

The P1 emotional system is characterised by:

1. Feelings of loneliness or panic if isolated from the group or feeling lonely. Studies

with mammals suggest brain areas involved in driving tribal belonging include areas of the diencephalon, including the thalamus and preoptic area, with stimulation of these structures eliciting panic and distress vocalisations (Klein, 2006). Corticotrophin-releasing hormone (CRH) is released into the blood by the hypothalamus in response to stress, including social isolation and promotes cortisol release from the adrenal cortex. While this response mobilises the body's energy stores and reduces inflammation [the 'fight or flight' response], prolonged activation is associated with many illnesses, and CRH has also been associated with a sense of loneliness and even panic (Klein, 2006). Prolonged administration of exogenous CRH can promote depressive responses (Panksepp, 1998).

2. Neutrality/Homeostasis. Serotonin modulators and anxiolytics (including the benzodiazepines, e.g. Valium) increase the ability of GABA inhibitory neurons to reduce excitatory transmission, particularly within the amygdala (Panksepp, 1998). "...drugs such as morphine that powerfully reduce [separation-induced] anxiety are also powerful alleviators of grief and loneliness in humans" (Panksepp, 1998, p. 263). Genetic abnormalities in serotonin transporters (and consequent changes to brain anatomy and physiology) are associated with higher levels of trait anxiety, particularly 'neuroticism' and 'harm avoidance' (Hariri & Holmes, 2006).

3. Positive emotions associated with social acceptance and belonging. Endorphins, naturally occurring opium-like compounds that stimulate well-being, are released in the brain in positive social situations. Lowered endorphin levels resulting from lack of stimulation can be compensated with alcohol, sweets and recreational drugs (Klein, 2006).

P1 THINKING ASPECT

1. Frontal cortex and left pre-frontal cortex (LPFC) are linked to three kinds of self control:

   - Suppressing/disrupting unwanted cognitive, affective or behavioural responses.

   - Involved in boosting the strength of weaker, but contextually appropriate, representations and action plans

   - The LPFC, along with the frontopolar region of the pre-frontal cortex (PFC), can flexibly combine symbolic representations using propositional rules to consider novel courses of action and, ultimately, set one in motion. (Eisenberger & Lieberman, 2009)

2. Ventromedial pre-frontal cortex (VMPFC). Linked with ensuring pro-social

behaviour by enabling the individual to 'fast forward' and play scenario options in a given social situation and then choose an appropriate one based on past similar situations and the best and worst emotional outcomes that have been experienced in the past (Damasio, 1999).

3. VMPFC also correlates well with several studies investigating moral reasoning. This area shows increased activity when healthy individuals are engaged in moral reasoning, and those with lesions in this area are more willing and faster to judge personal moral violations as acceptable behaviour. Lesions to the VMPFC in childhood impair the development of moral knowledge and the ability to make ethical judgements (Ciaramelli, 2007).

4. The striatum, cerebellum and brain stem are important in implicit and procedural learning, including priming, conditioning and skill-learning tasks (Richmond & Nelson, 2007).

5. Rapid eye movement (REM) sleep has been shown to be critical to consolidating episodic and declarative memories (linked to I1 and I2), but not procedural memory. Rasch et al., (2009) reported that preventing the REM phase during sleep (using selective serotonin reuptake inhibitors) improved, rather than inhibited, the consolidation of simple motor tasks.

Slow Ritualised Behaviour of P1

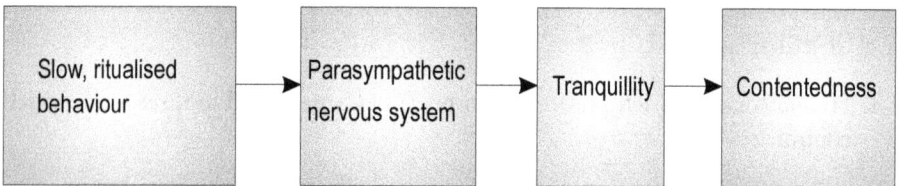

Adapted from Nataraja (2008)

Summary of the Key Neurobiological Systems of C1 (Expression)

THE EVOLUTIONARY SOCIAL BRAIN FUNCTION OF C1

The C1 system enables:

- Adaptation to novel situations by thinking laterally or creatively, using creativity to problem-solve and resolve conflict with others.

- Maintaining positive expectations for the future (Klein, 2006).

- Motivation to repeat constructive activities. Natural rewarding activities are necessary for survival and appetitive motivation ('pleasure'), usually governing beneficial biological behaviours like eating, sex, and reproduction and behaviour directed towards hedonic or pleasurable processes. Social contacts can further facilitate the positive effects exerted by pleasurable experiences (Esch and Stefano, 2004).

- Aversive motivation (pain) or getting away from hedonically unpleasant experiences of food, recreational drugs, sex and the like (Esch & Stefano, 2004).

- The experience of pleasure, the state of feeling happiness and satisfaction resulting from an experience that one enjoys (Esch & Stefano, 2004).

- The experience of extraversion and subjective well-being (Pavot et al., 1990).

- Satisfaction of the body returning to homeostatic conditions ('sensory alliesthesia'; Burgdorf & Panksepp, 2006).

DISTINGUISHING 'PLEASURE' (C1) FROM 'REWARD' (P2)

While much of neuroscientific research has historically blurred the distinction between external and internal rewards, each of these components is distinct. Where P2 relates to external rewards, goals and motivations, C1 involves the pursuit of pleasure resulting in internal neurochemical rewards arising from activation of dopaminergic pathways.

As Burgdorf & Panksepp (2006, p. 184) surmise:

> There appear to be at least two distinct classes of positive affect (PA) states represented in the brain, with separate but overlapping neuroanatomical substrates. An appetitive PA system, devoted to foraging and reward-

seeking, associated in part with the effects of psychostimulants such as cocaine and amphetamine is dependent in part on the ventral striatal dopamine system. [This is the P2 goal- and reward-oriented system.] A nearby PA system involved in processing sensory pleasure such as pleasurable touch and hedonic tastes, involves the opiate and GABA system in the ventral striatum and orbital frontal cortex. [This is the C1 pleasure-oriented system.] These classical distinctions between appetitive and consummatory processes have been encapsulated in motivational theories which distinguish the brain substrates of expectancy type processes, such as seeking and wanting, from consummatory reward processes… and are well illustrated by the work of Jurgens (1976), in which electrical brain stimulation revealed two distinct brain rewarding brain circuits that elicited two separate call types.

C1 SOMATIC ASPECT

Key neurobiological components in the C1 system:

1. [When C1 is engaged] the blood pulses faster (three to five heartbeats a minute faster than their normal state) skin temperature rises by about a tenth of a degree centigrade. This stimulation causes the skin to become somewhat damper, and skin conductance drops. Even the fingers tremble, though not in a jerky way (Klein, 2006).

2. When you feel good, the muscles relax and become more flexible. In addition, since happiness also shifts our hormonal balance, changes take place that we don't feel directly. The zygomatic muscle, which pulls the mouth upward, tenses slightly. The orbicularis oculi muscle with its crow's feet has also contracted slightly. By contrast, the corrugator supercilii muscle, which creates expressions of disgust, sadness and fear by pulling up the eyebrows, is relaxed (Klein, 2006).

3. Every feeling has its own corresponding pattern of brain activity, including both limbic and cortical components, and some parts of the brain are activated in both positive ('happy') and negative ('sad') feelings. Data arrives from the body through the brainstem, activating many regions of the mid-brain. The cerebellum processes impulses from the brainstem and gives orders to the muscles (e.g. the command to laugh when we are amused). Above the cerebellum, the diencephalon is activated to release emotional excitement. In the cerebrum, the pre-frontal cortex is especially active, converting emotions to plans and actions (Klein, 2006; Damasio, 2003).

4. The pleasure and pain centre in the brain is linked to the limbic system, which is made up of the limbic lobe and certain additional structures. The limbic lobe surrounds the corpus callosum and consists of the cingulate gyrus and the parahippocampal gyrus. The hippocampus, which is in the floor of the temporal horn of the lateral ventricle and is closely linked to memory processing, is also included in the limbic lobe. Additional structures incorporated in the limbic system are the dentate gyrus, amygdala, hypothalamus (especially the mamillary bodies), septal area (in the basal forebrain) and thalamus (anterior and some other nuclei). "Functionally, the 'hippocampal formation' consists of the hippocampus, the dentate gyrus and most of the parahippocampal gyrus. Neurobiologists have long known that the euphoria induced by drugs or abuse, sex or other things we enjoy arises because all these factors ultimately boost the activity of the brain's pleasure and reward systems" (Esch & Stefano, 2004, p. 236).

5. Reward pathways are evolutionarily ancient, like limbic structures, and the two share common mechanisms and morphologies. In fact, integral central nervous system (CNS) components involving reward and motivational processes are of limbic origin. Pre-frontal or orbito-frontal cortices, cingulate gyrus, amygdala, hippocampus and nucleus accumbens all participate in reward physiology. Thus pleasure, the limbic system and reward circuitry seem to be biologically connected. Memories of the pleasure of wellness, i.e. 'remembered wellness', are accessible to this circuitry through hippocampal mechanisms (Esch & Stefano, 2004).

6. Natural rewards can be modulated by the activity of the brain's reward and motivation circuitry. Feeding, sexual activity or maternal behaviour can be facilitated by opiate activation of the reward system. The origin of the ventral tegmental dopamine system (including the ventral tegmental area/VTA) seems to provide an important neurochemical interface where exogenous opiates and endogenous opioid peptides can activate a CNS mechanism involved in appetitive motivation and [internal neurochemical] reward… the VTA serves as an appetitive motivation system for diverse behaviours, since it controls both normal and pathological behaviours (Esch & Stefano, 2004).

C1 EMOTION/FEELING ASPECT

Because of the ascending interactions with higher brain areas, there is no emotion without a thought, and many thoughts can evoke emotions. Because of the lower interactions, there is no emotion without a physiological or

*behavioural consequence, and many of the resulting bodily changes can also
regulate the tone of emotional systems in a feedback manner.*

(Panksepp, 1998, p. 27)

In addition to areas that directly receive sensory input, parts of the brain are dedicated to representational maps of the body's condition, giving rise to our senses of proprioception and interoception (the awareness of 'how you feel'). What we experience as emotions are strongly related to the physiological state of our bodies, as represented in these areas and interpreted by the frontal lobe. These maps are located in parts of the somatosensory cortex (specifically the insular cortex and SII), the hypothalamus and nuclei in the brain stem tegmentum (Damasio, 2003) and, in particular, the anterior insular and cingulate cortices (Craig, 2009). "Almost all recent imaging studies of emotion report joint activation of the AIC [anterior insular cortex] and the ACC [anterior cingulate cortex] in subjects experiencing emotional feelings, including [C1 emotions]... happiness and sexual arousal" (Craig, 2009, p. 60).

Damasio (2003) reports that positive feelings (i.e. 'happiness') give rise to significant increases in activity of the pre-frontal cortex, while negative feelings 'sadness') give rise to marked deactivation in pre-frontal cortices, consistent with a loss of cognitive fluency in those who are distressed. In the C1 emotional circuit, this includes positive feelings of excitement, happiness and the anticipation of pleasure.

The C1 emotional system can be characterised by:

1. **Dopamine:** While oxytocin, vasopressin and beta-endorphin play important roles in desire, contentment and sexual attraction, however, the C1 system is dominated by dopamine (Klein, 2006).

2. **The Pleasure Pathway:** Amphetamines are one of many ruinously addictive drugs available throughout the world, including cocaine, crack, heroin, opium, etc. They all work by supplying dopamine to the tegmentum-nucleus accumbens (or 'pleasure pathway'), similar to the effects shown in sensation seekers. The mechanism of addiction is the activation and high reactivation potential of the neural pathways that cause a person to find a particular drug pleasurable. This makes sense: you anticipate how pleasurable it will be and come back for more (Department of Psychology, Florida State University, 2007).

3. Neuroscientist Bejjani triggered the sudden onset of mirth in 1999 by stimulating the **nucleus accumbens**. Until recently the dopamine pathway to the nucleus

accumbens was largely considered to be the key brain substrate for pleasure (Burgdorf and Panksepp, 2006).

4. In humans, the anticipation of an **imminent and highly predictable reward** elicits positive affect (Burgdorf & Panksepp, 2006).

5. Berridge (2003) suggests that the areas linked with positive affective reactions in the brain are **pre-frontal and cingulate cortex, the nucleus accumbens and its mesolimbic projection, lateral hypothalamus** and other structures associated with brain stimulation reward, **the ventral pallidum, and the brain stem** (especially the parabrachial nucleus).

C1 THINKING ASPECT

1. The left pre-frontal cortex (LPFC) is linked to cheerfulness and optimism (Klein, 2006).

2. The orbital frontal cortex (OFC) has been found to be activated in fMRI brain imaging of positive emotional states related to taste-induced positive arousal, olfactory-induced positive arousal, as well as somatosensory-induced positive arousal. Positive arousal states induced by music as well as mothers viewing pictures of newborn babies have also been shown to increase orbital frontal activity. In non-human primates, a subset of orbital frontal cortex neurons are activated specifically by taste stimuli that are palatable to the species (Burgdorf & Panksepp, 2006).

3. Divergent or creative thinking, the "...general process underlying the fluent production of alternative ideas during creative problem-solving", is characterised by strong increases in the complexity of EEG recordings within the frontal cortex, "... reflecting higher degrees of freedom in the competitive interactions among cortical neuron assemblies" (Molle et al, 1996).

Summary of the Key Neurobiological Systems of P2 (Leading the Pack)

THE EVOLUTIONARY SOCIAL BRAIN FUNCTION OF P2

The P2 system enables:

1. Survival through goal directed behaviour and independent action (Berkman & Lieberman, 2009).

2. Motivation and drive to push the mind and behaviour to stay on track for the achievement of purposeful goals that may involve competition with other members of the group for individual reward. Specifically, this involves attention, motor control, response inhibition and progress monitoring (Decety et al., 2004).

3. Prioritisation of options so that the individual can achieve the greatest benefit with minimum cognitive, somatic or emotional effort.

4. A sense of urgency and independence; a sense of willpower and ego.

DISTINGUISHING 'PLEASURE' (C1) FROM 'REWARD' (P2)

While much of neuroscientific research has historically blurred the distinction between external and internal rewards, each of these components is distinct. Where P2 relates to external rewards, goals and motivations, C1 involves the pursuit of pleasure resulting in internal neurochemical rewards arising from activation of dopaminergic pathways.

As Burgdorf & Panksepp (2006, p. 184) surmise:

There appear to be at least two distinct classes of positive affect (PA) states represented in the brain, with separate but overlapping neuroanatomical substrates. An appetitive PA system, devoted to foraging and reward-seeking, associated in part with the effects of psychostimulants such as cocaine and amphetamine is dependent in part on the ventral striatal dopamine system. [This is the P2 goal- and reward-oriented system.] A nearby PA system involved in processing sensory pleasure such as pleasurable touch and hedonic tastes, involves the opiate and GABA system in the ventral striatum and orbital frontal cortex. [This is the C1 pleasure-oriented system.] These classical distinctions between appetitive and consummatory processes have been encapsulated in motivational theories which distinguish the brain substrates of expectancy type processes, such as seeking and wanting, from consummatory reward processes... and are well illustrated by the work of Jurgens (1976), in which electrical brain stimulation revealed two distinct brain rewarding brain circuits that elicited two separate call types.

P2 SOMATIC ASPECT

Key neurobiological components in the P2 system:

1. **Motor Control.** Literature on the neural bases of goal pursuit observes the importance of brain regions related to motor control, including primary motor cortex, supplementary motor area, premotor cortex, cerebellum and basal ganglia (Berkman & Lieberman, 2009). This reflects recruitment of P1 motor circuits to enable execution of behaviours to achieve a set goal (P2).

2. **The orientation association area.** This area in the parietal lobe establishes a three-dimensional sense of 'self', creating a boundary between 'self' and 'non-self' that orientates us in physical space and time. The construction of an arbitrary boundary line between 'self' and 'non-self' is clearly essential to our ability to interact with our physical world. Our ability to move around without bumping into things, for example, requires the formation of a mental map that contains details about the environment in terms of how far away objects are and what relevance they have. In many ways, therefore, the sense of 'self' can be viewed as an artefact of our interaction with the physical world (Nataraja, 2008, pp. 82-83).

P2 SOMATIC MARKERS[2]: CHOOSING ACTION TO PROMOTE SUCCESS

Somatic markers give the individual access to information about the likely best way forward based on past experience. "When circuits in posterior sensory cortices and in temporal and parietal regions process a situation that belongs to a given conceptual category, the pre-frontal circuits that hold records pertinent to that category become active. Next comes activation of regions that trigger appropriate emotional signals such as the ventromedial pre-frontal cortices, courtesy of an acquired [that is, learned] link between that category of event and past emotional-

---

2   Damasio's somatic marker theory has recently been the subject of much debate. While it hasn't been discredited, it will be interesting to see the direction in which these ongoing directions take us.

feeling responses" (Damasio, 2003, p. 147). This 'feeling'-based activation of behaviour shortens the window of time required to choose a response that has previously proved successful in similar situations.

For P2, somatic markers prompt decision-making focused on previous experiences where there has been success or achievement. Actions are selected that give the greatest chance of achieving success.

P2 EMOTION/FEELING ASPECT

> *Because of the ascending interactions with higher brain areas, there is no emotion without a thought, and many thoughts can evoke emotions. Because of the lower interactions, there is no emotion without a physiological or behavioural consequence, and many of the resulting bodily changes can also regulate the tone of emotional systems in a feedback manner.*
>
> (Panksepp, 1998, p. 27)

In addition to areas that directly receive sensory input, parts of the brain are dedicated to representational maps of the body's condition, giving rise to our senses of proprioception and interoception (the awareness of 'how you feel'). What we experience as emotions are strongly related to the physiological state of our bodies, as represented in these areas and interpreted by the frontal lobe. These maps are located in parts of the somatosensory cortex (specifically the insular cortex and SII), the hypothalamus and nuclei in the brain stem tegmentum (Damasio, 2003) and, in particular, the anterior insular and cingulate cortices (Craig, 2009). "Almost all recent imaging studies of emotion report joint activation of the AIC [anterior insular cortex] and the ACC [anterior cingulate cortex] in subjects experiencing emotional feelings, including [P2 emotions]… anger, fear and indignation" (Craig, 2009, p. 60).

Damasio (2003) reports that positive feelings (i.e. 'happiness') give rise to significant increases in activity of the pre-frontal cortex, while negative feelings ('sadness') give rise to marked deactivation in pre-frontal cortices, consistent with a loss of cognitive fluency in those who are distressed. In the P2 emotional circuit, this includes positive feelings of success, and negative feelings of failure or frustration arising from external constraint.

P2 goal-oriented feelings include:

1. **High motivation to succeed.**

2. **Anger and frustration.** Anger is associated with activation of the left orbital frontal cortex, right anterior cingulate cortex, and bilateral anterior temporal poles (Dougherty et al., 1999).

3. **Power and perception of strength and dominating behaviour.** Testosterone is linked to aggressive behaviour in animals, and engaging in competitive tasks increases blood testosterone levels in human males (Nelson & Trainor, 2007). Cortisol, released during the fight or flight response, mobilises energy reserves and suppresses the immune system, contributing to increased short-term performance.

4. **Urgency or impatience.** Adrenaline and testosterone. Recent studies have suggested considerable overlap in the neural circuitry activated by rewards in the social (e.g. praise and status) and economic (e.g. money) domains (Saxe & Haushofer, 2008).

P2 THINKING ASPECT

1. **The attention association area.** "Across the different contemplative disciplines, various techniques are used to focus the mind to single-pointed attention, including mantras, chanting, images and repetitive movement. All these techniques trigger activity in the attention association area in the pre-frontal cortex. The neurons in this area of the brain are associated with goal-directed behaviour; both physical and psychological. Navigation through a crowded train station, for example, requires activity in this part of the brain, as we filter out redundant sensory information and focus only on those elements that can guide our path through the station. Similarly, in order to examine a thought properly or come up with a plan of action, we need to focus on the issue at hand and filter out redundant thoughts" (Nataraja, 2008, pp. 82-83).

2. **Pre-frontal cortex.** Areas of the pre-frontal cortex (PFC) are involved in the generation and maintenance of goal representation, as well as response inhibition in the service of maintaining action towards those goals. "Many forces pull us away from or against our goals, and a major role of the PFC is to guide our attention and behaviour through this gauntlet in a 'top-down' or executive manner, in a process that is known as Top-Down Excitatory Biasing (TEB). Within a goal

pursuit context, TEB can be thought of as a form of attentional control that serves to focus our cognitive resources on a goal or goal-relevant behaviour to the exclusion of other temptations or distractions. The PFC is involved in top-down regulation of both motor and non-motor responses such as cognitions and emotions" (Berkman & Lieberman, 2009).

Rapid Ritualised Behaviour Fosters P2

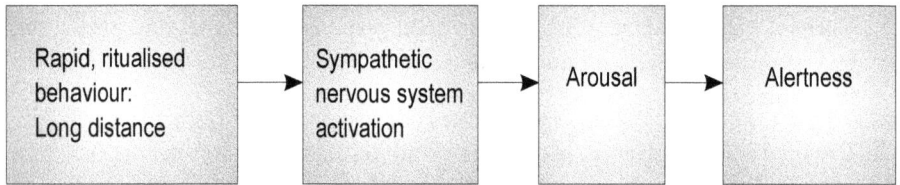

| Rapid, ritualised behaviour: Long distance | → | Sympathetic nervous system activation | → | Arousal | → | Alertness |

Adapted from Nataraja (2008)

Summary of the Key Neurobiological Systems of I2 (Interpersonal Connection)

THE EVOLUTIONARY SOCIAL BRAIN FUNCTION OF I2

The I2 system enables an individual to:

1. Survive through understanding and empathising with others, and through connection and loving friends and family.

2. Empathise with others and provide support and comfort during both good and bad times (attachment).

3. Best guess how others will react through Theory of Mind being able to guess what somebody else is thinking about you and others. This can be described as a process by which most healthy human adults:

   a. attribute unobservable mental states to others (and under certain circumstances, to the self); and

   b. integrate these attributed states into a single coherent model that can be used to explain and predict the target's behaviour and experiences (Saxe & Wexler, 2005).

4. Form lasting and meaningful relationships through romantic (pair bonding) and maternal love (Dêbiec, 2007).

I2 SOMATIC ASPECT

Key neurobiological components in the I2 system:

1. **Maternal Love:** Mothers viewing their own child showed increased activation of the orbital frontal cortex (OFC), periaqueductal grey, anterior insular cortex, and dorsal and ventrolateral parts of the putamen (Noriuchi, Kikuchi & Senoo, 2008).

2. **Attachment and Pair Bonding** recruit the medial insular cortex, anterior cingulate cortex and hippocampus and, in the subcortex, parts of the striatum and nucleus accumbens which together constitute core regions of the reward system (Zeki, 2007).

3. **Mirror Neurons** give us the ability to have mindsight or empathetic attunement.

These neurons are found within the pre-frontal cortex and Broca's area and fire when another individual is observed engaging in a specific behaviour. Empathy is thought to emerge when the facial expressions and posture of another individual activate similar sensory-motor circuits in an observer. These motor systems, in turn, are assumed to activate networks of emotion in the observer associated with such actions (Rizzolatti & Craighero, 2004; Wolf, Gales, Shane & Shane, 2000; 2001).

4. **Spindle Neurons** (also known as Von Economo Neurons) that are shared by humans with only a few species of higher primates, whales and elephants, are located in layer V of both the anterior paracingulate cortex (Gallagher & Frith, 2003) an orbito-frontal cortex (particularly the fronto-insular cortex, FI; Phillips, 2004). These large, high velocity neurons are currently the focus of intense research for their role in social cognition and emotions. John Allman from the California Institute of Technology has argued for the place of spindle neurons in distinguishing between two (of several) behavioural circuits in the brain:

   One is more deliberating, thinking about issues of fairness, punishment, moral judgements and the like. [This is the logical and moral reasoning encompassed in the P1 thinking style.] The second, faster system mediated by spindle cells controls more intuitive behaviour during social interactions. If you love someone, you know instantly how to react to them. You don't have to think. This is where spindle cells are important, Allman believes. "The main thing [spindle cells] do is to adjust your behaviour in a rapid real-time interaction in a complex social environment," he says.

   (Cited in Phillips, 2004)

5. **Visual system** – for when we see the face of someone we love, namely the cerebral cortex, orbital frontal cortex, anterior cingulate, cerebellum, insula, posterior hippocampus, caudate nucleus and putamen (Zeki, 2007).

6. **Romantic love.** Includes the activation of the frontal, parietal and middle temporal cortex as well as a large nucleus located at the apex of the temporal lobe, known as the amygdala (Zeki, 2007).

7. **Regions of the brain linked to either maternal or romantic love.** The anterior cingulate cortex, the ventral, caudate nucleus, insula, striatum, (consisting of putamen, cordate nucleus and globus pallidus) periaqueductal (central) grey and hippocampus (Zeki, 2007).

I2 EMOTION/FEELING ASPECT

Because of the ascending interactions with higher brain areas, there is no emotion without a thought, and many thoughts can evoke emotions. Because of the lower interactions, there is no emotion without a physiological or behavioural consequence, and many of the resulting bodily changes can also regulate the tone of emotional systems in a feedback manner.

(Panksepp, 1998, p. 27)

In addition to areas that directly receive sensory input, parts of the brain are dedicated to representational maps of the body's condition, giving rise to our senses of proprioception and interoception (the awareness of 'how you feel'). What we experience as emotions are strongly related to the physiological state of our bodies, as represented in these areas and interpreted by the frontal lobe. These maps are located in parts of the somatosensory cortex (specifically the insular cortex and SII), the hypothalamus and nuclei in the brain stem tegmentum (Damasio, 2003) and, in particular, the anterior insular and cingulate cortices (Craig, 2009). "Almost all recent imaging studies of emotion report joint activation of the AIC [anterior insular cortex] and the ACC [anterior cingulate cortex] in subjects experiencing emotional feelings, including [I2 emotions]… maternal and romantic love... and empathy" (Craig, 2009, p. 60).

Damasio (2003) reports that positive feelings (i.e. 'happiness') give rise to significant increases in activity of the pre-frontal cortex, while negative feelings 'sadness') give rise to marked deactivation in pre-frontal cortices, consistent with a loss of cognitive fluency in those who are distressed. In the I2 emotional circuit, this includes positive feelings of love and compassion and negative feelings of disconnection, disassociation and lack of generosity.

Emotional components of the I2 system include:

1. **Happiness, motherliness, joy, warmth, love, calmness, excitement** (Noriuchi et al., 2008). These feelings are made possible through areas of the brain that are rich in oxytocin and vasopressin receptors. Both are produced in the hypothalamus and released from the pituitary (Zeki, 2007).

2. **Love and attachment** are made possible through neuro-hypophyseal peptides oxytocin and vasopressin (Débiec, 2007; Zak, Stanton and Ahmadi, 2007). The receptors for both are distributed in many parts of the brain stem and are activated during both romantic and maternal love. Dopamine is released by the hypothalamus,

which is deep within the brain and functions as a link between the nervous and endocrine systems (Zeki, 2007).

3. **Love is associated with the deactivation of a common set of regions associated with negative emotions, social judgement and 'mentalising'** that is the assessment of other people's intentions and emotions (Zeki, 2007). This coincides with decreased levels of serotonin (Zeki, 2007).

4. **Generosity.** Treating individuals with oxytocin leads to greater demonstrated generosity, or 'liberality in giving', in tasks that require splitting of money with a stranger (Zak et al., 2007).

12 THINKING ASPECT

1. **Theory of Mind (TOM) or mentalising.** The four generally accepted brain regions that make TOM possible are the right tempo-parietal junction for the attribution of mental states, the left temporo-parietal junction posterior cingulate and medial pre-frontal cortex (Saxe & Wexler, 2005).

2. **Deactivated parts of the brain when in love.** The amygdala, related to fear, areas of the frontal and parietal cortices and parts of the temporal lobe are all commonly involved with negative emotions and cognitions. These areas are deactivated when faced with pictures of loved ones. Specifically this includes: the middle temporal cortex, occipital parietal junction, temporal pole, lateral pre-frontal cortex. "States of 'romantic love' involve 'a suspension of judgement or a relaxation of judgemental criteria by which we assess other people" (Zeki, 2007).

Summary of the Key Neurobiological Systems of I1 (Seeing the Facts)

THE EVOLUTIONARY SOCIAL BRAIN FUNCTION OF I1

The I1 system enables:

1. Survival through the recognition of objects and recall of information associated with them (Creem & Proffitt, 2001).

2. Communication with themselves internally and externally and with others through language.

3. Learning new things about the world and the formation of declarative memory.

4. The ability to identify patterns: in behaviour (both one's own and others'); the seasons; and dangerous situations.

I1 SOMATIC ASPECT

Key neurobiological components in the I1 system:

1. **Visual information** that is received by the visual cortex is distributed to cortical areas that perform specialised visual processing functions. This system includes: the posterior parietal lobe, temporal cortex, parietal cortex, V1 through V2, V3, the middle temporal area, medial superior temporal area, and posterior parietal cortex (Creem & Proffitt, 2001).

2. **Two visual processing streams** are classically defined, responsible for 'what' (ventral stream) and 'where' (dorsal stream) processing, respectively (Creem & Proffitt, 2001).

3. **The ventral stream**, projecting from V1 to the inferior temporal lobe, is responsible for object discrimination; the dorsal stream is responsible for object localisation in space (Creem & Proffitt, 2001).

4. **Information from the visual processing pathways** provides inputs to the prefrontal cortex, which plays a critical role in working memory (LeDoux, 1998).

5. **The hippocampus** is involved in the creation and retrieval of declarative (factual) memories (Creem & Proffitt, 2001).

6. **The medial temporal lobe and the pre-frontal cortex** (Bontempi & Durkin, 2007) including the hippocampus and parahippocampal cortex (Richmond & Nelson, 2007).

7. **Language-based communication** depends on healthy functioning of **Broca's region**, including BA44, BA45, and other areas involved in semantic, phonological, and syntactic verbal fluency (Heim, Eickhoft & Amunts, 2008; Davis et al., 2006; Cozolina, 2002).

I1 EMOTION/FEELING ASPECT

> *Because of the ascending interactions with higher brain areas, there is no emotion without a thought, and many thoughts can evoke emotions. Because of the lower interactions, there is no emotion without a physiological or behavioural consequence, and many of the resulting bodily changes can also regulate the tone of emotional systems in a feedback manner.*

(Panksepp, 1998, p. 27)

In addition to areas that directly receive sensory input, parts of the brain are dedicated to representational maps of the body's condition, giving rise to our senses of proprioception and interoception (the awareness of 'how you feel'). What we experience as emotions are strongly related to the physiological state of our bodies, as represented in these areas and interpreted by the frontal lobe. These maps are located in parts of the somatosensory cortex (specifically the insular cortex and SII), the hypothalamus and nuclei in the brain stem tegmentum (Damasio, 2003) and, in particular, the anterior insular and cingulate cortices (Craig, 2009). "Almost all recent imaging studies of emotion report joint activation of the AIC [anterior insular cortex] and the ACC [anterior cingulate cortex] in subjects experiencing emotional feelings, including [I1 emotions]... sadness... and aversion." (Craig, 2009, p. 60)

Damasio (2003) reports that positive feelings (i.e. 'happiness') give rise to significant increases in activity of the pre-frontal cortex, while negative feelings 'sadness') give rise to marked deactivation in pre-frontal cortices, consistent with a loss of cognitive fluency in those who are distressed. In the I1 emotional circuit, this includes positive feelings of curiosity and fascination.

I1 emotions include:

1. **Fascination:** Intense interest, a love of learning (if turned up too high this can

lead to greed or addiction). This fascination is driven by mid-brain dopaminergic regions that are engaged during learning (Poldrack & Foerde, 2008). If turned up too high this can lead to greed or addiction.

2. **Withdrawal:** Wanting to move back to get perspective and look or watch from a safe place (Damasio, 2003).

THINKING ASPECT OF I1 – CREATING SHORT- AND LONG-TERM MEMORIES

1. **The process of creating a memory:** After the information is perceived by the posterior cortex, the pre-frontal cortex captures and stores it in working memory for a while. "After a few minutes the frontal lobe washes its hands of the memory, and the hippocampus has to be recruited in order to retrieve it. When a memory is recalled with the help of the hippocampus, it is placed back in working memory in the frontal lobe. [In many ways, working memory is analogous to computer random-access memory (RAM)]. This is crucial for holding and manipulating words and our special representation. These functions fit roughly into the two components proposed by Allan Baddely, the phonological loop and the visuospatial sketchpad. A few years after the memory is acquired, the frontal lobe can access it directly without help from the hippocampus" (Ratey, 2002, p. 197).

2. **The process of long-term potentiation (LTP):** Memory is a set of distributed pieces that are pulled together on demand – they are literally created in the moment. Each new experience causes the neuronal firing across some synapses to strengthen and others to weaken. The pattern of change represents an initial memory of the experience. The memory will weaken and even disappear unless made stronger by LTP, which at a cellular level causes synapses to strengthen their connection to each other, coding the data as a series of connections. When such a memory is made, LTP blazes a trail along a series of neurons making it easier for subsequent messages along the same path.

3. **CREB** (cAMP Responsiveness Element Binding protein), an enzyme that regulates DNA transcription in neurons, enables the brain to produce proteins that are critical to synapse formation and the ability to move memories from short-term to long-term stores (Ratey, 2002).

Summary of the Key Neurobiological Systems of C2 (Hope for the Future)

C2 INTRODUCTION – THE MIND'S WIFI

The C2 system enables the individual to 'download' new ideas, paradigms or concepts that reflect a fundamentally changing world requiring a new map of understanding. C2 is a difficult system of the mind to chart and neuroscience is still not clear about exactly how the C2 Intelligence works. fMRI research on the neural pathways linked to meditation gives us the best current insight into how C2 may function.

> *Human characteristics such as inspiration and creativity are not determined by activity in a distinct and identifiable region of the brain; they emerge through the coordinated behaviour of large collections of neurons, spread over different regions of the human brain.*
>
> *If we are to gain a better understanding of some of our more elusive cognitive skills, our brain's emergent properties, we must examine them at the level of the whole brain.*
>
> *With the advent of non-invasive imaging techniques, such as Magnetic Resonance Imaging (MRI), we can study and measure activity across groups of neurons, even across the whole brain, and watch it in real time...*
>
> *This has revealed the different areas of the brain involved in specific tasks, the sequence in which activity in different brain regions changes during a particular task, and the impact of lifestyle factors and disease on brain function.*
>
> *Combining this new knowledge with detailed studies of individual neurons, their connections and their chemical signals, offers a more complete picture of how the brain works and responds, and is allowing us slowly to unravel the neural basis of human experience.*
>
> (Nataraja, 2008, pp. 72-73).

One controversial line of research into C2 states by Persigner attempted to use transcranial magnetic stimulation to induce mystical experiences by activating areas in the right parietal and temporal lobes (Khamsi, 2004).

"In John Horgan's book, Rational Mysticism, Persinger states that his helmet – sensationally named the 'God machine' by the media – has, as yet, not been able to induce a religious or mystical experience in its creator. Persinger attributes this lack of effect to his generally sceptical and scientific state of mind. As higher levels of temporal lobe lability are associated with right-brained thinking, individuals who are predominantly left-brained thinkers can be assumed to have lower levels of temporal lobe lability and therefore a reduced likelihood of a religious or mystical experience on temporal lobe stimulation" (Nataraja, 2008, p. 79).

"Interestingly, people with higher temporal lability were also found to be associated with predominately right-brained – intuitive rather than rational – thinking. Stimulation of the right temporal lobe was reported to produce more pleasant experiences than those evoked by stimulation of the left temporal lobe" (Nataraja, 2008).

"Through their research, Newberg and d'Aquili have shown that mystical experiences are associated with specific patterns of brain activity not limited to the temporal lobes. Whereas spontaneously evoked religious experiences appear to involve circuitry that lies within the temporal lobe, mystical experiences evoked by meditation appear to involve circuitry throughout the entire brain" (Nataraja, 2008, p. 81).

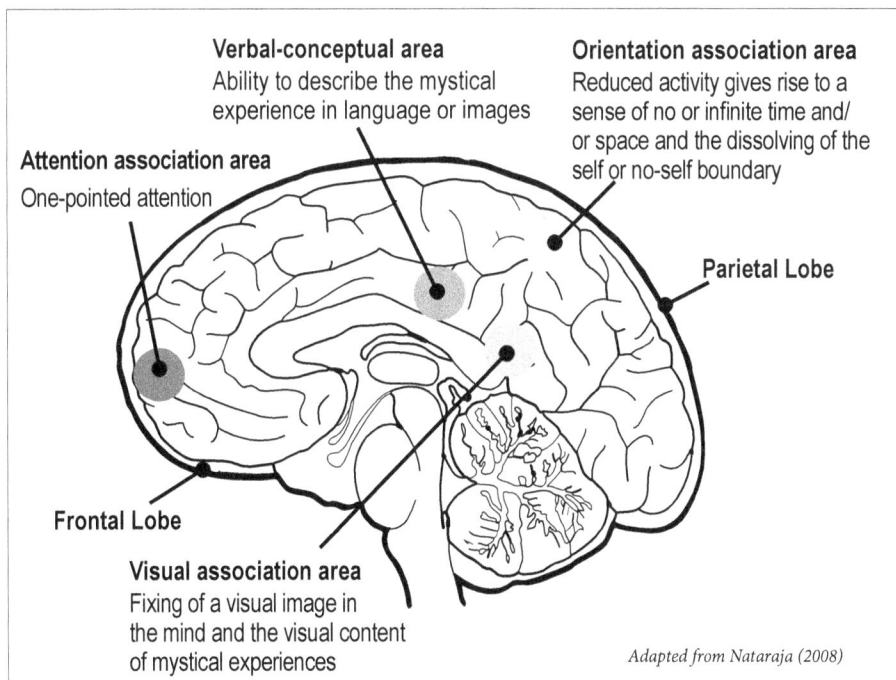

Verbal-conceptual area
Ability to describe the mystical experience in language or images

Orientation association area
Reduced activity gives rise to a sense of no or infinite time and/ or space and the dissolving of the self or no-self boundary

Attention association area
One-pointed attention

Parietal Lobe

Frontal Lobe

Visual association area
Fixing of a visual image in the mind and the visual content of mystical experiences

Adapted from Nataraja (2008)

Changes in the frontal and parietal lobes during mindfulness meditation

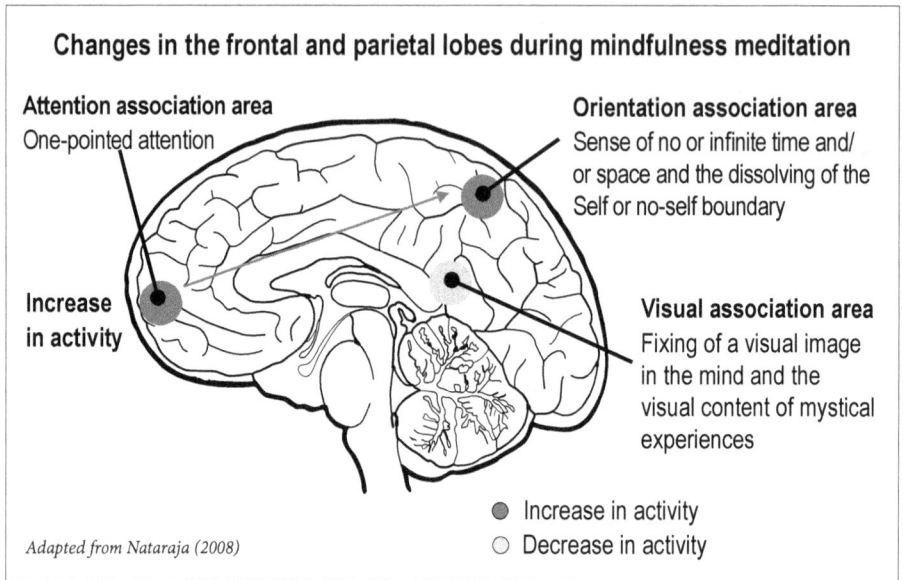

Attention association area
One-pointed attention

Orientation association area
Sense of no or infinite time and/ or space and the dissolving of the Self or no-self boundary

Increase in activity

Visual association area
Fixing of a visual image in the mind and the visual content of mystical experiences

Adapted from Nataraja (2008)

● Increase in activity
○ Decrease in activity

CHANGES IN THE FRONTAL AND PARIETAL LOBES DURING PASSIVE MEDITATION

Meditator: "Periodically, throughout the day, I become consciously aware of the fact that my mind is not focused on the now - instead, I'm fretting about some potential experience in the future. As I become aware of this, I bring my mind to focus on whatever I'm doing. This might be writing a letter or something as mundane as doing the washing up. With this intention my body relaxes and there is a conscious decision to focus my attention on experiencing the moment. Thoughts spontaneously pop into my head -something I forgot during a recent trip to the supermarket, a comment from a work colleague earlier in the day - but after acknowledging them I just return to the present-now. Slowly, over time, the gap between these interrupting thoughts gets longer and it takes no effort to focus my attention on the task at hand".

Neuroscientist: "At this point, there is an increase in activity in the attention association area and a decrease in activity in the surrounding areas of the frontal cortex and, from time to time, there are short bursts of activity in neurons in the frontal cortex. This reflects random thoughts arising and then dissipating. As the activity in the attention association area increases even further, with persistent one-focused attention, the short bursts of activity are eventually dampened and thoughts become more infrequent and less interrupting" (Nataraja, 2008, pp. 85-94).

Overall chain of brain processes during mindfulness meditation

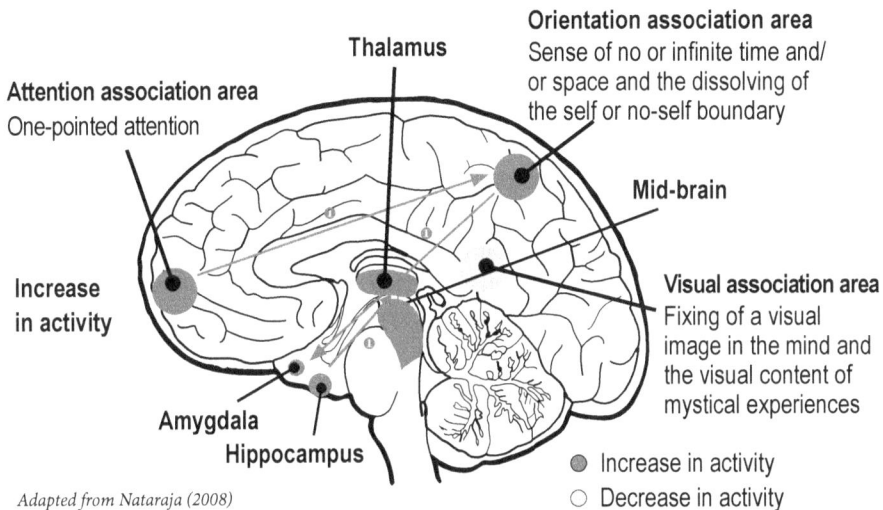

Orientation association area
Sense of no or infinite time and/
or space and the dissolving of
the self or no-self boundary

Thalamus

Attention association area
One-pointed attention

Mid-brain

Increase in activity

Visual association area
Fixing of a visual
image in the mind and
the visual content of
mystical experiences

Amygdala

Hippocampus

● Increase in activity
○ Decrease in activity

Adapted from Nataraja (2008)

Changes in the frontal and parietal lobes during active meditation

Attention association area
One-pointed attention

Orientation association area
Sense of no or infinite time and/
or space and the dissolving of
the self or no-self boundary

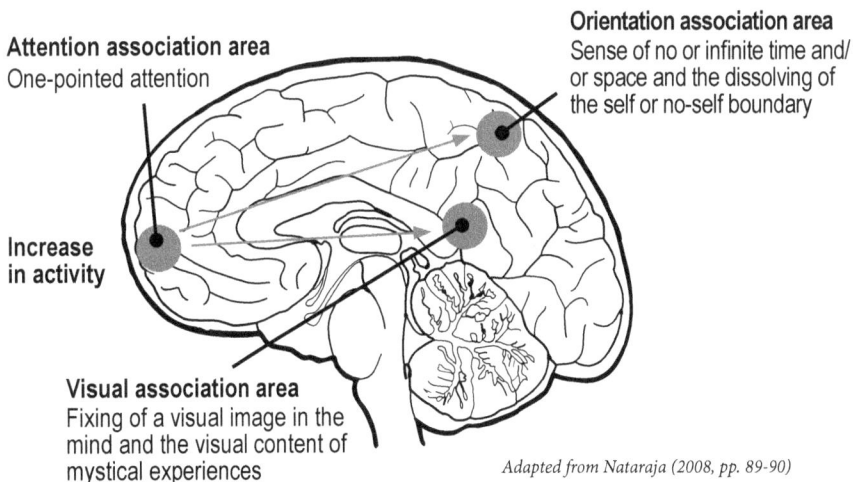

Increase in activity

Visual association area
Fixing of a visual image in the
mind and the visual content of
mystical experiences

Adapted from Nataraja (2008, pp. 89-90)

Meditator: "My awareness of my surroundings recedes into the background. At times I lose myself in the present-now, and time passes during which I'm not aware of my surroundings, not aware of my body or the ache in my back that was troubling me earlier, not really aware of where I begin and where I end. I feel a union with something much greater than myself, something much more expansive than my restricted and rigid sense of self."

Neuroscientist: "A decrease in activity in the orientation association area has occurred. Through one-pointed focus, the individual effectively filters out any so-called redundant information, including information from the sensory elements that build up an internal body image. As a result, the body image becomes blurred, and the boundary between body and everything else also becomes blurred. This gives rise to the sensation of unity with something that is greater than 'self'" (Nataraja, 2008, pp. 85-94).

Meditator: "As my awareness of the unity that lies beyond my restricted sense of self grows, my whole body appears to respond. A wave of bliss washes over me, like the sun emerging from a cloud and bathing me in light. I feel tremendous peace and union with all. Sometimes, at this point, an image or memory might appear and, with it, strong emotions. This can be enough to pull me back to myself as I delight in the image or replay the memory. But sometimes I manage to merely acknowledge the image or memory, storing it away for future examination, and then return to the present-now experience. Other times, I remain

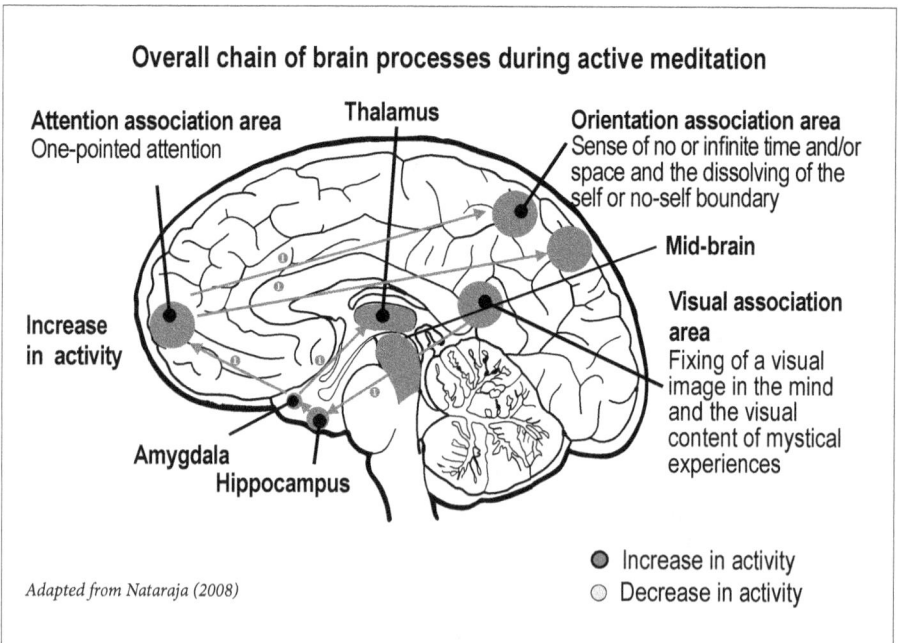

Overall chain of brain processes during active meditation

Attention association area
One-pointed attention

Thalamus

Orientation association area
Sense of no or infinite time and/or space and the dissolving of the self or no-self boundary

Mid-brain

Visual association area
Fixing of a visual image in the mind and the visual content of mystical experiences

Increase in activity

Amygdala

Hippocampus

● Increase in activity
○ Decrease in activity

Adapted from Nataraja (2008)

in this peaceful state for an indeterminable amount of time before emerging from my meditation. Sometimes, I become aware of a clarity of mind I don't normally experience in everyday life. From time to time, this clarity provides me with an insight or the answer to a question I'd been thinking about earlier in the day. I just seem to know the answer without being sure of the source. It's hard to explain. It appears to defy logic." (Nataraja, 2008, pp. 85-94)

Neuroscientist: "The decrease in activity in the orientation association area produces an autonomic nervous system response. This gives rise to the feelings of bliss that accompany the dampening of activity in both the right and left parietal lobe. The right-brain function stemming from meditation gives the individual access to right-brained 'big picture' thinking and right-brain vivid and accurate memories. The lack of activity in the left parietal lobe explains why knowledge gained during meditation is seen to stem from something greater than self." (Nataraja, 2008, pp. 85-94)

Meditator: "I settle down for meditation in a relaxed, upright position, and slowly relax my body, from the toes of my feet to the top of my head. At the same time I focus my attention on an image of the Virgin Mary. Thoughts appear, interrupting and demanding attention. However, I just return to the image and these thoughts disappear. I try to build up the image in my mind, seeing every single detail, and slowly it becomes clearer and it becomes easy to hold the image in the stillness. The Virgin Mary is fixed in my mind."

Neuroscientist: "At this point, there is an increase in activity in the attention association area and a decrease in activity in the surrounding areas of the frontal cortex. This is accompanied by an increase in activity in both the visual and orientation association areas. These areas are necessary to fix an object in the mind. As activity in the parietal lobe decreases, the individual's ability to see the boundary between 'self' and 'object' also decreases. This accounts for the sense of absorption into the object" (Nataraja, 2008, pp. 85-94).

CHANGES IN THE FRONTAL AND PARIETAL LOBES DURING PASSIVE MEDITATION

Meditator: "After a while the boundary between myself and the image slowly seems to dissolve. It's a strange feeling; losing my sense of self and being in the embrace of something boundlessly infinite. I'm absorbed into the image; the distinction between it and me becomes blurred, irrelevant. A wave of blissful peace washes me from head to foot in light and love (later I interpret this to be an overwhelming sense of the Virgin Mary's love for us all). As I emerge from meditation, I'm often struck by a clarity and presence of mind I don't associate with my normal waking life. In these moments sometimes images, vivid memories, or even profound insights, surface, along with strong emotions."

Neuroscientist: "At this point, the decrease in activity in the orientation association area in the parietal lobe produces an autonomic nervous system response. As before, this accounts for the wave of peaceful bliss passing through the individual's body. The autonomic nervous system also triggers the clarity of mind, however, as it is accompanied by a dampening of activity in both the right and left parietal lobes, there is a corresponding decreased awareness of 'self' during this meditative experience, so the individual is unlikely to become aware of this clarity until after the meditative session" (Nataraja, 2008, pp. 85-94).

BEGINNER'S MIND AND THE BENEFITS OF MEDITATION PRACTICE

The term 'beginners mind' refers to a receptive and open attitude, a willingness to see things as they are rather than how we think they are.

By the time we reach adulthood, many of us have developed fairly firm ideas about life, the universe and everything. This can leave us closed off to the new experiences, thoughts and behaviour that are so essential to our personal development.

Mindfulness-based Stress Reduction encourages the cultivation of 'an open mind', experiencing everything as if it were occurring for the very first time with no preconceptions or expectations. In this open mind there is space for new ideas, new ways of thinking and behaving; a readiness to see things from a different, less restrictive perspective.

(Nataraja, 2008, p. 196)

APPENDIX 14

Neuro-Limbic Type Body Shapes

Type One and Body Shape

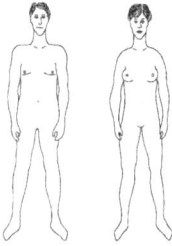

Type Two and Body Shape

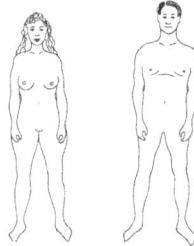

Type Three and Body Shape

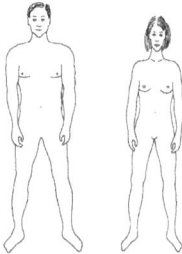

Type Four and Body Shape

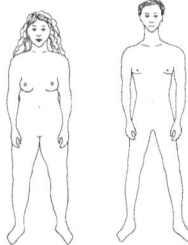

Type Five and Body Shape

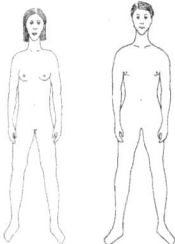

Type Six and Body Shape

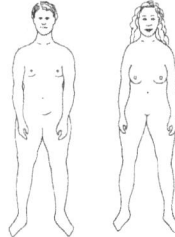

Type Seven and Body Shape

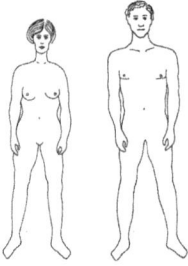

Type Eight and Body Shape

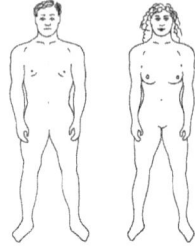

Type Nine and Body Shape

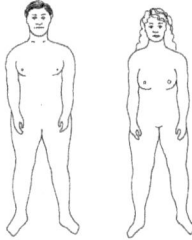

APPENDIX 15

Article: When Good Teams Make Bad Decisions

How Cognitive Bias and Group-think Undermine Judgement

BY PETER BUROW

Complex strategic decisions involving judgement, interpretation and complex trade-offs are at the centre of effective teamwork at senior levels of organisations. Yet leadership teams find it difficult to get it right. Perhaps this is because our brains have developed problem-solving processes that rely heavily on past experiences which significantly bias our beliefs today. The core beliefs that each of us hold have a major impact on the information we perceive, believe and remember. When left unchecked, the assumptions we make based on these core beliefs give rise to faulty thinking and biased decision-making. Moreover, because these are based in the brain's primitive emotional system and linked to survival impulses, we become so convinced we are right that we are willing to do whatever it takes to win the point. In teams, this leads to 'below-the-line' politics, lobbying, power games, white-anting and both aggressive and passive-aggressive behaviour.

In a study conducted by McKinsey of more than 1000 major investments, it emerged that when leadership teams understand how to mediate their biases in decision-making they achieved returns of up to seven percentage points higher. (For more on this study, see *The Case for Behavioural Strategy*, McKinsey Quarterly, March 2010.) Cognitive bias is real and alive in most leadership teams. In this article I will outline the top 20 decision-making biases that derail executive teams, how to detect which of these most impact your team and how to minimise their effect.

We all like to think that we make decisions logically and objectively. Neuroscientists working with economists are discovering, however, that our decision-making isn't as rational as we believe. In fact, the way our brains function means that we all have blind spots and biases that influence the choices we make. By learning how to spot the most common blind spots, both in yourself and in your team you can increase the effectiveness of your decisions.

Decision-making is one of the most important responsibilities of a leadership team. It's also often the hardest and riskiest part of the job. Poor decisions can damage the business and careers - sometimes permanently. Take the recent example of the Deepwater Horizon oil spill crisis in the US; bad luck or bad decision-making?

Of course it will be some time before the situation is fully analysed and properly understood, so any discussion is necessarily limited to theory or conjecture. But it's certainly an interesting case. From one perspective, it could be argued that BP CEO Tony Hayward presided over an organisational culture that permitted risk-taking, ignored expert advice, disregarded warnings about safety issues and hid facts. What if BP's failure to respond to the disaster itself with sufficient speed and attention was also a direct consequence of this flawed culture?

Tony Hayward's comments throughout the process are revealing: Hayward's apparent inability to understand public reaction to his comments makes him appear at best, defensive and out of touch with the reality of the situation and, at worst, weak, petty and selfish.

But how could someone so senior with a team of top advisors be so blind? To find out, we need to look at the role blind spots play in how decisions are made.

THE WAY OUR BRAIN WORKS CAN SABOTAGE OUR DECISIONS

As leaders, we are constantly called upon to deal with complexity. Faced with the need to process vast amounts of information in order to make decisions, we resort to unconscious routines. These mental shortcuts (also known as heuristics, or decision rules which are simple for the brain to compute) enable us to make decisions and avoid both 'information overload' and 'analysis-paralysis'. In general, heuristics are very useful when making most routine decisions or when time is of the essence, but they can also lead to severe and systematic errors in judgement.

Researchers at INSEAD, Harvard, Oxford and Stanford Universities have identified a whole series of such flaws in the way we think when making decisions (besides heuristics, others include 'motivational factors' and 'social influence'). Of course, what makes these blind spots so dangerous is their invisibility. Because they are biases that are hardwired into our brains, we fail to recognise them and repeatedly make the same mistakes. These blind spots effectively create holes in our reasoning ability which, over time, produce recurring patterns of erroneous decision-making. In a group, the combined, overlapping biases of the individuals in the team reinforce and amplify biases. This can result in disastrous decisions.

While no one can entirely rid his or her mind of these ingrained patterns, it is possible to learn strategies to compensate for bias. The best approach is always awareness and the first step is to understand how these blind spots are formed. Executives who familiarise themselves with these blind spots and the diverse forms they take can consciously adapt their decision-making processes to ensure that the decisions they make are sound.

HOW EMOTIONS COLOUR OUR THINKING – OUR CORE BELIEFS AT WORK

While neuroscientists continue to grapple with the complex ways that emotions interact with and influence the cognitive skills involved in decision-making, one thing is clear: emotions play a crucial role. In fact, we actually can't make decisions without them. By informing our desires, preferences and aversions, emotions shape our rational calculations. This is useful and necessary, because if we didn't have an emotional response to something (one way or another) we wouldn't be motivated to make a decision about it. Complete apathy leads to total lack of interest – we 'tune out'.

Problems develop, however, because our emotional responses inform our rational

Over the course of our lives, each of us has developed a complex matrix of core beliefs that we believe will keep us 'safe' in the world.

decision-making in a way that perpetuates our own personal philosophy to life (our unique world view). Neuro-economics describe people who decide different things in identical situations as different 'types'. These types are described as having different decision rules or different core beliefs.

Core beliefs are deep-seated perceptions that everyone has about the world around them. Over the course of our lives, each of us has developed a complex matrix of core beliefs that we believe will keep us 'safe' in the world. These beliefs have evolved over millennia to help us respond quickly and unthinkingly to dangerous situations; they act as our survival strategies and are embedded in the most primitive parts of our brain.

SYSTEM 1 AND SYSTEM 2 – YOUR EMOTIONAL AND RATIONAL BRAIN

The interaction of our emotion-based core beliefs and our rational brain is illustrated in Diagram 15.1 - 'How the Brain Makes Decisions'. It shows how the two cognitive systems in our brain interact to make decisions and ultimately produce behaviour.

As Daniel Kahneman (who won a Nobel Prize for his work in the area of neuro-economics) explains, these two systems differ in speed, flexibility and operation.

The operations of System 1 (our emotional and most primitive brain – where our core beliefs live) are typically fast, automatic, effortless, associative, implicit (not available to introspection) and often emotionally charged; they are also governed by habit and therefore difficult to control or modify. The operations of System 2 (our rational, more evolved and modern brain) are slower, serial, effortful, more likely to be consciously monitored and deliberately controlled; they are also relatively flexible.

Both Systems 1 and 2 influence our judgements and choices - meaning that how we feel about something is as important as what our reasoning tells us about it. While this may conflict with our view of our own decision-making as highly rational, it often lines up with our experience of other people (who we see as occasionally irrational and emotional when we are arguing with them).

What makes this process particularly hard to track in ourselves is our tendency to rely on our primitive brain with its relatively simple (emotionally-charged core belief) evaluations to arrive at our decisions. We do this because it's so much easier and requires far less effort than using our rational brain. We then retrospectively justify (or post-rationalise) our core belief-based decisions using our rational brain and see them as rational choices.

In this way, each core belief's survival strategy filters out important data. This produces blind spots in System 1's emotional responses that influence what otherwise seem to be System 2's rational decisions. They are therefore linked to the many forms of what psychologists call 'cognitive bias', which is a tendency to draw incorrect conclusions in certain circumstances based on partial evidence.

An understanding of your own core beliefs is a great asset for any current or aspiring

Diagram A15.1 How the Brain Makes Decisions

1. Input enters brain and the limbic system reacts emotionally, based on existing Core Beliefs – System 1.

   a. If the situation is not 'out of the ordinary' (or 'novel'), an habitual response is invoked and translates into immediate behaviour.

   b. If the situation is novel, then the information moves to System 2. Here it is assessed and matched against the individual's conscious world view and analytical style to reach a decision.

2. The trial decision from System 2 is checked by the limbic system:

   a. If it lines up with past experience (i.e. a similar decision has been made previously and the outcome is familiar) the individual will feel 'comfortable' with the trial decision, which will be embraced and translated into action.

   b. If no similar decision has been made previously and the anticipated outcome is unfamiliar, a feeling of discomfort will arise and the trial decision will then be sent back to System 2 for further thought.

3. This moving between the two systems will continue until a balance is reached and both systems are comfortable with the trial decision. Only then will it be translated into behaviour.

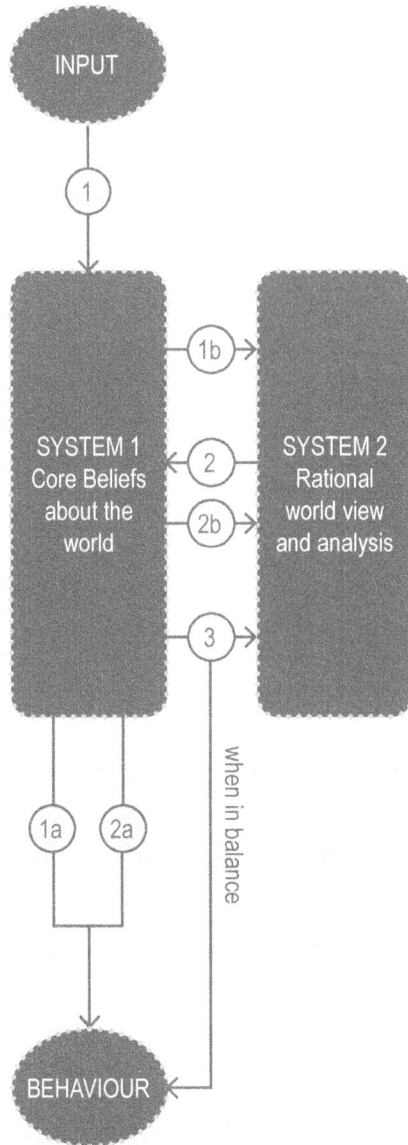

leader because it enables you to predict and therefore circumvent likely cognitive biases, thereby increasing the effectiveness of your decision-making.

In the same way, insights about core beliefs and how they drive our decision-making can also be applied in a team context; by understanding the core belief profiles of the team, it becomes possible to predict the most likely accumulative and amplified cognitive biases that the team will experience in group decision-making processes.

Furthermore, because emotion is so central to our decision-making, the impact of our core belief-driven survival strategies vary according to our level of stress (see Diagram 15.2).

At best, when everything is proceeding 'business-as-usual' and we are experiencing healthy levels of stress, our core beliefs help us make timely decisions. While these decisions may be correct, they are inherently biased. With awareness, we can learn to manage these biases using our rational brain.

As we become slightly stressed, our core beliefs encode the sorts of things that are likely to trigger us emotionally (based on whatever it is that we learnt to associate with survival when we were young). As the stress intensifies, we can get to an emotional tipping point, when we get triggered because we subjectively perceive (usually inaccurately) that our survival is being threatened. This explains why you might find something frustrating, annoying or infuriating, while others seem blissfully unaware it even happened - you simply have different core belief survival strategies that are wired to see different things as potential threats.

When something triggers you emotionally, you reach this emotional tipping point. This is also known as experiencing an emotional 'pinch'. Unfortunately, as your stress levels increase further, usually because the issue isn't addressed, the pinch can progress further to a second, much more dramatic tipping point called a 'crunch'. This highly emotional state often causes damage to relationships, both personal and professional, and leads to very poor decisions.

In most work contexts, it's considered socially inappropriate to show how you're

Diagram A15.2 The Core Belief Continuum: From Best to Worst

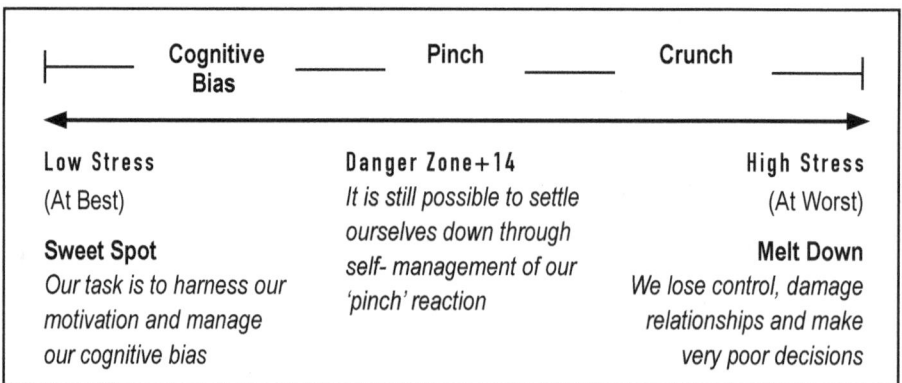

├──── Cognitive Bias ────	Pinch ────	Crunch ────┤
Low Stress	**Danger Zone+14**	**High Stress**
(At Best)	*It is still possible to settle ourselves down through self- management of our 'pinch' reaction*	(At Worst)
Sweet Spot		**Melt Down**
Our task is to harness our motivation and manage our cognitive bias		*We lose control, damage relationships and make very poor decisions*

feeling and so we usually do everything we can to avoid saying what we feel. Neuroscientists call this masking and, unfortunately, it comes at a cost. When we mask, the rational parts of the brain (in the frontal lobes) have to work overtime to keep the emotional parts of the brain under control. Matthew Lieberman and his team at the University of California in Los Angeles have found that doing this can lead to massive reductions in cognitive capacity - when you're masking, you lose your ability to think and remember. In teams, once the rational brain has become preoccupied with trying to control your emotional brain, the team loses its collective ability to create new and constructive solutions to the big problems. Instead, we resort to more primitive, survival-driven strategies to further our own objectives, and group politics start to emerge within the team.

Fortunately, there is a solution. Lieberman and his team have used fMRI to study the brain's activity and shown that labelling unpleasant emotions has an immediate impact on how much they affect you. When you can find the right word to describe how you're feeling, the thinking part of the brain (in the prefrontal cortex) sends signals to settle down the emotional parts of the brain (including the amygdala). Learning how to express how you're feeling can be one of the quickest ways to help move past it and get back to peak performance.

The rest of this article will be focusing on the cognitive bias aspect of the continuum rather than the pinch or crunch tipping points. While it assumes at least a basic understanding of the core belief profiles in making the links to different cognitive biases, that's certainly not necessary to grasp the key concepts we'll be discussing. As an introduction, Table A15.3 provides a brief overview of the nine core beliefs types. If you're interested, you can find out more information about the core beliefs – and start the process of identifying your own and those of your team – by reading the book 'Core Beliefs: Harnessing the Power' (Burow, 2010).

UNDERSTANDING COGNITIVE BIAS

Researchers agree there are at least 20 distinct cognitive biases that can be tracked and measured both in individuals and collectively in teams. This does not include biases caused by an inability to understand and work with numbers - also known as innumeracy

Table A15.3 The Nine Core Belief Types

Each of us has three of these core beliefs:

Core Belief Profile 1 — Perfectionists | Focus: Integrity/Clarity
Driven by the belief that you must be good and right to be worthy. Consequently, are conscientious, responsible, improvement-oriented and self-controlled, but also can be critical, resentful and self-judging.

Core Belief Profile 2 — Helpers | Focus: Influence
Driven by the belief that you must give fully to others to be loved. Consequently, are caring, helpful, supportive and relationship-oriented, but also can be prideful, overly intrusive and demanding.

Core Belief Profile 3 — Achievers | Focus: Achieving Results
Driven by the belief that you must accomplish and succeed to be loved. Consequently, are industrious, fast-paced, goal-focused and efficiency-oriented, but also can be inattentive to feelings, impatient and image-driven.

Core Belief Profile 4 — Artists | Focus: Elite Standards
Driven by the belief that you must obtain the longed-for ideal relationship or situation to be loved. Consequently, are idealistic, deeply feeling, empathetic and authentic to self, but also dramatic, moody and sometimes self-absorbed.

Core Belief Profile 5 — Analysts | Focus: Analysis/Depth of Technical Knowledge
Driven by the belief that you must protect yourself from a world that demands too much and gives too little to assure life. Consequently, are self-sufficiency seeking, non- demanding, analytical/thoughtful and unobtrusive, but also can be withholding, detached and overly private.

Core Belief Profile 6 — Loyal Sceptics | Focus: Loyalty/Scepticism
Driven by the belief that you must gain protection and security in a hazardous world you just can't trust. Consequently, are themselves trustworthy, inquisitive, good friends and questioning, but also can be overly doubtful, accusatory and fearful.

Core Belief Profile 7 — Epicures | Focus: New Opportunities
Driven by the belief that you must keep life up and open to assure a good life. Consequently, are optimistic, upbeat, possibility- and pleasure-seeking and adventurous, but also can be pain-avoidant, uncommitted and self-serving.

Core Belief Profile 8 — The Boss | Focus: All or Nothing
Driven by the belief that you must be strong and powerful to assure protection and regard in a tough world. Consequently, are justice seeking, direct, strong and action-oriented, but also overly impactful, excessive and sometimes impulsive.

Core Belief Profile 9 — Peacemakers | Focus: Minimising Conflict
Driven by the belief that to be loved and valued you must blend in and go along to get along. Consequently, are self-forgetting, harmony-seeking, comfortable and steady, but also conflict avoidant and sometimes stubborn.

Table A15.4 How Core Beliefs Lead to Individual Cognitive Bias in Decision-making

Category of Biases	Cognitive Bias	1	2	3	4	5	6	7	8	9
PATTERN RECOGNITION BIASES	**Saliency Bias:** Giving disproportionate weight to recent dramatic events, thereby exaggerating the probability of rare but catastrophic occurrences	✓	✓		✓		✓			✓
	Confirmation Bias: Seeking information that confirms an existing perspective and ignoring evidence that supports alternative views	✓	✓	✓	✓	✓	✓	✓	✓	✓
	False Analogies Bias: Relying on comparisons with situations that are not directly comparable	✓	✓	✓			✓			
	Champion Bias: Evaluating options on the basis of the track record of the individual who suggests it rather than on the facts	✓	✓					✓	✓	
	Availability Bias: Overestimating the risks of an event that can be imagined vividly, while leaving oneself exposed to less vivid risks		✓		✓		✓		✓	
ACTION-ORIENTED BIASES	**Over Confidence Bias:** Overestimating one's ability to affect future outcomes, taking credit for past outcomes and minimising the role of chance. Also overestimating our skill level relative to others			✓				✓	✓	
	Unfounded Optimism Bias: Being excessively optimistic about the future and unrealistic about the likelihood of positive/ negative events			✓				✓	✓	
	Competitor Neglect Bias: Planning without factoring in competitive responses	✓			✓	✓				✓
	Over Cautiousness Bias: Focusing on worst case analysis and failing to take any appropriate action at all (i.e. the 'Prudence Trap')	✓	✓		✓	✓	✓			✓
	All or Nothing Bias: Failing to take a portfolio risk and instead seeking complete protection (i.e. putting all the eggs in one basket and then watching the basket)	✓			✓			✓	✓	

Category of Biases	Cognitive Bias	Core Belief Profile								
		1	2	3	4	5	6	7	8	9
STABILITY BIASES	**Status Quo Bias:** Favouring options that perpetuate the status quo (to avoid both taking action/responsibility and opening oneself to criticism/risk)	✓	✓		✓	✓	✓			
	Sunk Costs Bias: Making choices that justify past flawed decisions, thereby avoiding acknowledgement of a past error	✓		✓	✓		✓		✓	✓
	Anchoring Bias: Giving disproportionate weight to the first information received		✓	✓				✓	✓	
	Loss Aversion Bias: Being motivated to avoid potential losses even when this involves taking unnecessary risks	✓	✓		✓	✓	✓			✓
INTEREST BIASES	**Misaligned Perception Bias:** Choosing options that align with one's individual perception of the hierarchy or relative weight of goals pursued by the organisation (rather than on an agreed understanding of the hierarchy/weight)				✓	✓		✓	✓	
	Inappropriate Attachment Bias: Preferring options that support or are linked to one's emotional attachment to certain individuals or elements of the business		✓	✓			✓	✓	✓	✓
SOCIAL BIASES	**Herding Instinct Bias:** Conforming to the dominant views of the group	✓	✓	✓						✓
	Sunflower Management Bias: Aligning with the views of the leader or ultimate decision-maker (whether expressed or assumed)	✓	✓	✓			✓			✓
	False Consensus Bias: Over-estimating the extent to which others share our views, beliefs and experiences	✓		✓				✓	✓	
	Default Bias: Defaulting to an existing strong social norm	✓	✓	✓		✓	✓			✓

biases (see Table A15.4).

The balance of the biases can be grouped into five main categories:

1. **Pattern recognition biases:** Misinterpreting conceptual relationships or identifying patterns where there are none
2. **Action-orientated biases:** The drive to take action too quickly
3. **Stability biases:** The tendency toward inertia in the presence of uncertainty
4. **Interest biases:** Arising in the presence of conflicting incentives (including non-monetary and even purely emotional ones)
5. **Social biases:** The preference for harmony over conflict

COGNITIVE BIAS IN ACTION: POOR DECISION-MAKING AT BP

Returning to the BP situation, the initial information available suggests that there were the apparent elements of underestimating risk, ignoring advice, disregarding warnings about safety issues and post-rationalising. These are all classic markers of Confirmation Bias.

This suggests that BP's decision-making may have been biased towards confirming existing beliefs by seeking only information that confirmed preconceptions and by ignoring evidence in support of other viewpoints. Unchecked, Confirmation Bias results in ill-informed, narrow and partial decisions most commonly seen in situations of 'Groupthink'.

Groups with this bias often exhibit a degree of 'we're right, you're wrong' certainty that is often unwarranted. In the BP case, this may help explain the wildly inaccurate early estimates regarding the environmental impact of the disaster.

BP's actions also showed signs of three other biases: Unfounded Optimism Bias (being excessively optimistic about the future and unrealistic about the likelihood of positive/negative events), Over Confidence Bias (overestimating their ability to affect future outcomes in the cleanup process) and False Consensus Bias (overestimating the extent to which others shared BP's perspective on the disaster and instead assuming that everyone else thinks the same way they do).

Each of these biases is common to the Core Belief Profile 3. Perhaps the team had too many Core Belief Profile 3's in its composition, or perhaps they had a number of Core Belief Profile 3 advisors. Or the BP culture may reflect the legacies of Core Belief Profile 3's in the past.

While we can hypothesise about the decision-making factors that contributed to the accident, it's important to note that BP is not alone in experiencing biased decision-making.

When we work with Australian leadership teams and boards that are facing highly stressful situations (e.g. shareholder outrage at poor performance), they can often track back the seeds of the situation they are facing to a long line of poor decisions that reflect the primary biases of the team. Unchecked, cognitive bias leads to poor commercial performance, because the crucial decisions from the top are flawed.

Awareness is the key to counteracting bias and overcoming decision-making blind spots

Highly complex and important decisions are the most prone to distortion by cognitive bias because they tend to involve the most assumptions, the most estimates, and the most inputs from the greatest number of people. And, of course, the higher the stakes, the higher the risk of falling prey to one or more psychological biases because we are stressed and by nature therefore more emotional.

Even if teams can't eradicate the distortions ingrained in the way their members' minds work, they can build tests and discipline into their decision-making process that can uncover errors in thinking before they become errors in judgement and lead to disastrous decisions.

COGNITIVELY BALANCING COGNITIVE BIAS

In a team context, the most effective way to minimise the impact of cognitive bias on group decisions is to create awareness of the team's bias and to use key questions to balance the bias. When I work with leadership teams, we enhance and sharpen the focus of this awareness by identifying the exact Core Belief Profiles in the team using a tool called the Core Beliefs Inventory and then cross tabulate this with the 20 biases (see Table A15.4). With this information, it is possible to tally which of the 20 cognitive biases will have the greatest influence over the team. The questions outlined in Table A15.5 can be used to counteract the team's biases and drive more effective decision-making. Calculate key high priority biases within your team and then workshop the relevant questions.

Decision-making, either as a leader or as part of a team, is never an easy process. Unfortunately, as the stakes increase, so too does the likelihood that the outcome will be driven by cognitive bias, rather than the reality of the situation. The good news is that with awareness and questioning, you can significantly reduce cognitive bias. And once done, the effectiveness of your decisions will increase – to the benefit of both you and your team.

Checklist for countering your team's decision-making bias

- Use the Core Beliefs Inventory to identify the Core Belief Profiles of your team members.
- Use Table A15.4 to calculate the highest Cognitive Biases in the team.
- Use questions that balance up the Cognitive Biases (sample questions in Table A15.5) to shape decision-making.
- Monitor team meetings to ensure you maintain the rage against faulty decision-making caused by cognitive bias.

Table A15.5 Sample Questions to Counteract Cognitive Bias

	Cognitive Bias	Questions for bringing the bias into consciousness
Pattern Recognition Biases	Saliency Bias	If we knew for certain that everything would go smoothly over the next 12 months, and that no rare but catastrophic events are about to occur, what might you decide to do differently?
	Confirmation Bias	What information can you find that does not support the current way of thinking?
	False Analogies Bias	What differences can you find between the current challenge and the past situations that have been referenced in the decision-making process? List as many differences as possible.
	Champion Bias	If this option were being proposed by an unknown person from outside the team, how would you objectively assess its merits?
	Availability Bias	If you knew that none of the major risks you've already identified would eventuate, would that change your decision? What additional unlikely risks can you think of?
Action-oriented Biases	Over Confidence Bias	Assuming you have little ability to control all future outcomes, what role would you say chance could play in future success?
	Unfounded Optimism Bias	If you were to look at this situation from a pessimistic viewpoint, what might you see that could go wrong?
	Competitor Neglect Bias	How are your competitors likely to respond to the implementation of your plan? How might that affect its efficacy?
	Over Cautiousness Bias	What is the best case scenario in terms of outcome? For that situation to eventuate, what would you need to do now?
	All or Nothing Bias	How else could you apply at least some of your resources across a number of portfolios?
Stability Biases	Status Quo Bias	How could we approach this issue in a completely new way? What benefits would this bring?
	Sunk Costs Bias	If you were an external expert, and knew nothing about the history of this issue to date, what would you recommend? If there were no financial issues to consider (i.e. the financial slate were wiped clean) what approach would you adopt?
	Anchoring Bias	How many different sources of information have been considered on this issue? How many experts have been consulted? What was the trend of the last batch of information received? What did the information suggest on balance?
	Loss Aversion Bias	Are we so concerned with avoiding losses here that we are blind to the risks associated with our decision?

	Cognitive Bias	Questions for bringing the bias into consciousness
Interest	Misaligned Perception Bias	Which of the organisation's goals does this approach further? Would everyone agree that this is a high priority?
	Inappropriate Attachment Bias	If this decision were about a different part of the business/involved different people, how might your approach be different?
Social Biases	Herding Instinct Bias	If this were a decision that was solely your responsibility and for which you alone would be held accountable, what would you do?
	Sunflower Management Bias	If this decision were being made anonymously and knew that no one – including both the leader and ultimate decision-maker – knew what you had decided, what would you do?
	False Consensus Bias	How are the drivers of the different stakeholders different from our drivers? What stakeholders will be disadvantaged by this decision and why? What would need to happen for the key stakeholder groups to consider the decision outstanding?
	Default Bias	If a team at one of your major competitors was faced with this challenge, what would they do?

APPENDIX 16

Article: Building Trust with the Nine Core Beliefs Types

Becoming a good advisor takes more than having good advice to offer. There are additional skills involved, ones that no one ever teaches you, that are critical to your success.

Most importantly, we have learned the hard way that you don't get the chance to employ advisory skills until you can get someone to trust you enough to share their problems with you. No one ever taught us how to do that either. Yet we had to learn it. Somehow.

The key is to understand that the seeds of trust are not just technical mastery of one's discipline (which is, of course, essential), but also the ability to work with clients in such a way as to earn their trust and gain their confidence.

Why invest in learning to become a Trusted Advisor?

Based on 50 years of collective research and experience, Maister, Green and Galford found that the more clients trust you the more they:

1. Reach for your advice

2. Are inclined to accept and act on your recommendations

3. Bring you in on more advanced, complex, strategic issues

4. Treat you as you wish to be treated

5. Respect you

6. Share more information that helps you to help them, and improves the quality of the service you provide

7. Pay your bills without question

8. Refer you to their friends and business acquaintances (client advocacy)

9. Lower the level of stress in your interactions

10. Give you the benefit of the doubt

11. Forgive you when you make a mistake

12. Protect you when you need it (even from their own organisation)

13. Warn you of dangers that you might avoid

14. Are comfortable and allow you to be comfortable

15. Involve you early on when their issues begin to form, rather than later in the process (or maybe even call you first!)

16. Trust your instincts and judgements (including those about other people such as your colleagues and theirs)

Adapted from *Maister et al.* (2004)

Introduction

WHY ARE CORE BELIEFS RELEVANT TO BUILDING TRUST?

Maister et al.'s Trust Equation radically advanced our understanding of the scope of professional skills needed to be a good advisor. Based on their professional experiences, they determined a simple model that identified four key variables that shape whether a technical advisor can make the transition to being a Trusted Advisor to his or her clients: credibility, reliability, intimacy and self-orientation. They argued that by providing sound advice, being reliable, showing an ability to handle sensitive information, and demonstrating a principle focus on the client's interests, each of us can become a Trusted Advisor.

The Trusted Advisor equation has been validated by its successful implementation by many people across industries in markets around the world.

So why is it that sometimes - inexplicably - it can fail? Why is it that with the best of intentions and with sincere effort, our attempts to build relationships with clients can still occasionally backfire? The cause often lies in a clash between your Core Beliefs and those of your client.

Core Beliefs are deep-seated perceptions that we all have about the world in which we live, work and play. Built through experience in early life and embedded within the brain's primitive emotional system (or 'limbic system'), they act as perceptual filters that enable us to simplify complex situations so that we can convert oceans of data into concrete action.

Core Beliefs challenge the idea that we all see and recall the same facts. In fact, we each see what our Core Beliefs allow us to see- and everything else falls into a 'blind spot'.

This is important, because we fall into the trap of assuming that our clients see the world the same way that we do and will therefore interpret our intentions accurately. In fact, the opposite is far more likely to be true- research based on 20,000 individuals over 20 years has shown us that when we communicate in a way that contradicts an individual's Core Beliefs we will be seen as sincerely wrong, lying or incompetent. Needless to say, this undermines trust!

TREATING OTHERS THE WAY THEY WOULD LIKE TO BE TREATED - NOT THE WAY YOU WOULD

Applied cognitive neuroscience (the study of how the brain works) now enables us to take the Trusted Advisor model to the next level. It does this by giving us powerful insights into how different people assess the variables that contribute to

Technically Competent
(High Rational Engagement)

Technical Expert	*Trusted Advisor*
Poor Supplier	*Charismatic Salesman*

Fails to Engage with Client's Core Belief
(Low Emotional Engagement)

Engages with Client's Core Belief
(High Emotional Engagement)

Technically Incompetent
(Low Rational Engagement)

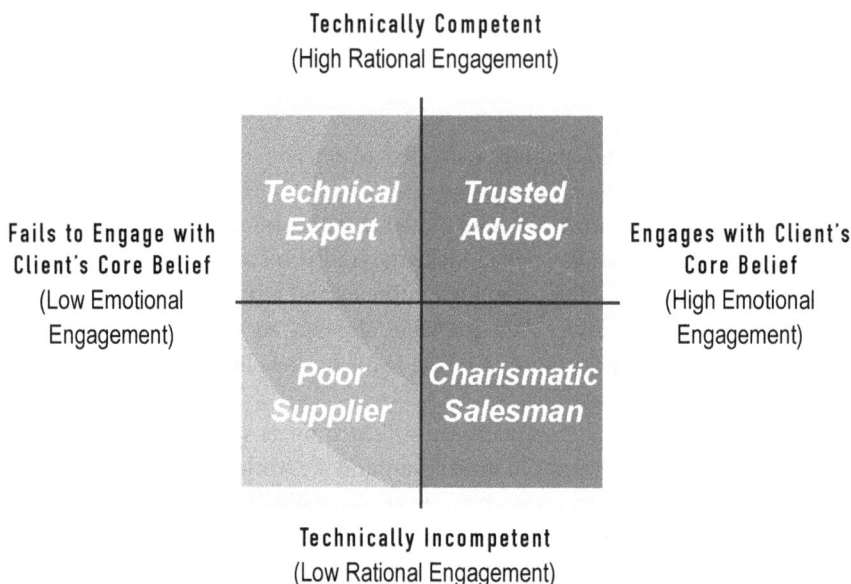

trustworthiness. We now know that the way an individual judges the components of the Trust Equation (credibility, reliability, intimacy and self-orientation) varies predictably according to an individual's emotional Core Beliefs.

Take **credibility**, for example. Many of us are suspicious by nature. We avoid risks and are constantly on the lookout for hollow boasting and deceit. For individuals with this Core Belief (the Core Belief Profile 6, or CBP6), the neurochemical cortisol and an overactive amygdala (the part of the brain that processes fear) creates an underlying anxiety that pushes us to avoid risks. As a Trusted Advisor to these types, your credibility rests on your ability to be realistic about the risks and limitations associated with your advice and to demonstrate through your actions and explanations that you are on your client's side.

However, others of us are very different. The CBP8, for example, starts with Core Belief that when you're trying to get a job done, bigger is always better. Driven by testosterone and adrenaline, they use their own strength and conviction to get the job done and will judge your credibility by the same standards. For these people, uncertainty reflects weakness, which will erode their trust in you. This means that to build credibility as a advisor, you need to be able to show that you have tackled big projects in the past, that your organisation has the size to handle anything and that you personally have the courage to see things through.

Understanding the Core Beliefs of your client and how these shape their expectations is critical to helping you build trust by matching your experience and abilities to what your client wants from the relationship (and what, therefore, they will look for when they judge whether to trust you).

The following pages are therefore dedicated to describing in detail how credibility, reliability, intimacy and self-orientation are assessed by each of the nine key Core Belief Profiles, and how you can respectfully manage your own behaviour to align with these implicit expectations. In doing so, you will more effectively build relationships with your clients based on mutual respect and trust, thereby increasing your ability to deliver exceptional client outcomes.

Table A16.1 The Chancellor Levels of Development

Core Belief Profile	Motivation to Seek Advice	Their Preferred Advisor Will Be	TO BUILD TRUST — To establish CREDIBILITY	To be perceived as RELIABLE	To be trusted with INTIMACY (i.e. confidential information)	To strike the right balance of SELF-ORIENTATION	How this profile will be wanting to receive advice
CBP1 The Perfectionist	Wants assistance to determine the most appropriate and 'correct' course of action from an acknowledged expert- wants all the information so they can make the responsible decision	✓ Qualified ✓ Pillar of the Industry ✓ Conservative	• Articulate your relevant qualifications and specific experience that directly relates to the area in which you are advising them- CBP1s trust due process and large institutions, so you need to show them that you are amongst the most respected within your field • Be well prepared to explain the rationale behind your thinking in a clear, structured way • Reference established models and first principles	• Always follow the rules • Clearly outline your role and their role • Always be punctual with all commitments - CBP1s are fixated on sticking to schedule and if you are late they are unlikely to quickly forget • Do play by the rules- if you change your mind often the CBP1 will lose respect for you • Always do what you say you will do; if you can't, then call them well before the deadline with a simple and clear explanation and the most appropriate way forward • Detail every expense with receipts, billed to the dollar (rather than rounding)	• Do express yourself politely and with consideration- CBP1s believe in etiquette and manners. This includes showing respect to, for example, your competitors even when they are not present • Discuss both yours and their Code of Conduct and standards of ethical behaviour. Explore and negotiate these to make sure there is alignment between the two of you • Keep the discussion on-topic and avoid straying into what may appear to be unrelated topic areas • Avoid name-dropping and de-identify case studies before you share them	• Relate professional expertise, credentials and years of experience • Always be polite and follow culturally appropriate etiquette • Do be neat at all times and take pride in your appearance -it counts for a great deal (this applies to both you and your work) • Show modesty and demonstrate through your actions (rather than words) that you have high personal standards and a strong personal work ethic	• In written form and with a bare minimum of 'presentation' • Written materials should be clear, uncluttered and consistent in language and formatting, but should not be flashy or feel too 'designed'; black and white printing rather than colour; preferably no more than one page • CBP1s will want advice with succinct recommendations on the most appropriate course of action that are clearly justified • Suggested structure: describe the Situation; outline a Recommended Course of Action; and provide a Rationale

Core Belief Profile	Motivation to Seek Advice	Their Preferred Advisor Will Be	TO BUILD TRUST To establish CREDIBILITY	To be perceived as RELIABLE	To be trusted with INTIMACY (i.e. confidential information)	To strike the right balance of SELF-ORIENTATION	How this profile will be wanting to receive advice
CBP4 The Artist	Wants to make an exceptional difference in their area of the business. Wants to find a tailored solution that is a 'perfect fit' for the existing situation. Wants to be supported in championing elite standards within their organisation	✓ Driven by values and focusing on a particular segment or niche area with a unique cluster of skills	• Take the time to experience the nuances of their situation before offering a way forward • Don't try to sell them 'cookie-cutter' solutions that have been used in other places - CBP4s want a unique solution that is based on them and their unique needs • Share examples of relevant personal experience that show you understand your field and its complexity • Demonstrate that you have gained wisdom in your field by 'learning the hard way' • Show how you have tailored the proposed solution to meet their unique situation • Be prepared to acknowledge challenges and hardship that may arise from your proposed solutions and acknowledge any flaws • Do let the CBP4 have detailed input into developing the end result- provide them with a process rather than a rigid goal; ask them to 'paint you a picture' of what the ideal outcome would look like	• Maintain regular contact • Provide regular assurances of your commitment to them - the CBP4 will be on constant look out for the possibility of abandonment • Be aware that the CBP4 often relies on their intuition when evaluating options and so keep an eye on their non-verbals to see how they are tracking. If it looks like they're unhappy, uncertain or disengaged then you need to go back and reengage them by focusing in on their values or hearing their perspective • Understand that the CBP4 has a keen eye for detail and will notice when things are out of place or inaccurate	• Appreciate that for the CBP4, important conversations take time • Do try to empathise with them rather than exclusively focusing on attempting to assist them • Go out of your way to acknowledge and in some cases even praise CBP4s for their unique perspective and insight- 'their personal touch' • Do acknowledge their creative ideas and communicate that they have been received, understood and appreciated	• Be prepared to relate your own personal experience beyond the specific scope of the problem as well as your personal feelings about situations and suggestions • Don't pretend to understand their situation if you don't -they will see through it. Instead, acknowledge that you want to understand their situation at a deeper level and take the time to listen	• In face-to-face meetings with a focus on how the way forward aligns with their values • Show the way forward is the best approach; CBP4s are very comfortable with short-term pain for long-term gain • Provide a phased approach detailed on a few pages that you walk through with them during the meeting • Make sure you include key numbers

Core Belief Profile	Motivation to Seek Advice	Their Preferred Advisor Will Be	TO BUILD TRUST — To establish CREDIBILITY	To be perceived as RELIABLE	To be trusted with INTIMACY (i.e. confidential information)	To strike the right balance of SELF-ORIENTATION	How this profile will be wanting to receive advice
CBP7 The Epicure/	Wants to explore new and exciting ideas to relieve pain points and generate energy, enthusiasm and momentum within their area. Wants to find an ingenious or clever solution to their current problem. Wants a fresh perspective on the situation	✓ Someone they've met socially or whom they like personally	• Be prepared to meet them in a coffee shop or somewhere informal - the CBP7 often feels claustrophobic in an enclosed office • Do present problems as interesting opportunities to solve something • Frame your experience with an emphasis on the quick and painless ways in which you have helped clients in the past - CBP7s care less about your qualifications and more about whether you can solve the problem quickly • Do prepare for rapid give and take on issues - CBP7s think and talk quickly • Be prepared to follow their tangents and discuss related topics before returning to your original point • Understand that the CBP7 is constantly moving towards new frameworks and ideas and they are attracted to the cutting edge for its excitement and 'wow' factor. Avoid becoming yesterday's news by having multiple tools and methodologies at your disposal and always keeping up with the latest developments and trends. You will impress them most by sharing a great new tool that everyone's talking about but that they haven't heard of yet	• Be able to turn deliverables around quickly. Whatever you discuss today will be old news in a week, so keep the momentum going at their pace otherwise you will be left behind • Understand that CBP7s love ideas but have very little interest in execution, so always offer to do the work for them - once a decision has been made they will want to move on to something else and leave someone else to do the follow-up work • Never say 'No' to a CBP7- say 'Yes, if we can...' and explore the conditions that would need to be met for that to work (even if unrealistic). Then you can co-create an alternative option that would match what their current suggestion achieves and exceeds it • Always be prepared to discuss and change the strategy as the work progresses • Once you have settled on a strategy, accept that the CBP7 will see it as their idea and will want to take the credit for it. Don't compete for the limelight • Be aware that CBP7s talk a lot but may not actually be committing. CBP7s love exploring ideas, but if you want commitment, get it in writing	• Do align with their dream - let the CBP7 share their enthusiasm with you and highlight how you can help them make it even better • CBP7s naturally seek advice and prefer to bounce ideas off other people rather than consider things alone • However, they will unconsciously avoid people they perceive as having a negative outlook on life, so to be trusted with sensitive information you need to show an ability to turn lemons into lemonade (that is, to take problems and turn them into opportunities). Your role as an advisor is to give them the right advice, but it needs to be framed in a way that gives the CBP7 a positive way forward • CBP7s feel uncomfortable with excessive seriousness and so will often lighten the mood with humour even when things are looking bad. • Be prepared to engage with the humour and read between the lines to hear the underlying issue. If you just play along with the jokes you risk being caught by surprise	• Keep the conversation cheerful and fast-paced • Understand that CBP7's are attracted to successful, optimistic people both at home and at work • The CBP7 will enjoy hearing about exciting things that are happening in your business and/ or your personal life (e.g. major changes, travel etc) but speak no more than a few minutes. As a rule CBP7s tend to want about 70% of the airtime • The CBP7 will feel uncomfortable hearing about unpleasant and/or painful experiences so avoid sharing those • Don't try to pin them down, impose your values on them or get them to commit	• Provide a topline summary that outlines key points in no more than a page plus a more detailed report as an appendix. • Your advice should focus on the positive and rephrase challenges as opportunities • Describe issues as briefly as possible and always provide the solution or positive next steps • CBP7s like new, exciting, colourful and designed materials so consider a range of visual ways to convey your message

Core Belief Profile	Motivation to Seek Advice	Their Preferred Advisor Will Be	TO BUILD TRUST To establish CREDIBILITY	To be perceived as RELIABLE	To be trusted with INTIMACY (i.e. confidential information)	To strike the right balance of SELF-ORIENTATION	How this profile will be wanting to receive advice
CBP2 The Helper	Wants to discuss options and decide with someone how to resolve an issue	✓ An advisor to the influential, significant and powerful	• Show that you can take complex ideas and express them in the CBP2's metaphors and language - it demonstrates that you are listening to them and that you respect them • Discuss the impact of your proposed solutions on all the stakeholders involved, including their direct reports and customers • Acknowledge their people skills and their generosity • Do not expect them to acknowledge their own needs - this is their blind spot. As a result, reframe both problems and solutions through the lens of other people's needs (e.g. their customers, their team, their superiors etc)	• Be flexible with where and when you meet with them, preferably over coffee or a meal face-to-face • Be willing to discuss mutual acquaintances, family and show you are willing to go the extra mile to help them • Be prepared to accept their generosity but never take them for granted - CBP2s enjoy helping others but will snap unexpectedly if there are signs you are taking advantage of them • Do find ways to make deposits in their favour bank and help them expand their sphere of influence	• Spend the time to provide a great deal of personal contact - face-to-face is best • Show how the information they share will help the quality of your conversation and the final outcome • Consistently show an interest in them as a person, their family, life and work • Be willing to share family pictures and stories of your own • Don't rush or 'fit them in' to your schedule - always take time to work within their constraints	• Focus almost entirely on them, their needs, preferences and priorities • You can mention high-profile/influential companies or people you are working for • Relate how delighted you are to focus on addressing their needs	• In personal face-to-face meetings where all the information is shared and then discussed • Clearly articulate your role and theirs in implementing the recommendations and follow-up afterwards to see how they are travelling • Written recommendations should be very simple, preferably no more than three to five dot points and no longer than a page. Include an action plan that clearly outlines who is going to do what

Core Belief Profile	Motivation to Seek Advice	Their Preferred Advisor Will Be	TO BUILD TRUST — To establish CREDIBILITY	To be perceived as RELIABLE	To be trusted with INTIMACY (i.e. confidential information)	To strike the right balance of SELF-ORIENTATION	How this profile will be wanting to receive advice
CBP5 The Analyst	Wants to consult with a specialist in a given field to give them access to additional information or to compare and contrast the conclusions they have come to personally with those of acknowledged or respected specialist	✓ A published specialist	• Show that you have deep knowledge of the relevant field - CBP5s respect expertise and distrust generalists • Demonstrate your expertise through appropriate use of technical language but avoid empty jargon and sharing opinions where you lack knowledge CBP5s will see through this • Be precise, focus on the detail, speak with specific examples and always avoid generalisations • When discussing trends, patterns and models, make sure you have detailed examples and data to support them • Show an interest in building your own knowledge and experience by understanding the detail of the organisational systems that operate within the CBP5's environment • Demonstrate a systems-based understanding of the topic in question	• Follow meetings with a summary of the key discussion points and outlining agreed next steps with responsibilities • When promising additional information like website links or detailed analysis or studies, provide them within the agreed timeframe. • When quoting for work, give them a menu of options to choose from, be prepared to break the quotation into the different aspects of the value chain, be willing to pare the service back to the utilitarian deliverable (rather than the value-added service) • When billing, break any quotation or bill down into all its constituent parts and provide greater than usual detail on time spent (by whom, doing what) • Demonstrate how you will or have used time and resources cleverly by applying your expertise • Keep emotion and conflict to a minimum in meetings - always discuss the issue rather than the person and maintain a calm and dispassionate tone • Provide space for CBP5s to make decisions after the meeting rather than during it- don't spring important decisions on them at short notice	• To be trusted with any information, you must first show the CBP5 how you will protect the information they share with you. Safeguard the data and ensure that it does not go further than the CBP5 is comfortable with. Always make it explicit exactly what you will and will not do with the information • Appreciate that CBP5s find most face-to-face meetings unnecessary -make sure you provide them with an agenda and relevant information beforehand, include any detailed reports (they will usually be the only ones who read them) • More than any other profile, CBP5s value sensitive information and will be extremely reluctant to share it • Therefore, be prepared to work only with the information you absolutely need. If you need to request additional information, show directly how it will improve the result or reduce costs and time associated with the work you are doing	• Listen carefully for the framework they use for the topic that you are discussing and then use that as the basis for presenting data and insight back to them (and comparing it with data and insight they have already collected) • They have a love of learning, so embody a love of learning as you discover their framework, their insights and their concerns • Don't try to compare your preferred framework with theirs or to persuade them that yours is better • Focus on the data, the framework and the issue, rather than the people, the family and the feelings in any situation	• In writing, electronically, supported by key studies and reports with references to all sources • Short emails related to specific events that give a topline of the advisor's assessment of the situation are highly valued by the CBP5 • Long abstract documents about general theories are not valued

Core Belief Profile	Motivation to Seek Advice	Their Preferred Advisor Will Be	TO BUILD TRUST				How this profile will be wanting to receive advice
			To establish CREDIBILITY	To be perceived as RELIABLE	To be trusted with INTIMACY (i.e. confidential information)	To strike the right balance of SELF-ORIENTATION	
CBP8 The Boss	Wants the biggest or the best to tackle a major problem	✓ The biggest or most powerful in the market	• Show that your organisation has the size and strength to deliver on their large-scale plans • Meet with them for the first time in the boardroom, not the coffee shop • Focus on clear, simple actions and demonstrate how you are powerful enough to drive the achievement of the CBP8's key objectives • Talk in black and white terms and aim for simplicity rather than complexity - CBP8s have little tolerance for subtlety or philosophical context • Tell them straight away when they are making mistakes or making you angry (they prefer to know)	• Do acknowledge their power but demonstrate your own -they respect strength, not weakness • Avoid appearing weak by backing down at the first sign of conflict. CBP8s do not trust those who cannot hold their own in an argument • Do expect turf wars- on each occasion, ask yourself 'is this clause/point essential?'- if it is, tell the CBP8 it is a deal breaker and be prepared to back it up • Do ensure that you always turn up when they want you there • Be prepared to scale projects up at short notice • Understand that while the CBP8 appreciates honest advice and feedback, once they have made a decision you are expected to show loyalty and support that decision in public. Continuing to question or challenge their decision in front of others will be seen as a betrayal	• Do communicate confidently - CBP8s appreciate all news (good and bad) straight up and to the point • Be respectful at all times, but be prepared to call a spade a spade • Do not talk about them behind their back or discuss issues with a third party instead of with them - CBP8s are always on the alert for signs of disloyalty • Build your relationship with the CBP8 by spending time away from the office or work context. CBP8s often do not trust someone until they've gotten to know them in a physically challenging environment • Recognise that they will feel more comfortable sharing their true perspective with you one-on-one over dinner than during a meeting with many others	• Take pride in your actions and meet the CBP8s strength and confidence with your own • Understand that to become their trusted advisor you need to be a self-contained asset who will help them succeed in their chosen battlefield. If they are the army general, then you are the colonel who assists and advises but does not need their help get things done • Avoid apologising unnecessarily- this will be interpreted as weakness • Emphasise your motivation to help them achieve their objectives	• Face-to-face with an action plan as an outcome • Simple, clear and to the point • Good and bad news clearly explained right up front • No more than a one page summary

Core Belief Profile	Motivation to Seek Advice	Their Preferred Advisor Will Be	TO BUILD TRUST To establish CREDIBILITY	To be perceived as RELIABLE	To be trusted with INTIMACY (i.e. confidential information)	To strike the right balance of SELF-ORIENTATION	How this profile will be wanting to receive advice
CBP3 The Achiever	Wants to avoid looking incompetent. Wants to turn the situation into an action plan as quickly as possible and, if possible, leverage success from the situation	✓ Personally successful. Fast moving and practical in their advice	• Do come straight to the point and be well organised for all meetings • Do establish clear parameters that define success – be explicit about what you will achieve • Break service delivery into small and discrete projects with clear timeframes, fees, estimates and outcomes • Think of ways you can save them time and money • Do expect them to want immediate action and be prepared to deliver • Demonstrate how you respect them by valuing their time and resources • Move to action as fast as possible • Be willing to look after the situation for them	• Ensure that you are scheduled into their appointment list before making contact – they will be busy and so will need to include you amongst the things to get done • Provide short range plans and milestones, then follow up with updates on your progress • Keep the project cycle tight • Do deliver on what you promise – the CBP3 is committed to completion so you need to be as well • Write short emails and letters that focus on actions that need to be taken – less is more since the time they spend reading what you have written stops them from doing other work • Understand that for the CBP3, the ability to advance personally contributes greatly to deciding whether the project has been successful - they will reject a great solution to a problem if they can't see a way to get their key stakeholders (including their superiors) over the line. So to be perceived as reliable make sure that your advice considers the internal politics of the CBP3's environment	• Be willing to listen to and respect their time constraints • Show how key information they can share can help inform your action plans • Avoid criticising the organisation they work for - particularly based on sensitive information they have shared. CBP3s often see the company they work for as a direct reflection of themselves so to criticise their company for poor decisions means you are also criticising them. Reframe challenges presented by the data as opportunities • Understand that the CBP3 is highly focused on their own personal success and the success of the project. Don't compete for the limelight - let them take the credit	• You do need to demonstrate that you are personally successful and, if possible, have worked with companies or individuals in the same class or higher than the client • You want to be perceived as a prestigious advisor, so being clear and proud of your success at the beginning sends the right message • CBP3s understand and respect 'win-win' situations so establish why you value the ongoing relationship with them and how it helps you to succeed • Focus on turning every discussion into an Action Plan with clear deliverables and timeframes	• Efficiently • Initial meeting and then as much that can be done online and supported by phone and email the better • Presentation is as important as content, so paper quality, graphic design, layout and the overall image of your document containing the content is important • Frame up solutions in terms of making the most of opportunities and use negative framing as little as possible • Focus on action - what you will do and how this will help them do what they need to do • Restate the objectives and create line-of-sight between the proposed activity and the goals of the project

Core Belief Profile	Motivation to Seek Advice	Their Preferred Advisor Will Be	TO BUILD TRUST / To establish CREDIBILITY	To be perceived as RELIABLE	To be trusted with INTIMACY (i.e. confidential information)	To strike the right balance of SELF-ORIENTATION	How this profile will be wanting to receive advice
CBP6 The Loyal Sceptic	• Wants to resolve their uncertainty by finding the best solution and managing any risks associated with it. • Wants to feel reassured by getting honest advice from someone who understands all the risks involved	✓ A friend of the family or part of their local community ✓ An ex-colleague or recommended expert	• Do not try to sell them a 'perfect solution' - CBP6s are deeply suspicious of silver bullets. • Do make your allegiances/interests clear as they like to know what is in it for you • Do intersperse the positive with negatives when you are communicating to them – they see this as being realistic and honest • Avoid setting up clear polarities - having to choose between two opposing options significantly slows progress • Always provide a clear recommended course of action and explain the rationale behind it. Provide source material to show how you have come to your conclusions. Acknowledge the risks, uncertainties and assumptions associated with their proposed course of action and show how these have been managed or can be addressed moving forward • Understand that the CBP6 is highly focused on internal politics within the organisation, so get up to speed as quickly as you can and show them that your advice has taken into account how others in the CBP6's organisation are likely to respond	• Do keep to your explicit word – nothing will help them more than having a sense that you mean what you say and they can trust you • Do only commit to what you know you can deliver and then ensure that you keep to this commitment • Do be honest when you have made a mistake • Demonstrate your personal loyalty to them through actions • Be willing to explore best and worst-case scenarios	• Be willing to share your weaknesses or concerns • Be willing to discuss contingency plans and negative scenarios • Demonstrate that the relationship is important to you - show an interest in them personally	• Focus on sharing time discussing internal and external threats • Be willing to share how things have gone badly for you in the past, what you have learnt from that and how this insight can be applied to the current situation • Emphasise that you are available to support them 24/7	• A clear one-page summary with detailed reference material attached • A slick presentation and appearance is not as important as 'authenticity' and accuracy - the headers and footers, page numbers, referencing and logos are taken as signs that you do this work for a living • Make a phone call to contextualise why you are sending information, send an email with the detail and set up a meeting to discuss the detail and agree on next steps

Core Belief Profile	Motivation to Seek Advice	Their Preferred Advisor Will Be	TO BUILD TRUST To establish CREDIBILITY	To be perceived as RELIABLE	To be trusted with INTIMACY (i.e. confidential information)	To strike the right balance of SELF-ORIENTATION	How this profile will be wanting to receive advice
CBP9 **The** **Peacemaker**	Doesn't have the technical expertise or doesn't want to have to think through the issue	✓ Someone older and more experienced who has spent a lifetime in that industry	• Understand that CBP9s naturally contextualise any question within a range of broader situational issues, challenges and opportunities, so don't try to jump straight to the solution • Show them that you can consider multiple contingencies and interrelationships - the world of the CBP9 is based on the belief that you need to understand all the elements before you can get to a solution • Demonstrate the depth of your personal experience and wisdom by being able to focus on both the hard numbers and the people issues involved in equal measure • Realise that asking a CBP9 for their opinion is helpful in getting them on board - showing them respect by listening and learning from them is critical	• Provide a CBP9 with regular meetings - a CBP9 may not assert themselves, but the relationship will work best when you give them your undivided attention • Establish clear goals - they tend to get fuzzy when it comes to agreements because they are willing to amend their approach if the situation changes, so it is good to have things written down • Do understand that CBP9s resist making fixe short-term commitments — you will need to confirm decisions and the steps you want them to follow	• Always take the time to listen to what they have to say - it says that you respect them. Absolutely never cut-them-short, talk over the top of them, or dismiss their perspective with firs taking time to consider it • Understand that the CBP9 will need time to reflect on new information or questions before they respond, and that once they have thought about it their responses are often highly insightful • Avoid being aggressive or forcing them into positions that they seem to be resisting - CBP9s have a strong dislike for bullies and 'pushy people' and the harder you push the more they will resist • Be willing to invest in the relationship	• Take time to understand their situation and their systems and then clearly advocate the best way forward for them • Don't self-promote or focus on brands, success or efficiency - it usually angers the CBP9. They are quite comfortable with you sharing so long as you are not big-noting yourself • Focus on establishing the context and depthing your understanding of the situation	• Meet face-to-face to discuss the big picture, philosophy or broad brush approach • Provide a one-page summary of key insights and recommendations • Include as much referencing as possible - they may not read it but they want to know it's there if they decide to

Bibliography

Abrahamson, E. (2000). Change without pain. *Harvard Business Review, July-August.*

Adams, R.D., Victor, M., & Ropper, A.H. (1997). *Principles of neurology.* New York: McGraw-Hill.

Ader, R., Felton, D., & Cohen, N. (1991). *Psychoneuroimmunology, 2nd edition.* San Diego: Academic Press.

Ahern, G. L., Schomer, D. L., Kleefield, J., Blume, H., Rees Cosgrove, G., Weintraub, S. et al. (1991). Right hemisphere advantage for evaluating emotional facial expressions. *Cortex, 27,* 193-202.

Ainsworth, M. D. S., Blehar, M. C., Waters, E., & Walls, S. (1978). *Patterns of attachment: A psychological study of the strange situation.* Hillsdale: NJ: Erlbaum.

Alexander, C., Harung, H. S., & Heaton, D. P. (1999). *Evolution of organizations in the new millennium, 20* (4). MCB University Press: The Leadership and Organization Development Journal.

Amodio, D.M., & Frith, C.D. (2006). Meeting of minds: The medial frontal cortex and social cognition. *Nature Reviews Neuroscience, 7,* 268-277.

Amodio, D., Shah, J., Sigelman, J., Brazy, P., and Harmon-Jones, E (2004). Implicity regulatory focus associated with frontal cortical activity, J. Exp. Soc. Psychol 40, 225-232.

Anik, L. Aknin, L.B., Norton, M.I., & Dunn, E.W (2009). Feeling Good about Giving: The Benefits (and Costs) of Self-Interested Charitable Behavior. *Harvard Business School. Working Paper 10-012.*

Anticevic, A., Repovs, G., & Barch, D.M. (2010). Resisting emotional interference: Brain regions facilitating working memory performance during negative distraction. *Cognitive, Affective, & Behavioral Neuroscience, 10 (2), 159-173.*

Argyris, C., & Schön, D. (1995). *Organisational Learning* (2nd edition). Harlow: Addison-Wesley.

Aristotle, translated by Ernest Barker, revised by R.F. Stalley. (1995). *The Politics*. Oxford: Oxford.

Ashkanasy, N.M., Härtel, C.E.J., & Zerbe, W.J. (Eds.) (2000). *Emotions in the work place: Theory, research, and practice*. Westport, CT: Quorum Books.

Aspinwall, L.G. (1998). Rethinking the role of positive affect in self-regulation. Motivation and Emotion, 22, 1-32.

Astin, J.A., & Forys K. (2004). *Psychosocial Determinants of Health and Illness: Integrating Mind, Body and Spirit*. Advances.

Badaracco, J.L. (1998). The discipline of building character. *Harvard Business Review, March-April*.

Baird, A., Scheffer, I.E., & Wilson, S.J. (2011). Mirror neuron system involvement in empathy: A critical look at the evidence. *Social Neuroscience, 6 (4), 327–335*.

Baltes, P.B., & Staudinger, U.M. (2000). *Berlin Wisdom Paradigm*.

Bakermans-Kranenburg, M.J. et al., (2012). Oxytocin decreases handgrip force in reaction to infant crying in females without harsh parenting experiences. *Social Cognitive and Affective Neuroscience, 7 (8), 951-957*.

Bandura, A. (1982). Self-efficacy mechanism in human agency. *The American Psychologist, 37*(2), 122 - 147. Baron, 1988.

Baron-Cohen, S. (1995). *Mindblindness: An essay on autism and theory of mind*. Cambridge, MA: MIT Press.

Bartz, J.A. et al., (2010). Effects of oxytocin on recollections of maternal care and closeness. *PNAS 107 (50) 21371–21375*.

Bartz, J.A. et al., (2010). Oxytocin Selectively Improves Empathic Accuracy. *Psychological Science, 21(10) 1426–1428*.

Bartz, J.A., Zaki, J., Bolger, N., Oschsner, K.N. (2011). Social effects of oxytocin in humans: context and person matter. *Trends in Cognitive Sciences, 15 (7), 301-309*.

Bateson, M.C. (1979). The epigenesis of conversational interaction: A personal account of research development. In M. Bullowa (Ed.), *Before speech: The beginning of human communication* (pp. 63-77). Cambridge, UK: Cambridge University Press.

Bauer, P. J. (1996). What do infants recall of their lives?: Memory for specific events by one- to two-year-olds. *American Psychologist, 51*, 29-41.

Baxter, L.R., Schwartz, J.M., Bergman, K.S., Szuba, M.P., Guze, B.H., Mazziotta, J.C. et al. (1985). Caudate glucose metabolic rate changes with both drug and behavior therapy for obsessive-compulsive disorder. *Archives of General Psychiatry, 40*, 681-689.

Baxter, L.R., Schwartz, J.M., Phelps, M.E., Mazziotta, J.C., Guze, B.H., Selin, C.E. et al. (1989). Reduction of prefrontal cortex glucose metabolism common to three types of depression. *Archives of General Psychiatry, 46,* 243-350.

Bear, M.F., Connors, B.W., & Paradiso, M.A. (2001). *Neuroscience: Exploring the Brain.* Baltimore: Lippincott.

Beauregard, M., Paquette, V. (2006). Neural correlates of a mystical experience in Carmelite nuns. *Neuroscience Letters 405, 186–190.*

Bechara, A., Damasio, H., Tranel, D., & Damasio, A. (1997). Deciding advantageously before knowing the advantageous strategy. *Science, 275,* 1293-1295.

Beck, D.E., & Cowan, C.C. (1996). *Spiral Dynamics.* Oxford: Blackwell Publishing.

Beer, J. S., John, O. P., Scabini, D., & Knight, R. T. (June 2006). Orbitofrontal Cortex and Social Behavior: Integrating Self-monitoring and Emotion-Cognition Interactions. *Journal of Cognitive Neuroscience, 18* (6) , 871-879.

Benoit, D., & Parker, K. C. H. (1994). Stability and transmission of attachment across three generations. *Child Development, 65,* 1444-1456.

Benson, F. D. (1994). *The Neurology of Thinking.* New York: Oxford University Press.

Berkman, E., & Lieberman, M. D. (2009). The neuroscience of goal pursuit: Bridging gaps between theory and data. In G. Moskowitz & H. Grant (Eds.) *The Psychology of Goals* (98-126). New York, NY: Guilford Press.

Berkowitz, L., & Lutterman, K. (1968). The traditionally socially responsible personality. Public Opinion Quarterly, 32, 169-185.

Berne, E. (1975). *Games People Play: The basic handbook of transactional analysis.* Ballantine Books.

Berne, E. (1970). *Sex in Human Loving.* Simon & Schuster.

Berne, E. (1986). *Transactional Analysis in Psychotherapy.* Ballantine Books; Reissue edition.

Berne, E. (1975). *What do you do after you say hello?* London: Corgi Books.

Bernick, C. (2001). When your Culture Needs a Makeover. *Harvard Business Review, June.*

Berridge, K.C. (2003). Pleasures of the brain. *Brain and Cognition, 52,* 106-128.

Billington, J., Baron-Cohen, S., & Bor, D. (2008). Systemizing influences attentional processes during the Navon task: An fMRI study. *Neuropsychologia 46, 511–520.*

Bittel, L. R. (1989). *The McGraw-Hill 36-hour management course.* McGraw-Hill.

Blanchard, K. & Johnson, S. (1996). *The One Minute Manager.* Harper Collins Business.

Blanke, O., Ortigue, S., Landis, T., & Seeck, H. (2002). Stimulating Illusory Own-Body Perceptions. *Nature,* 419 (6904), 269-270.

Blonder, L. X., Bowers, D., & Heilman, K. M. (1991). The role of right hemisphere in emotional communication. *Brain, 114,* 1115-1127.

Bonda, E., Petrides, M., Frey, S., & Evans, A. C. (1994). Frontal cortex involvement in organized sequences of hand movements: Evidence from a positron emission tomography study. *Social Neuroscience Abstracts, 20* (7353).

Bontempi, B., & Durkin, T.P. (2007). *Dynamics of hippocampal-cortical interactions during memory consolidation: Insight from functional brain imaging.* Heidelberg: Springer-Verlag.

Bowlby, J. (1969). *Attachment.* New York: Basic Books.

Bowlby, J. (1988). *A secure base: Parent-child attachment and healthy human development.* New York: Basic Books.

Bracha, V., Zhao, D.A., Wunderlich, S.J., Morrissy, S.J. & Bloedel, J.R. (1997). Patients with cerebellar lesions cannot acquire but are able to retain conditioned eyeblink reflexes. *Brain, 120,* 1401-1413.

Bradshaw, J. (1990). *Homecoming: Reclaiming and championing your inner child.* New York: Bantam.

Brannon, L. & Feist, J. (2004). *Health Psychology* (5th ed). Thomson Wadsworth.

Bretherton, I. (1992). Social referencing, international communication, and the interfacing of minds in infancy. In S. Feinman (Ed.), *Social referencing and the social construction of reality in infancy* (pp. 57-77). New York: Plenum Press.

Bretherton, I. (1993). From dialogue to internal working models: The co-construction of self in relationships. In C. A. Nelson (Ed.), *Minnesota Symposia on Child Psychology: Vol. 26. Memory and affect in development* (pp. 237-264). Hillsdale, NJ: Erlbaum.

Brodsky, M., & Lombroso, P. J. (1998). Molecular mechanisms of developmental disorders. *Development and Pschopathology, 10.*

Bromberg-Martin, E. S., & Hikosaka, O. (2009). Midbrain Dopamine Neurons Signal Preference for Advance Information about Upcoming Rewards. *Neuron 63, 119–126.*

Brown, S. L. et al. (2009). Social closeness increases salivary progesterone in humans. *Hormones and Behavior 56, 108–111.*

Bucke, R. (1974). *Cosmic Consciousness, A Study in the Evolution of the Human Mind.* New York: Causeway Books.

Buckingham, M., & Clifton, D. (2001). *Now Discover Your Strengths.* The Free Press.

Burgdorf, J. & Panksepp, J. (2006). The neurobiology of positive emotions. *Neuroscience and Biobehavioral Reviews, 30,* 173-187.

Burns, R., & Gallini, J. (1983). The relation of cognitive and affective measures to achievement during an instructional sequence. *Instructional Science, 12,* 103-120.

Burow, P. (2007). *Core Beliefs: Harnessing the power.* Melbourne: Copernicus

Publishing.

Cacioppe, R. (2000). *Creating Spirit at work: Re-visioning Organisation Development and Leadership – Part 1.* MCB University Press, Leadership and Organization Development Journal 21/2.

Cacioppe, R. (2000). *Creating Spirit at work: Re-visioning Organisation Development and Leadership - Part 2.* MCB University Press, Leadership and Organization Development Journal 21/2.

Cacioppo, J.T., & Bernston, G.C. (1992). Social psychological contributions to the decade of the brain: Doctrine of multilevel analysis. *American Psychologist, 47*(8), 1019-1028.

Cahill, L., et al. (1994). *Beta-adrenergic Activation and Memory for Emotional Events.* Nature.

Capra, F. (1984). *The Tao of physics: An exploration of the parallels between modern physics and eastern mysticism.* New York: Bantam. Capra, F. (1996). *The web of life.* New York: Doubleday.

Capra, F., & Steindl-Rast, D. (1975). *Belonging to the Universe.* San Francisco: Harper.

Casti, J.L. (2000). *Paradigms regained.* New York: William Morrow.

Cavanna, A. E., & Trimble, M. R., (2006). The precuneus: a review of its functional anatomy and behavioral correlates. *Brain (2006), 129, 564–583.*

Chalmers, D.J. (1996). *The conscious mind.* New York: Oxford University Press.

Chapman, E. et al. (2007). Fetal testosterone and empathy: Evidence from the Empathy Quotient (EQ) and the "Reading the Mind in the Eyes" Test. *Social Neuroscience, 1* (2), 135-148.

Chatzkel, J.L. (2003). *Knowledge capital.* Oxford: Oxford University Press.

Chiron, C., Jambaque, I., Nabbout, R., Syrota, A., & Dulac, O. (1997). The right brain is dominant in human infants. *Brain, 120* (6), 1057-1065.

Chopra, D. (1993). *Ageless body, timeless mind: The quantum alternative to growing old.* New York: Harmony.

Chopra, D. (1989). *Quantum healing: Exploring the frontiers of mind/body medicine.* New York: Bantam.

Chopra, D. (2003). *Synchro Destiny.* Harmony Books.

Christman, S. D. (1994). The many side of the two sides of the brain. *Brain and Cognition, 26.*

Ciaramelli, E., Muccioli, M., Làdavas, E., & di Pellegrino, G. (2007). Selective deficit in personal moral judgment following damage to ventromedial prefrontal cortex. *Scan, 2,* 84-92.

Clark L. (1997). *Essential Celtic Mythology*. San Francisco: Thorsons.

Cogill, S. R., Caplan, H. L., Alexandra, H., Robson, K. M., & Kumar, R. (1986). Impact of maternal postnatal depression on cognitive development of young children. *British Medical Journal, 292* (6529), 1165-1167.

Colby, A., Kohlberg, L., Gibbs, J., & Lieberman, M. (1983). *A longitudinal study of moral judgment. Monographs of the Society for Research in Child Development*, 48, Nos. 1-2.

Colin, V. L. (1996). *Human attachment*. New York: McGraw-Hill.

Colinvaux, P. (1980). *The fate of nations: A biological theory of history*. New York: Simon and Schuster.

Collins, J. C., & Porras, J. I. (1996). Building your company's vision. *Harvard Business Review, September-October*.

Cope, M. (2000). *Know your value? Manage your knowledge and make it pay*. London: Prentice Hall.

Cordoso, C. (2012). *Acute Intranasal Oxytocin Improves Positive Self-Perceptions of Personality*. A Thesis in the Department of Psychology. Presented in Partial Fulfillment of the Requirements for the Degree of Master of Arts (Psychology) at Concordia University, Montreal, Quebec, Canada.

Covey, S. (1992). *Principle Centred Leadership*. New York: Fireside.

Covey, S. R. (1990). *Principle Centred Leadership*. New York: Fireside.

Covey, S.R.W. (1989). *The seven habits of highly effective people*. New York: Free Press.

Cozolina, L. J. (2002). *The neuroscience of psychotherapy: Building and rebuilding the human brain*. New York: WW Norton and Company.

Craig, A.D. (2002). How do you feel? Interoception: the sense of the physiological condition of the body. *Nature Reviews Neuroscience, 3*, 655-666.

Craig, A.D. (2009). How do you feel – now? The anterior insula and human awareness. *Nature Reviews Neuroscience, 10*, 59-70.

Creem, S.H. & Proffitt, D.R. (2001). Defining the cortical visual systems "What", "Where" and "How". *Acta Psychologica, 107*, 43-68.

Crick, F. (1994). *The astonishing hypothesis: The scientific search for the soul*. New York: Scribner's Sons.

Crowe, E., & Higgins, T., (1997). Regulatory Focus and Strategic Inclinations: Promotion and Prevention in Decision-Making. *Organizational Behavior and Human Decision Processes, 69, No. 2, 117–132*. Academic Press.

Csíkszentmihályi, Mihály (1990). *Flow: The Psychology of Optimal Experience*. New York: Harper and Row.

Damasio, A. R. (1994). *Descartes' error.* New York: Putnam.

Damasio, A. R. (1999). *The feeling of what happens.* New York: Harcourt Brace.

Damasio, A. R. (2003). *Looking for Espinoza.* Harcourt Inc.

Daniels, D. & Price, V. (2000). *The Essential Enneagram: The Definitive Personality Test and Self-Discovery Guide.* HarperCollins: San Francisco. Daruna, J.H. (2004). *Psychoneuroimmunology.* Elsevier .

Davis, C., Kleinman, J.T., Newhart, M., Heidler-Gray, J. & Hillis, A.E. (2006). Speech and language functions that depend on Broca's area. *Brain and Language, 99,* 8-219.

Dawes, R.M. (1988). *Rational Choice in an Uncertain World.* Harcourt Brace Jovanovich.

Dawkins, R. (1976). *The Selfish Gene.* Oxford University Press

Dawson, G., Panagiotides, H., Klinger, L. G., & Hill, D. (1992). The role of frontal lobe functioning in the development of self-regulatory behavior. *Brain and Cognition, 20.*

Dêbiec, J. (2007). From affiliative behaviors to romantic feelings: a role of nanopeptides. *Federation of European Biochemical Societies Letters, 581,* 2580-2586.

Decety, J. (1994). Mapping motor representations with positron emission tomography. *Nature, 371.*

Decety, J., Jackson, P.L., Sommerville, J.A., Chaminade, T., & Meltzoff, A.N. (2004). The neural bases of cooperation and competition: an fMRI investigation. *NeuroImage, 23*(2), 744-751.

Decety, J. et al. (2008). Children Are Naturally Prone To Be Empathic And Moral. Who caused the pain? *An fMRI investigation of empathy and intentionality in children. Neuropsychologia;* DOI: 10.1016/j.neuropsychologia.2008.05.026

Decety, J. (2010). Dissecting the Neural Mechanisms Mediating Empathy. *Emotion Review, 3 (1), 92–108.*

Demartini, J. F. (2002). *The breakthrough experience.* Carlsbad: Hay House.

Department. Of Psychology, Florida State University. (2007). *Junkies, Adrenaline Junkies, and Pleasure, 10.1371/journal.*

Descartes, R. (1984). *The philosophical writings of Descarts* (J. Cottingham, R. Stoothoff, & D. Murdock, Trans.). Cambridge: Cambridge University Press.

De Waal, F. (1989). *Peacemaking among primates.* New York: Penguin.

Dennett, D. C. (1991). *Consciousness Explained.* Boston: Little, Brown.

Desimone, R. (1991). Face-selective cells in the temporal cortex of monkeys. *Journal of Cognitive Neuroscience, 3.*

DiAngi, L. (2002). *The Magic is in the Extra Mile.* Erie: Larry DiAngi Productions.

Diamond, J. (1979). *Behavioral Kinesiology.* New York: Harper and Row.

Diamond, J. (1979a). *Your Body Doesn't Lie.* New York: Warner Books.

Diamond, M. C., Krech, D., & Rosenweig, M. R. (1966). The effects of enriched environment on the histology of the rat cerebral cortex. *Journal of Comparative Neurology, 123.*

Diamond, M. C., Scheibel, A. B., Murphy, G. M., & Harvey, T. (1985). On the brain of a scientist: Albert Einstein. *Experimental Neurology, 88.*

Dickerson, S. & Kemeny, M. (2004). Acute Stressors and Cortisol Responses: A Theoretical Integration and Synthesis of Laboratory Research. *Psychological Bulletin, 130, No. 3, 355–391.*

Diversi, T. (2006). *The Correlation between HOS Types and Body Shape.* (unp).

Doidge, N. (2007). *The brain that changes itself.* Melbourne: Scribe Publications.

Dolan, R. J. (1999). On the neurology of morals. *Nature Neuroscience, 2*(11).

Doughty, D.D., Shin, L.M., Alpert, N.M., Pitman, R.K., Orr, S.P., Lasko, M. et al. (1999). Anger in Healthy Men: A PET study using Script-Driven Imagery. *Society of Biological Psychiatry, 46, 466-472.*

Dowse, R. & Ehlers, M. (2005). Medicine labels incorporating pictograms: Do they influence understanding and adherence?, *Patient Education and Counseling, 58, (1).*

Drake, R. A., & Seligman, M. E. P. (1989). Self-serving biases in casual attributions as a function of altered activation asymmetry. *International Journal of Neuroscience, 45.*

Duhaime-Ross, A. (2013). Empathy and Disgust Do Battle in the Brain: An injured rat helps us understand the struggle between empathy and disgust. *Scientific American, June 15, 2013.*

Dunphy, D., Turner, D. & Crawford, M. (1997). Organizational learning as the creation of corporate competencies. *Journal of Management Development, 16* (4).

Dunn, E. W. et al. (2008). Spending Money on Others Promotes Happiness. Science 319, 1687-1688.

Easterlin, R.A., & Crimmins, E.M. (1991). Private materialism, personal self-fulfillment, family life, and public interest: The nature, effects, and causes of recent changes in the values of American youth. Public Opinion Quarterly, 55, 449-533.

Edelman, G. (1992). *Bright air, brilliant fire.* New York: Basic Books.

Eddington, K. M., Dolcos, F., Cabeza, R., Krishnan, K. R., & Strauman, T. J. (2007). Neural correlates of promotion and prevention goal activation: An fMRI study using an idiographic approach. *Journal of Cognitive Neuroscience, 19, 1152–1162.*

Eddington, K. M., Dolcos, F., McLean, A. N., Cabeza, R., Krishnan, K. R. R., and

Strauman, T. J. (2009). Neural correlates of idiographic goal priming in depression: goal-specific dysfunctions in the orbitofrontal cortex. *Soc.Cogn.Affect.Neurosci. 4,* 238–246.

Eggert, N. (1998). *Contemplative Leadership for Entrepreneurial Organizations: Paradigms, Metaphors, and Wicked Problems.* Westport: Quorum Books.

Ehlers, A., & Margraf, J. (1987). Anxiety induced by false heart rate feedback in patients with panic disorder. *Behavior Research and Therapy, 26.*

Eisenberg, N.I., & Lieberman, M.D. (in press). *Why it hurts to be left out: the neurocognitive overlap between physical and social pain.* Submitted to *Trends in Cognitive Science.*

Eisenberger, N.I., & Lieberman, M.D. *Conflict and Habits: a social cognitive neuroscience approach to the self. 4004.* CRC Press.

Eisenberger, N.I., Lieberman, M.D., & Williams, K.D. (2003). Does rejection hurt? An fMRI study of social exclusion. *Science, 302,* 290-292.

Eisenberger, N.I., & Lieberman, M.D. (2004). Why rejection hurts: a common neural alarm system for physical and social pain. *Trends in Cognitive Sciences, 8(7),* 294-300.

Eisenhardt, K.M., Kahwajy, J. L., & Bourgeois, L. J. (1997). How management teams can have a really good fight. *Harvard Business Review, July-August.*

Emde, R. (1990). Mobilising fundamental modes of development: Empathic availability and therapeutic action. *Journal of the American Psychoanalytic Association, 38,* 881-913.

Epstein, D. (1994). *The 12 stages of healing: A network approach to wholeness.* San Rafael, CA: Amber-Allen Publishing.

Esch, T., & Stefano, G.B. (2004). The neurobiology of pleasure, reward processes, addiction and their health implications. *Neuroendicronology Letters, 25(4),* 235-251.

Esch, T., & Stefano, G. B. (2005). The Neurobiology of Love. *Neuroendocrinology Letters 26(3):175-192.*

Eslinger, P. J. (1998). Neurological and neuropsychological bases of empathy. *European Neurology, 39,* 193-199.

Farrer, C., & Frith, C. D. (2002). Experiencing Oneself vs Another Person as Being the Cause of an Action: The Neural Correlates of the Experience of Agency. *NeuroImage 15, 596–603.*

Fast, N., Gruenfeld, D. K., Sivanathan, N., & Galinsky, A. (2009). Illusory Control: A Generative Force Behind Power's Far-Reaching Effects. *Psychological Science.* Downloaded from pss.sagepub.com at UQ Library on July 14, 2013

Feist, G.J. (1998). A meta-analysis of the impact of personality on scientific and artistic creativity. *Personality and Social Psychological Review, 2,* 290-309.

Feldman, R., Greenbaum, C. W., & Yirimiya, N. (1999). Mother-infant affect synchrony as an antecedent of the mergence of self-control. *Developmental Psychology, 35* (1), 223-231.

FeldmanHall, O., Mobbs, D., & Dalgleish, T. (2012). Deconstructing the brains moral network: dissociable functionality between the temporoparietal junction and ventro-medial prefrontal cortex. doi:10.1093/scan/nss139. Oxford University Press.

FeldmanHall, O., Dalgleish, T., & Mobbs, D., (2013). Alexithymia decreases altruism in real social decisions. *SciVerse ScienceDirect, Cortex 49, 899-904.*

Fellows, L. K., & Farah, M. J., (2003). Ventromedial frontal cortex mediates affective shifting in humans: evidence from a reversal learning paradigm. *Brain, 126, 1830-1837.*

Fenwick, P. (2011). The Neuroscience of Spirituality. Royal College of Psychiatrists.

Field, T. M., Healy, B., Goldstein, S., Perry, S., & Bendell, D. (1988). Infants of depressed mothers show 'depressed' behavior even with non depressed adults. *Child Development, 59* (6), 1569-1579.

Field, T. M. (1997). The treatment of depressed mothers and their infants. In L. Murry & P. J. Cooper (Eds.), *Postpartum depression and child development* (pp. 221-236). New York: Guilford.

Fields, C. (2011). From "Oh, OK" to "Ah, yes" to "Aha!": Hyper-systemizing and the rewards of insight. *Personality and Individual Differences 50 (2011) 1159–1167.*

Filoteo, J. V., et al., (in press). Cortical and Subcortical Brain Regions Involved in Rule-Based Category Learning. *NeuroReport.*

Fischer, H., Wik, G., & Fredrikson, M. (1997). Extraversion, Neuroticism and Brain Function: a PET study of personality. *Person. individ. Diff. 23 (2), 345-352.*

Fisher, B. (1988). Wandering in the wilderness: The search for women role models. Signs: Journal of Women in Culture and Society, 13, 211–233.

Fisher, C.D. & Ashkanasy, N. M. (2000). The emerging role of emotions in working life: An introduction. Journal of Organizational Behavior, 21, 123-129.

Fisher, H. (2004). *Why We Love.* New York: Henry Holt.

Fivush, R., & Hudson, J. A. (1990). *Knowing and remembering in young children.* New York: Cambridge University Press.

Fivush, R. (1994). Constructing narrative, emotion, and self in parent-child conversations about the past. In U. Neisser & R. Fivush (Eds.), *The remembered self: Construction and accuracy in the self-narrative* (pp. 136-157). New York: Cambridge University Press.

Fliessbach, K. et al., (2007). Social Comparison Affects Reward-Related Brain Activity in the Human Ventral Striatum. *Science, 318, 1305-1308.*

Focquaert, F., et al., (2007). Empathizing and systemizing cognitive traits in the sciences and humanities. *Personality and Individual Differences 43, 619–625.*

Focquaert, F., et al., (2010). Mindreading in individuals with an empathizing versus systemizing cognitive style: An fMRI study. *Brain Research Bulletin 83, 214–222.*

Fogassi, L., & Rizzolatti, G. (2013). The Mirror Mechanism as Neurophysiological Basis for Action and Intention Understanding. I*s Science Compatible with Free Will?: Exploring Free Will and Consciousness in the Light of Quantum Physics and Neuroscience, DOI 10.1007/978-1-4614-5212-6_9, Springer Science & Business Media, LLC, 117-134.*

Fonagy, P., Steele, M., Steele, H., Moran, G. S., & Higgitt A.C. (1991). The capacity to understand mental states: The reflective self in parent and child and its significance for security of attachment. *Infant Mental Health Journal, 12*(3), 201-218.

Fontana, D. (1993). *The Secret Language Of Symbols.* London: Pavilion Books.

Forrester, J. (1994). *Learning through systems dynamics as preparation for the 21st century.* MIT Systems Dynamics Education Project.

Forrester, J. (1956). *The beginning of systems dynamics.* MIT Systems Dynamics Education Project.

Foster, B. & Seeker, K. (1997). *Coaching for Peak Performance.* San Francisco: Jossey-Bass Pfeiffer.

Fox, N. A. (1994). Dynamic cerebral processes underlying emotion regulation. In N. A. Fox (Ed.), *The development of emotion regulation: Biological and behavioral considerations. Monographs of the Society for Research in Child Development, 59* (2-3, Serial No. 240).

Frackowiak, R.S.J. (Ed.). (2004). *Human brain function, 2nd edition.* San Diego: Elsevier Academic.

Freyd, J. J. (1987). Dynamic mental representations. *Psychological Review, 94,* 427-438.

Frijda, N. H. (1986). *The Emotions.* Cambridge, UK: Cambridge University Press.

Frith, C. (2002). Attention to action and awareness of other minds. *Consciousness and Cognition, 11,* 481-487.

Frith, C.D., & Frith, U. (1999). Interacting minds: A biological basis. *Science, 286,* 1692-1695.

Fritz, R. (1984). *The Path Of Least Resistance.* New York: Fawcett Columbine.

Gaillard R, Dehaene S, Adam C, Clémenceau S, Hasboun D, et al. (2009). *Converging Intracranial Markers of Conscious Access.* PLoS Biol 7(3): e1000061. Doi:10.1371/

journal.pbio.1000061.

Gallagher, H.L. & Frith, C.D. (2003). Functional Imaging of Theory of Mind. *Trends in Cognitive Sciences, 7,* 51-96.

Gallese, V., Fadiga, L., Fogassi, L., & Rizzolatti, G. (1996). Action recognition in the premotor cortex. *Brain, 119,* 593-609.

Gauther, I., et al., (1999). Activation of the middle fusiform 'face area' increases with expertize in recognizing novel objects. *Nature Neuroscience 2 (6), 568-573.*

George, C., & Solomon, J. (1996). Representational models of relationships: Links between caregiving and attachment. *Infant Mental Health Journal, 17* (3), 198-216.

Gigerenzer, (1996). The psychology of good judgment: Frequency formats and simple algorithms. *Journal of Medical Decision Making, 16.*

Goel, V., Grafman, J., Sadato, N., & Halletta, M. (1995). Modelling other minds. *NeuroReport, 6,* 1741-1746.

Goldenfeld N., Baron-Cohen, S., & Wheelwright, S. (2005). Empathizing and Systemizing in Males, Females and Autism. *Clinical Neuropsychiatry 2 (6), 338-345.*

Goldberg, E. (1999). *The 9 Ways of Working.* Marlowe & Company.

Goldberg, E. (2001). *The Executive Brain.* Oxford University Press.

Goldberg, E. (2005). *The wisdom paradox.* London: Pocket Books.

Goldberg, E., & Costa, L. D. (1981). Hemispheric differences in the acquisition and use of descriptive systems. *Brain and Language, 14.*

Goleman, D. (1995). *Emotional Intelligence.* New York: Bantam Books.

Goleman, D. (2000). Leadership That Gets Results. *Harvard Business Review, March-April .*

Goleman, D. (1998). *Working with emotional intelligence.* London: Bloomsbury Publishing.

Goleman, D. (2006). *Social intelligence: The new science of human relationships.* New York, NY: Bantam Books.

Goleman, D., Boyatzis, R., & McKee, A. (2002). *Primal leadership: realizing the power of emotional intelligence.* Boston: Harvard Business School Press.

Gonzalez-Liencres, C. Shamay-Tsoory, S. G. & Brune, M. (2013). Review Towards a neuroscience of empathy: Ontogeny, phylogeny, brain mechanisms,context and psychopathology. *Neuroscience and Biobehavioral Reviews 37, 1537– 1548.*

Goodworth, C. (1988). *The secrets of successful leadership and people Management.* Heinman Professional Publishing.

Grafton, S. T., Arbib, M. A., Fadiga, L., & Rizzolatti, G. (1996). Localisation of grasp representations in humans by positron emission tomography. 2: Observation

compared with imagination. *Experimental Brain Research, 112* (1), 103-111.
Graham, G. (2002). If you want honesty, break some rules. *Harvard Business Review, April.*

Graham, A. M., Fisher, P. A., & Pfeifer, J. H. (2013). What Sleeping Babies Hear: An fMRI Study of Interparental Conflict and Infants' Emotion Processing. *Psychol Sci. 24(5): 782–789. doi:10.1177/0956797612458803.* NIH-PA Author Manuscript.

Greene, R. & Elffers, J. (1998). *48 Laws of Power*, New York: Viking Press.

Greenfield, S. (2000). *The private life of the brain.* London: Penguin Books.

Grisaru, N., Chudakov, B., Yaroslavsky, Y., & Belmaker, R. H. (1998). Transcranial magnetic stimulation in mania: A controlled study. *American Journal of Psychiatry, 155*(11).

Gunnar, M. R., & Stone, C. (1984). The effects of positive maternal affect on infant responses to pleasant, ambiguous and fear-provoking toys. *Child Development, 55,* 1231-1236.

Gunnar, M. R. (1992). Reactivity of the hypothalamic-pituitary-adrenocortical system to stressors in normal infants and children. *Pediatrics, 90* (3), 491-497.

Gurdjieff, G. (1950). *Beelzebub's Tales To His Grandson.* London: Broadway house.

Han, S., & Northoff, G. (2009). Understanding the self: a cultural neuroscience approach. *Progress in Brain Research, 178, 203-212.*

Hanson, J. L., et al., (2012). Structural Variations in Prefrontal Cortex Mediate the Relationship between Early Childhood Stress and Spatial Working Memory. *The Journal of Neuroscience, 32(23):7917–7925.*

Harackiewicz, J. M., Barron, K. E., & Elliot, A. J. (1998). Rethinking achievement goals: When are they adaptive for college students and why? *Educational Psychologist, 33,* 1-21.

Harbaugh, W. T. et al. (2007). Neural Responses to Taxation and Voluntary Giving Reveal Motives for Charitable Donations. *Science 316, 1622-1625.*

Hariri, A. R., & Holmes, A. (2006). Genetics of emotional regulation: the role of the serotonin transporter in neural function. *Trends in Cognitive Sciences, 10*(4), 182-191.

Hariri, A.R. et al. (2000). Modulating Emotional Response: Effects of a Neocortical Network on the Limbic System. *NeuroReport, 8,* 11-43.

Harlow, J. (1868). Recovery from the passage of an iron bar through the head. *Publication of the Massachusetts Medical Society, 2.*

Harris, M., & Butterworth, G. (2002). *Developmental Psychology.* London: Psychology Press.

Harris, T. (1976). *I'm OK - You're OK: A practical guide to transactional analysis.* London: Pan Books.

Harter, S., Bresnick, S., Bouchey, H. A., & Whitsell, N. R. (1997). The Development of multiple role-related selves during adolescence. *Development and Psychopathology, 9,* 835-854.

Hasselmo, M. E., Rolls, E. T., & Baylis, G. C. (1989). The role of expression and identity in the face-selective responses of neurons in the temporal visual cortex of the monkey. *Behavior Brain Research, 32* (3), 203-218.

Hawkins, D.R. (1995). *Power versus Force: An Anatomy of Consciousness.* Carlsbad: Hay House.

Heim, S., Eickhoff, A.B. & Amunts, K. (2008). Specialisation in Broca's region for semantic, phonological, and syntactic fluency? *NeuroImages, 40,* 1362-1368.

Herald, J. (2004). *What are you waiting for?* Crows Nest: Allen & Unwin.

Hesse, E. (1999). The adult attachment interview: Historical and current perspectives. In J. Cassidy & P. R. Shaver (Eds.), *Handbook of attachment: theory, research, and clinical applications* (pp. 395-433). New York: Guilford.

Hill, G. W. (1982). Groups versus individual performance: Are N+1 heads better than one? *Psychological Bulletin, 91.*

Hirschhorn, L. (2002). Campaigning for change. *Harvard Business Review, July.*

Hirosawa, T. et al., (2012). Oxytocin attenuates feelings of hostility depending on emotional context and individuals' characteristics. *Scientific Reports, 2, 384. DOI: 10.1038/srep00384*

Hofer, M. A. (1994). Hidden regulators in attachment, separation, and loss. *Monographs of the Society for Research in Child Development, 59* (2-3), 192-207.

Horney, K. (1945). *Our Inner Conflicts.* New York: Norton.

Houf, H. (1945). *What religion is and does: an introduction to the study of its problems and values.* New York: Harper and Brothers.

Hout, T. M., & Carter, J. C. (1995). Getting it done: New roles for Senior Executives. *Harvard Business Review, November-December.*

Howard, G. S. (1991). Culture tales: A narrative approach to thinking, cross-cultural psychology, and psychotherapy. *American Psychologist, 46*(3), 187-197.

Hoyle, R. L., Bromberger, B., Groversman, H. D., Klauber, M. R., Dixon, S. D., and Snyder, J. M. (1983). Regional anesthesia during newborn circumcision: Effect on infant pain response. *Clinical Pediatrics (Philadelphia), 22.* http://en.wikipedia.org/wiki/Neuroscience retrieved 20/5/2007.

Hubel, D.H. (1967). Effects of distortion of sensory input on the visual system of kittens.

Physiologist, 10(1), 17-45.

Hudson, K. (1999). *Transforming a Conservative Company - One Laugh at a Time*. Harvard Business School Press.

Hurlemann, R. et al., (2010). Oxytocin Enhances Amygdala-Dependent, Socially Reinforced Learning and Emotional Empathy in Humans. *The Journal of Neuroscience, 30(14):4999 –5007.*

Huskinson, L. (2004). *Nietzsche and Jung: The Whole Self in the Union of Opposites.* Hove.

Huxley, T. (1874). On the hypothesis that animals are automata. In *Collected Essays.* London, 1893-94.

Izuma K., Saito, D., & Sadato, N. (2008). Processing of Social and Monetary Rewards in the Human Striatum. *Neuron 58, 284–294, April 24, 2008.* Elsevier Inc.

Jack I. J., et al., fMRI reveals reciprocal inhibition between social and physical cognitive domains. *NeuroImage 66, 385–401.*

James, W. (1890). *The Principles of Psychology.* New York: Holt.

Janoff-Bulman, R. (1992). *Shattered assumptions: Towards a new psychology of trauma.* New York: Free Press.

Jantsch, E. (1975). *Design for Evolution.* New York: George Brazillier.

Jason, G., & Pajurkova, E. (1992). Failure of metacontrol: Breakdown in behavioral unity after lesions of the corpus callosum and inferomedial frontal lobes. *Cortex, 28.*

Jauch, J. M. (1968). *Foundations of Quantum Mechanics.* Reading, Mass.: Addison-Wesley.

Jaynes, J. (1976). *The origins of consciousness in the breakdown of the bicameral mind.* Boston: Houghton Mifflin.

Jeannerod, M., Arbib, M. A., Rizzolatti, G., & Sakata, H. (1995). Grasping objects: The cortical mechanism of visuomotor transformation. *Trends in Neuroscience, 18* (7), 314-320.

Jeffers, S. (1987). *Feel The Fear and do it Anyway.* Butler Bowdon.

Jeffers, S. (1992). *Dare to connect: Reaching out in romance, friendship and the workplace.* New York: Fawcett Columbine.

Jordan, J., Sivanathan, N., & Galinsky, A. (2012). Something to Lose and Nothing to Gain: The Role of Stress in the Interactive Effect of Power and Stability on Risk Taking. *Administrative Sceince Quarterly 2011 56: 530.* Sage Publications. http://asq. sagepub.com/content/56/4/530 retrieved 14/7/2013.

Johnson, Dr S. (1999). *Who moved my cheese?* London: Vermilion.

Johnson, M. (1987). *The body in the mind.* Chicago: University of Chicago Press.

Johnson, M., et al., (2006). Dissociating medial frontal and posterior cingulate activity during self-reflection. *SCAN 1, 56-64.* Oxford University Press.

Joseph, R. (1996). *Neuropsychiatry, neuropsychology, and clinical neuroscience.* Baltimore: Williams and Wilkins.

Judith, A. (1996). *Eastern body, western mind: Psychology and the chakra system as a path to the self.* Berkley, CA: Celestial Arts.

Jueptner, M., & Weiller, C. (1998). A review of differences between basal ganglia and cerebellar control of movements as revealed by functional imaging studies. *Brain, 121*(8), 1437-1449.

Jung, C. (1969). *Aion.* Princeton: Princeton University Press.

Kahneman, D. (2003). A perspective on judgment and choice: Mapping bounded rationality. *American Psychologist, 58*(9), 697-720. Kagan, J. (1994). *Galen's Prophecy,* New York: Basic Books.

Kalbe, E. et al. (2010). Dissociating cognitive from affective theory of mind: A TMS study. *ScienceDirect Cortex 46, 769–780.*

Kalin, N.H., Shelton, S.E., & Lynn, C.M. (1995). Opiate systems in mother and infant primates coordinate intimate contact during reunion. *Psychoneuroimmunology, 20,* 735-742.

Kaplan, R.S., & Norton, D.P. (1996). *The balanced scorecard: Translating strategy into action.* Boston: Harvard Business School Press.

Keenan, J.P., McCutcheon, B., Freund, S., Gallup, G.G. Jr, Sanders, G.,*Pascual-Leone, A. (1999). Left hand advantage in a self-face recognition task. *Neuropsychologia, 37*(12), 1421-1425.

Kehoe, P., & Blass, E.M. (1989). Opioid-mediation of separation distress in 10-day-old rats: Reversal of stress with maternal stimuli. *Developmental Psychobiology, 19*(4), 385-398.

Kekes, J. (1995). *Moral Wisdom and Good Lives.* Ithaca, NY: Cornell University Press.

Kelley, R. E. (1998). *How to be a star at work.* New York: Times Books.

Kelner, S., Rivers, C.A., & O'Connell K.H. (1996). *Managerial Style as a Behavioral Predictor of Organisational Climate.* Boston: McBer and Company.

Keltner, D., & Haidt, J . (2003). Approaching awe, a moral, spiritual, and aesthetic emotion. *Cognition and Emotion, 17,* 297-314.

Kemp, A. H. et al. (2012). Oxytocin Increases Heart Rate Variability in Humans at Rest: Implications for Social Approach-Related Motivation and Capacity for Social Engagement. *PLOS One 7 (8) e44014.*

Kehoe, P., & Blass, E. M. (1989). Conditioned opioid release in ten-day-old rats: Reversal of stress with maternal stimuli. *Developmental Psychobiology, 19*(4).

Kersey, D., & Bates, M. (1984). *Please Understand me (Sth Ed.).* Prometheus Nemesis

Books Co.

Keverne, E. B., Martens, N. D., & Tuite, B. (1989). Beta-endorphin concentrations in cerebrospinal fluid of monkeys are influenced by grooming relationships. *Psychoneuroendocrinology.*

Kim, D. (1993). *The Systems Thinker.* Pegasus Communications.

Klein, S. (2006). *The Science of Happiness.* Carlton North, Vic: Scribe publications.

Klein, E., Kreinin, I., Chistyakov, A., Koren, D., Mecz, L., Marmur, S. et al. (1999). Therapeutic efficacy of right prefrontal slow repetitive transcranial magnetic stimulation in major depression. *Archives of General Psychiatry, 56* (4), 315-320.

Knowles, P.A., Conner, R.L., & Panksepp, J. (1989). Opiate effects on social behavior of juvenile dogs as a function of social deprivation. *Pharmacology, Biochemistry and Behavior, 33* (3), 533-537.

Koban, L., Pichon, S., and Vuilleumier, P. (2013). Responses of medial and ventrolateral prefrontal cortex to interpersonal conflict for resources. Oxford University Press. doi:10.1093/scan/nst020

Koestler, A. (1967). *The Ghost in the Machine.* London: Hutchinson.

Kosfeld, M. et al. (2005). Oxytocin increases trust in humans. *Nature, 435, 673-676.*

Kotter, J. P. (1999). What Leaders Really Do. *Harvard Business Review.* Cambridge .

Kotter, J. P. (1995). Leading Change: Why Transformation Efforts Fail. *Harvard Business Review, March-April.*

Kouzes, J., & Posner, B. (1993). *Credibility, How Leaders Gain and Lose It, Why People Demand It.* San Francisco: Jossey-Bass.

Krapp, A., & Fink, B. (1992). The development and function of interests during the critical transition from home to preschool. In K.A Renninger, S. Hidi, & A. Krapp (Eds.), *The role of interest in learning and development* (pp. 397-430). Hillsdale, NJ: Lawrence Erlbaum.

Krause, D. (1995). *The Art of War for Executives.* Perigee Book.

Kretschmer, E. (1925). *Physique and Character. International Library of Psychology.* Routledge. Great Britain.

Kubler-Ross, E. (1970). *On Death and Dying.* New York: MacMillan.

Kuhn, T.S. (1962). *The Structure of Scientific Revolutions.* Chicago: University of Chicago Press.

Lamm, C., Decety, J., & Singer, T. (2010). Meta-analytic evidence for common and distinct neural networks associated with directly experienced pain and empathy for pain. *NeuroImage 54 (2011) 2492–2502.*

Langer, E. J. (1978). Rethinking the role of thought in social interaction. In J. H. Harvey, W. Ickes, & R. F. Kidd (Eds.), *New directions in attribution research, 2,* pp. 35-58).

Hillsdale, NJ: Erlbaum.

Lapid-Bogda, G., (2004). *Bringing Out the Best in Yourself at Work: How to Use the Enneagram System for Success.* Santa Monica: McGraw-Hill.

Larsen, R.J., Kasimatis, M., & Frey, K. (1992). Facilitating the furrowed brow: An unobtrusive test of the facial feedback hypothesis applied to unpleasant affect. *Cognition and Emotion, 6,* 321-338.

Le Doux, J. (1998). *The emotional brain.* Phoenix: Orion Books Ltd.

Lerner, J. S. & Keltner, D. (2000). Beyond valence: Toward a model of emotion-specific influences on judgement and choice. *Cognition and Emotion, 14 (4), 473-493.*

Levine, S., Haltmeyer, G. C., Karas, G. G., & Denenberg, V. H. (1967). Physiological and behavioral effects of infantile stimulation. *Physiology and Behavior, 2*(1).

Levy, J. (1969). Possible basis for the evolution of the human brain. *Nature, 224.*

Lewicki, P., Hill, T., & Czyzewska, M. (1992). Non-conscious acquisition of information. *American Psychologist, 47*(6).

Lewis, C.S. (1960). *Four Loves.* Harvest Books.

Lieberman, M.D., & Eisenberger, N.I. (2004). Conflict and habits: a social cognitive neuroscience approach to the self. In Tesser, A., Wood, J., Stapel, D. (Eds.), *On Building, Regulating and Defending the Self: a Psychological Perspective* (pp. 77-102). New York, NY: Psychology Press.

Lieberman, M.D., & Eisenberger, N.I. (2009). Pains and pleasures of social life. *Science, 323,* 890-891.

Lieberman, M.D., Gaunt, R., Gilbert, D.T., & Tope, Y. (2002). Reflexion and reflection: A social cognitive neuroscience approach to attributional inference. *Advances in Experimental Psychology, 34,* 199-249.

Lieberman, M.D., Schreiber, D., & Ochsner, K.N. (2003). Is political cognition like riding a bicycle? How cognitive neuroscience can inform research on political thinking. *Political Psychology, 24*(4), 681-704.

Lieberman, M. et al. (2005). A Pain by Any Other Name (Rejection, Exclusion, Ostracism) Still Hurts the Same: The Role of Dorsal Anterior Cingulate Cortex in Social and Physical Pain. In J. Cacioppo et al. (Eds.), *Social Neuroscience: People Thinking About Thinking People.* Cambridge, Mass.: MIT Press.

Liebert, R.M., & Liebert L.L. (1998). *Personality: Strategies & Issues Eighth Edition.* New York: Brooks Cole Publishing.

Liotti, M., & Tucker, D. M. (1992). Right hemisphere sensitivity to arousal and depression. *Brain and Cognition, 18,* 138-151.

Llinas, R. R. (1990). Intrinsic electrical properties of mammalian neurons and CNS function. *Fidia Research Foundation Neuroscience Award Lectures, 4.*

Loewenstein, G.F. (1994). The psychology of curiosity: A review and reinterpretation. *Psychological Bulletin, 116*(1), 75-98.

Lord, C. G., Ross, L., and Lepper, M. (1979). Biased assimilation and attitude polarisation: The effects of prior theories on subsequently considered evidence. *Journal of Personality and Social Psychology, 37* (11), 2098-2109.

Lorenz, E. N. (1963). *Deterministic nonperiodic flow.* J. Atmos. Sci. 20: 130–141.

Lowen, A. (1958). *Language of the Body.* New York: Collier Books.

Lupien, S. J., et al., (2009). Effects of stress throughout the lifespan on the brain, behavior and cognition. *Nature Reviews, Neuroscience, 10, 434-445.*

MacLean, P.D. (1985). Brain evolution relating to family, play, and the separative call. *Archives of General Psychiatry, 42,* 405-417.

MacLean, P. D. (1985). The psychobiological functions of dissociation. *American Journal of Hypnosis, 26*(2).

Maier, S.F., & Seligman, M.E.P. (1976). Learned helplessness: Theory and evidence. *Journal of Experimental Psychology: General, 105,* 3-46.

Main, M. (1995). Attachment: Overview, with implications for clinical work. In S. Goldberg, R. Muir, & J. Kerr (Eds.), *Attachment theory: Social , developmental, and clinical perspectives* (pp. 407-474). Hillsdale, NJ: Analytic Press.

Main, M., & Goldwyn, R. (1984). *Adult attachment scoring and classification system.* Unpublished manuscript, University of California at Berkeley.

Main, M., & Goldwyn, R. (1984). *Adult attachment scoring and classification system.* Unpublished manuscript, University of California at Berkeley.

Main, M., & Solomon, J. (1990). Procedures for identifying infants as disorganized/ disorientated during the Ainsworth Strange Situation. In M. T. Greenberg, D. Cicchetti, & E. M. Cummings (Eds.), *Attachment in the preschool years: Theory, research, and intervention* (pp. 121-160). Chicago: University of Chicago Press.

Main, M., Kaplan, N., & Cassidy, J. (1985). Security in infancy, childhood, and adulthood: A move to the level of representation. In I. Bretherton & E. Waters (Eds.), Growing points of attachment theory and research. *Monographs of the Society for Research in Child Development, 50* (1-2), 66-104.

Malinkowski, B. (1984). The role of myth in life. In A. Dundes (Ed.), *Sacred narrative* (pp.193-206). Berkeley: University of California Press.

Markovits, Y., et al., (2008). Regulatory foci and organizational commitment. *Journal of Vocational Behavior 73, 485-489.*

Martin-Araguz, A., Bustamante-Martinez, C., Fernandez-Armayor, A., & Moreno-

Martinez, J. (2002). Neuroscience in al-Andalus and its influence on medieval scholastic medicine. *Revista de neurología, 34* (9).

Maslow, A. H. (1964). *Toward a psychology of being.* Princeton, NJ: Van Nostrand.

Matthews, J. (1991). *The Celtic Shaman: A Practical Guide.* London: Rider.

McAndrew, F. T., (2009). The interacting roles of testosterone and challenges to status in human male aggression. *Aggression and Violent Behavior.* Elsevier Ltd.

McCarthy, G. (1995). Functional neuroimaging of memory. *The Neuroscientist, 1*(3).

McCaskey, M. B. (1979). The hidden messages managers send. *Harvard Business Review, November-December.*

McCraty, R. (2002). Influence of cardiac afferent input on heart-brain synchronization and cognitive performance. *International Journal of Psychophysiology, 45*(1-2), 72-73.

McCraty, R., Atkinson, R., & Tiller, W. (1999). The role of physiological coherence in the detection and measurement of cardiac energy exchange between people. Paper presented at the Tenth International Montreux Congress on Stress, Montreux, Switzerland.

McCraty, R., & Watkins, A. (1996). *Autonomic Assessment Report Interpretation Guide,* Boulder Creek, California: Institute of HeartMath.

Meaney, M., Aiken, D. H., Viau, V., Sharma, S., & Sarrieau, A. (1989). Neonatal handling alters adrenocortical negative feedback sensitivity and hippocampal type II glucocorticoid receptor binding in the rat. *Neuroendocrinology, 50.*

Meaney, M. J., Diorio, J., Francis, D., Weaver, S., Yau, J., Chapman, K., & Seckl, J. R. (2000). Postnatal handling increases the expression of CAMP-inducible transcription factors in the rat hippocampus: The effects of thyroid hormones and serotonin. *The Journal of Neuroscience, 20*(10).

Mehta, P. H., & Josephs, R. A., (2006). Testosterone change after losing predicts the decision to compete again. *Hormones and Behavior 50, 684–692.*

Melchizedek, D. (1990). *The Ancient Secret of the Flower of Life.* Flagstaff: Light Technology Publishing.

Meyer, M. (2009). How Culture Shapes Our Mind and Brain. Weblog *http://brainblogger. com/2009/10/10/how-culture-shapes-our-mind-and-brain.*

Meyers, C. A., Berman, S. A., Scheibel, R. S., & Hayman, A. (1992). Case report: Acquired antisocial personality disorder associated with unilateral left orbital frontal lobe damage. *Journal of Psychiatry and Neuroscience, 17*(3), 121-125.

Miller, H., Alvarez, V., & Miller, N. (1990). *The psychopathology and psychoanalytic psychotherapy of compulsive caretaking.* Unpublished manuscript.

Miller, P.J., & Sperry, R.W. (1988). Early talk about the past: The origins of conversational stories of personal experience. *Journal of Child Language, 15*(2), 293-315.

Mintzberg, H., Ahirstrand, B., and Lapel J. (1998). *Strategy Safari*. New York: The Free Press.

Mitchell, K. J., et al., (2009). Age-Group Differences in Medial Cortex Activity Associated with Thinking About Self-Relevant Agendas. *Psychol Aging. 2009 June ; 24(2): 438–449*. NIH Author Manuscript.

Moll, J., et al., (2005). The neural basis of human moral cognition. *Nature Reviews, Neuroscience, 6, 799-809.*

Mölle, M., Marshall, L., Lutzenberger, W., Pietrowsky, R., Fehm, H.L., & Born, J. (1996). Enhanced dynamic complexity in the human EEG during creative thinking. *Neuroscience Letters, 208*(1), 61-64.

Moore, T. (1992). *Care of the Soul.* HarperCollins Publishers.

Moore, T. (1994). *Soul mates: Honoring the mysteries of love and relationship.* New York: Harper Perennial.

Moskovitz & Grant (2009). *The Psychology of Goals.* New York: The Guildford Press

Moriguchi, Y., et al., (2006). Impaired self-awareness and theory of mind: An fMRI study of mentalizing in alexithymia. *NeuroImage 32, 1472 – 1482.*

Moriguchi, Y., et al., (2007). Empathy and Judging Other's Pain: An fMRI Study of Alexithymia. *Cerebral Cortex 17:2223-2234.*

Myss, C. (2002). *Sacred Contracts: Awakening Your Divine Potential.* Harmony.

Myss, C. (1996). *Anatomy of the spirit: The seven stages of power and healing.* New York: Crown Publishers.

Nataraja, S. (2008). *The blissful brain: Neuroscience and proof of the power of meditation.* London: Gaia Publications.

Nelson, C. A., (Eds.). (1993). *Minnesota symposia on child psychology: Vol.26. Memory and effect in development.* Hillsdale, NJ: Erlbaum.

Nelson, K. (1993). Events, narratives, memory: What develops? In C.A. Nelson (Ed.), *Minnesota Symposia in Child Psychology: Vol. 26. Memory and affect in development* (pp. 1-24). Hillsdale, NJ: Lawrence Erlbaum Associates, Inc.

Nelson, R. J. & Trainor, B. C. 2007. Neural mechanisms of aggression. *Nature Reviews Neuroscience, 8, 536-546.*

Nichols, K., & Champness, B. (1971). Eye gaze and the GRS. *Journal of Experimental Social Psychology, 7.*

Nichols, R. G., & Stevens, L. A. (1957). Listening to people. *Harvard Business Review, September-October.*

Nisbett, R. E., & Ross, L. D. (1980). *Human Inference: Strategies and Shortcomings of Social Judgment.* Englewood Cliffs, NJ: Prentice-Hall.

Nishitani, N., & Hari, R. (2000). Temporal dynamics of cortical representation for action. *Proceedings of the National Academy of Science, 97*(2), 913-918.

Nix, G. A., Ryan, R. M., Manly, J. B., & Deci, E. L. (1999). Revitalization through self-regulation: The effects of autonomous and controlled motivation on happiness and vitality. *Journal of Experimental Social Psychology, 35,* 266-284.

Noriuchi, M., Kikuchi, Y., & Senoo, A. (2008). The Functional Neuroanatomy of Maternal Love: Mother's Response to Infant's Attachment Behaviors. *Society of Biological Psychiatry, 63,* 415- 423.

O'Connel, B. (1997). *Mindreading.* Cox & Wyman Ltd.

O'Doherty, J., Kringelback, M. L., Rolls, E. T., Hornak, J., & Andres, C. (2001). Abstract reward and punishment representations in the human orbitofrontal cortex. *Nature Neuroscience, 4*(1), 95-102.

Oatley, K. (1992). Integrative action of narrative. In D. J. Stein & J. E. Young (Eds.), *Cognitive science and clinical disorders* (pp. 151-172), New York: Academic. Ochs, E., & Capps, L. (2001). *Living narrative: Creating lives in everyday storytelling.* Cambridge, MA: Harvard University Press.

Ochsner, K. et al. (2004). For Better or for Worse: Neural Systems Supporting the Cognitive Down- and Up-regulation of Negative Emotion. *NeuroImage, 23,* 483-99.

Ochsner, K. et al. (2006). How Thinking Controls Feeling: A Social Cognitive Neuroscience Approach. In P. Winkleman, & E. Harmon-Jones (Eds.), *Social Neuroscience.* New York: Oxford University Press.

Ochsner, K. N., Bunge, S. A., Gross, J. J., & Gabrieli, J. D. (2002). Rethinking feelings: an FMRI study of the cognitive regulation of emotion. *Journal of Cognitive Neuroscience, 14(8), 1215-1229.*

Oei, N. Y. L., et al., (2012). Stress shifts brain activation towards ventral affective areas during emotional distraction. *SCAN (2012) 7, 403-412.*

Oppenheim, D., Nir, A., Warren, S., & Emde, R.N. (1997). Emotion regulation in mother-child narrative co-construction: Associations with children's narratives and adaptation. *Developmental Psychology, 33,* 284-294.

Ornstein, R. (1997). *The right mind: Making sense of the hemispheres.* New York: Harcourt Brace.

Osman, M. (2012). The role of reward in dynamic decision making. *Frontiers in Neuroscience 6 (35).*

Overmier, J.B., & Seligman, M.E.P. (1967). Effects of inescapable shock upon subsequent escape and avoidance behavior. *Journal of Comparative and Physiological Psychology, 63*, 23-33.

Pagano, B., & Pagano, E. (2004). *Transparency Edge: How Credibility Can Make Or Break You In Business.* New York: McGraw-Hill.

Palmer, H. (1998). *Inner Knowing: Consciousness, Creativity, Insight, and Intuition.* New York: Jeremy Tarcher/Putnam.

Palmer, H. (1998). *The Enneagram Advantage: Putting the 9 Personality Types to Work in the Office.* New York: Harmony Books.

Palmer, H. (1995). *The Enneagram in Love and Work: Understanding Your Intimate & Business Relationships.* San Francisco: Harper/Collins.

Palmer, H. (1988). *The Enneagram: The Definitive Guide to the Ancient System for Understanding Yourself and the Others in Your Life.* San Francisco: Harper/SF.

Palmer, H. (1995). *The Pocket Enneagram.* San Francisco: Harper/SF.

Panksepp, J. (1998). *Affective neuroscience: The foundation of human and animal emotions.* New York: Oxford University Press.

Panksepp, J., Nelson, E., & Siviy, S. (1994). Brain opioids and mother-infant social motivation. *Acta Paediatrica Supplement, 397*, 40-46.

Parkes, C. M., Stevenson-Hinde, J., & Marris, P. (1991). *Attachment across the life cycle.* London: Routledge.

Pascarella, P. (2003). Workers Without Borders: Creating Bonds When Workers Have No Loyalty. In *Business: the Ultimate Resource.* China Citic Press.

Pascual-Leone, A., Nguyet, D., Cohen, L.G., Brasil-Neto, J.P., Cammarota, A., Hallett, M. (1995). Modulation of muscle responses evoked by transcranial magnetic stimulation during the acquisition of new fine motor skills. *Journal of Neurophysiology, 74*, 1037–1045.

Pascual-Leone, A., et al., (1996). The role of the dorsolateral prefrontal cortex in implicit procedural learning. *Exp Brain Res 107:479-485.* Springer-Verlag.

Pavot, W., Diener, E., & Fujita, F. (1990). Extraversion and happiness. *Personality and Individual Differences, 11*, 1299-1306.

Pearsall, P. (1999). *The heart's code: Tapping the wisdom and power of our heart energy.* London: Bantam.

Perls, F. S. (1969). *Ego, Hunger and Aggressio.* New York: Vintage Books.

Perner, J., & Ruffman,T. (1995). Episodic memory and autonoetic consciousness: Developmental evidence and a theory of childhood amnesia. *Journal of Experimental Child Psychology, 59*(3), 516-548.

Perry, A. et al., (2010). Intranasal oxytocin modulates EEG mu/alpha and beta rhythms during perception of biological motion. *Psychoneuroendocrinology (2010) 35, 1446—1453.*

Perry, B.D., Pollard, R.A., Blakley, T.I., Baker, W.L., & Vigilante, D. (1995). Childhood Trauma, the Neurobiology of Adaptation and 'Use-Dependent' *Infant Mental Health Development of the Brain* – How 'States' become 'Traits'. *Journal, 16* (4), Winter.

Peterson, C.I. & Seligman, M.E.P. (2004). *Character strengths and virtues: A handbook and classification.* Washington, DC: APA Press and Oxford University Press.

Phillips, H. (2004). The cells that make us human. *New Scientist, 2452*(19), 32-36.

Pierrehumbert, B., et al., (2012). Adult attachment representations predict cortisol and oxytocin responses to stress. *Attachment & Human Development, 14* (5), 453–476.

Pinel, J.P.J. (2009). *Biopsychology* (7th ed.). Boston, MA: Allyn and Bacon.

Plato. (2000). *The Republic.* Mineola, NY: Dover Publications.

Platt, M. L., & Glimcher, P. W. (1999). Neural correlates of decision variables in parietal cortex. *Nature, 400.*

Plotsky, P. M., & Meaney, M. J. (1993). Early, postnatal experience alters hypothalamic corticotropin-releasing factor (CRF) MRNA, median eminence CRF content and stress-induced release in adult rates. *Molecular Brain Research, 18.*

Poldrack, R.A., & Foerde, K. (2007). Category learning and the memory systems debate. *Neuroscience and Biobehavioral Reviews, 32,* 197-205.

Porges, S. W., Doussard-Roosevelt, J. A., & Maiti A. K. (1994). Vagal tone and the physiological regulation of emotion. *Monographs of the Society for Research in Child Development, 59* (2-3), 167-186.

Porter, M. (1998). *Competitive strategy: Techniques for analysing industries and competitors.* London: Free Press.

Radojevic, M. (1994). Mental representations of attachment among prospective Australian fathers. *Australian and New Zealand Journal of Psychiatry, 28.*

Raine, A., Buchsbaum, M. S., Stanley, J., Lottenberg, S., Abel, L., & Stoddard, J. (1994). Selective reductions in prefrontal glucose metabolism in murderers. *Biological Psychiatry, 36.*

Rameson, L.T., & Lieberman, M.D. (2009). Empathy: A social cognitive neuroscience approach. *Social and Personality Psychology Compass, 3*(1), 94-110.

Rasoal, C., Danielsson, H., & Jungert, T. (2012). Empathy among students in engineering programmes. *European Journal of Engineering Education, 37* (5): 427

Ratey, J. (2002). *A User's Guide to the Brain.* London: Vintage Books.

Recanzone, G. H., Schreiner, C. E., & Merzenich, M. M. (1993). Plasticity in the frequency representation of primary auditory cortex following discrimination training in adult owl monkeys. *Journal of Neuroscience, 13.*

Reich, Wilhelm. (1949). *Character Analysis*. New York: Farrar, Straus, and Giroux.

Richard, J. & Nelson, C.H. (2007)., *Accounting of change in declarative memory: a cognitive neuroscience perspective: Developmental Review, 27,* 349-373.

Richmond, J., & Nelson, C.H. (2007). Accounting for change in declarative memory: A cognitive neuroscience perspective. *Developmental Review, 27,* 349-373.

Rizzolatti, G., & Arbib, M. A. (1998). Language within our grasp. *Trends in Neuroscience, 21* (5), 188-194.

Rizzolati, G., & Craighero, L. (2004). The mirror-neuron system. *Annual Review of Neuroscience, 27,* 169-192.

Robbins, A. (1991). *Awakening the Giant Within*. New York: Simon & Schuster.

Robbins, S., Millet, B., Cacioppe, R., & Waters-Marsh T. (1998). *Organizational Behavior: Leading and Managing People In Australia and New Zealand*.

Roethlisberger, F. (1941). *Management and Morale*. Cambridge: Harvard University Press.

Rogers, C., and Farson, R. E. (1957). Active Listening. In R. G. Newman, M. A. Danziger, & M. Cohen (Eds.) (1987), *Communication in Business Today*. Washington C.C.: Heath and Company.

Rolls, E. T. (2000). The orbitofrontal cortex and reward. *Cerebral Cortex, 10*(3).

Ross, E. D., Homan, R. W., & Buck, R. (1994). Differential hemispheric lateralisation of primary and social emotions: Implications for developing a comprehensive neurology of emotions, repression, and the subconscious. *Neuropsychiatry, Neuropsychology and Behavioral Neurology, 7,* 1-19.

Rothbart, M. K., Taylor, S. B., & Tucker, D. M. (1989). Right-sided facial asymmetry in infant emotional expression. *Neuropsychologia, 27.*

Rowan, A. (2003). *The lore of the Bard*. St Paul: Llewellyn Publications.

Russek, L. G., & Schwartz, G. E. (1996). Energy cardiology: A dynamical energy systems approach for integrating conventional and alternative medicine. *Advance, 12.*

Sagi, A., van Ijzendoorn, M. H., Scharf, M. H., Koren-Karie, N., Joels, T., & Mayseless, O. (1994). Stability and discriminant validity of the adult attachment interview: A psychometric study in young Israeli adults. *Developmental Psychology, 30.*

Saling, L.L., & Phillips, J.G. (2007). Automatic behavior: efficient not mindless. *Brain Research Bulletin, 73,* 1-20.

Sassa, Y., et al., (2012). The correlation between brain gray matter volume and empathizing and systemizing quotients in healthy children. *NeuroImage 60, 2035–2041.*

Saxe, G. N., Chinman, G., Berkowitz, R., Hall, K., Leiberg, G., Schwartz, J., & van der Kolk, BA. (1994). Somatization in patients with dissociative disorders. *American*

Journal of Psychiatry, 151(9).

Saxe, R., & Haushofer, J. (2008). For love or money: A Common Neural Currency for Social and Monetary Reward. *Neuron, 58,* 164-165.

Saxe, R., & Wexler, A. (2005). Making sense of another mind: The role of the right temporo-parietal junction. *Neuropsychologia, 43*(10), 1391-1399.

Saxe, R. (2006). Uniquely human social cognition. *Current Opinion in Neurobiology, 16:235–239*

Schaefer, M. et al., (2013). Mirror-like brain responses to observed touch and personality dimensions. *Frontiers in Human Neuroscience., 7 (227).*

Schacter, D. L. (1996). *Searching for memory: the brain, the mind and the past.* New York: Basic.

Schacter, D. L., Alpert, N. M., Savage, C. R., Rauch, S. L., & Albert, M. S. (1996). Conscious recollection and the human hippocampal formation: Evidence from positron emission tomography. *Proceedings of the National Academy of Sciences USA, 93.*

Schacter, D. L. (1992). Understanding implicit memory: A cognitive neuroscience approach. *American Psychologist, 47.*

Schaffer, R. H. (1988). *Breakthrough Strategy.* New York: Harper Business.

Schedlowski, M. & Tewes, U. (1996). *Psychoneuroimmunology.* Kluwer Academic / Plenum Pub.

Schmitter, A. M. (2010). Ancient, Medieval and Renaissance Theories of the Emotions. 17th and 18th Century Theories of Emotions. *The Stanford Encyclopedia of Philosophy (Winter 2010 Edition).*

Schore, A. N. (1991). Early superego development: The emergence of shame and narcissistic affect regulation in the practicing period. *Psychoanalysis and Contemporary Thought, 14,* 187-250.

Schore, A. N. (1994). *Affect regulation and the origin of the self: The neurobiology of emotional development.* Hillsdale, NJ: Erlbaum.

Schore, A. N. (1997). Early organisation of the non-linear right brain and development of a predisposition to psychiatric disorders. *Development and Psychopathology, 9*(4), 595-631.

Schore, A.N. (2003). *Affect Regulation and the Repair of the Self.*

Schore, A.N. (2003). *Affect Regulation and Disorders of the Self.* Norton & Co. Ltd.

Schultheiss, O. C., Wirth, M. M., & Stanton, S. J. (2004). Effects of affiliation and power motivation arousal on salivary progesterone and testosterone. *Hormones and Behavior 46, 592– 599.*

Schuman, J. (1997). *The neurobiology of affect in language*, Malden, MA: Blackwell.

Scientific American, October, 1994.

Searle, J. R., *Minds, brains, and programs*, Behavioral and Brain Sciences, 3: 417-24, 1980.

Searle, J. R. (1984). *Minds, brains, and science.* Cambridge: Harvard University Press.

Searleman, A. (1977). A review of right hemisphere linguistic capabilities. *Psychological Bulletin, 84*(3), 503-528.

Seligman, M., & Peterson, C. (2004). *Character Strengths and Virtues: A Handbook and Classification.* Oxford University Press.

Seligman, M.E.P. (1975). *Helplessness: On depression, development, and death.* New York: Freeman.

Seligman, M.E.P., & Maier, S. F. (1967). Failure to escape traumatic shock. *Journal of Experimental Psychology, 74,* 1-9.

Senge, P. (1994). *The fifth discipline field book.* London: Nicholas Brealey Publishing.

Serven-Schreiber, D. (1996). *Healing Without Prozac.*

Serven-Schreiber, D. (2004). *Healing Without Freud or Prozac.* Rodale International. Servan-Schreiber, D. (2005). *Healing without Freud or prozac: Natural approaches to curing stress, anxiety and depression without drugs and without psychotherapy.* London: Rodale International.

Shamay-Tsoory, S. G., et al. (2009). Intranasal Administration of Oxytocin Increases Envy and Schadenfreude (Gloating). *Society of Biological Psychiatry 66:864–870.*

Sheldon, W.H. (1942). *The Varieties of Temperament: A Psychology of Constitutional Differences.* USA: Harper & Brothers.

Sheldon, W.H. (1954). *Atlas of Men.* USA: Harper & Brothers.

Shepard. G. M. (1994). *Neurobiology,* 3rd edition. Oxford University Press.

Shaw, G., Brown, R. & Bromley, P. (1998). *How 3M Is rewriting business planning, May-June.*

Sheldrake, R. (1981), *A New Science of Life: The Hypothesis of Formative Causation,* Los Angeles: JP Tarcher.

Shepherd, S. V. et al., (2009). Mirroring of attention by neurons in macaque parietal cortex. *PNAS 106 (23) 9489–9494.*

Sherman, G., et al., (2012). Leadership is associated with lower levels of stress. *PNAS Early Edition, 1-5.*

Shine, B. (1999). *The Infinite Mind.* Harper Collins Publishers.

Shnabel, N., et al., (in press). Demystifying Values-Affirmation Interventions: Writing

About Social Belonging Is a Key to Buffering Against Identity Threat. *Personality and Social Psychology Bulletin.* Downloaded from psp.sagepub.com at Columbia University on March 12, 2013.

Siegel, D. J. (1995). Perception and cognition. In B. Kaplan and W. Sadock (Eds.), *Comprehensive textbook of psychiatry,* (6th edition) (pp. 277-291). Baltimore: Williams & Wilkins.

Siegel, D. (1999). *The developing mind: How relationships and the brain interact to shape who we are.* New York: Guilford Press.

Sigelman, C., & Rider, E. (2006). *Lifespan human development* (5th ed.). Belmont, CA: Thompson Wadsworth.

Simon, H. A. (1983). Human Nature in Politics: The Dialogue of Psychology with Political Science. In (Jun., 1985), *The American Political Science Review, 79* (2), 293-304.

Simons, J. (2011). What really happened? Sharp memories tied to brain crease. *msnbc. com contributor.*

Smither, R., Houston, J., & McIntire, S. (1996). *Organisation Development, Strategies for Changing Environments.* New York, NY: Harper Collins.

Sperduti, M., et al., (2011). Different brain structures related to self- and external-agency attribution: a brief review and meta-analysis. *Brain Struct Funct, 216:151–157.*

Sperry, R. W. (1969). A modified concept of consciousness. *Psychological Review, 76,* 532-36.

Squire, L.R. (1987). *Memory and the brain.* New York: Oxford University Press.

Squire, L.R., & Zola-Morgan, S. (1991). The medial temporal lobe memory system. *Science, 253*(5026), 1380-1386.

Squire, L. R., Knowlton, B., & Musen, G. (1993).The structure and organisation of memory. *Annual Review of Psychology, 44.*

Stafford, L. D., et al., (2010). Bolder, happier, smarter: The role of extraversion in positive mood and cognition. *Personality and Individual Differences 48, 827–832.*

Stanovich, K.E., & West, R.F. (2000). Advancing the rationality debate. *Behavioral and Brain Sciences, 23,* 701-726.

Stapp, H. P. (1993). *Mind, matter, and quantum mechanics.* Berlin: Springer-Verlag.

Stich, S. (1990). *The Fragmentation of Reason.* Cambridge: MIT Press.

Strauman, T. J., et al., (2013). What shall I be, what must I be: neural correlates of personal goal activation. *Frontiers in Integrative Neuroscience, 6, Article 123.*

Szekely, E. B. (1973). *Creative Yoga, Karma Yoga.* San Diego: Academy Books.

Stuss, D.T., Gallup, G. G., & Alexander, M. P. (2001). The frontal lobes are necessary for 'theory of mind'. *Brain, 124*(2), 279-286.

Summerfield, C., et al., (2005). Mistaking a House for a Face: Neural Correlates of Misperception in Healthy Humans. *Cerebral Cortex doi:10.1093/cercor/bhi129.* Oxford University Press.

Sweeney, P. J., Matthews, M. D. & Lester, P. B (2011). *Leadership in Dangerous Situations.* Naval Institute Press: Annapolis, Maryland.

Tabibnia, G., and Lieberman, M. D. (2007). Fairness and Cooperation Are Rewarding: Evidence from Social Cognitive Neuroscience. *Ann. N.Y. Acad. Sci. 1118: 90–101. New York Academy of Sciences. doi: 10.1196/annals.1412.001*

Takeuchi et al. (2013). White matter structures associated with empathizing and systemizing in young adults. *NeuroImage 77, 222–236.* Elsevier Inc.

Takeuchi, H. et al. (2013). Resting state functional connectivity associated with trait emotional intelligence. *NeuroImage (in press).*

Takeuchi, H. et al., (2013). White matter structures associated with empathizing and systemizing in young adults. *NeuroImage, 77, 222-236.*

Tamir, D. I., & Mitchell, J. P. (2012). Disclosing information about the self is intrinsically rewarding. *PNAS Early Edition.* www.pnas.org/cgi/doi/10.1073/pnas.1202129109

Taylor, G. J. (2000). Recent developments in alexithymia theory and research. *Canadian Journal of Psychiatry, 45.*

Taylor, M. A. (1999). *The fundamentals of clinical neuropsychiatry.* Oxford, UK: Oxford University Press.

Taylor, S. E., & Brown, J. D. (1988). Illusion and well-being: A social psychological perspective on mental health. *Psychological Bulletin, 103*(2), 193-210.

Teneback, C. C., Nahas, Z., Speer, A. M., Molloy, M., Stallings, L. E., Spicer, K. M., Risch, S. C., & George, M. S. (1999). Changes in prefrontal cortex and paralimbic activity in depression following two weeks of daily left prefrontal TMS. *The Journal of Neuropsychiatry and Clinical Neurosciences, 11*(4), 426-435.

Thatcher, R. W., Walker, R. A., & Giudice, S. (1987). Human cerebral hemispheres develop at different rates and ages. *Science, 236*(4805), 1110-1113.

Thelen, E. (1989). Self-organisation in developmental processes: Can systems approaches work? In M. Gunnar & E. Thelen (Eds.), Minnesota Symposium on Child Psychology, 22, *Systems and development* (pp. 77-117). Hillsdale, NJ: Erlbaum.

Thibodeau, G.A., & Patton, K. T. (1997). *Structure and Function of the Body.*

Topps, M. (2009). Oxytocin: Envy or Engagement in Others? *Society of Biological Psychiatry 67:e5–e6.*

Tracy, B. (2004). *Goals! How to get everything you want – Faster than you ever thought possible*. San Francisco, CA: Berrett-Koehler Publishers, Inc.

Treffil, J. (1992). *Sharks have no bones*. New York: Simon and Schuster.

Tremblay, L., & Schultz, W. (1999). Relative reward preference in primate orbitofrontal cortex. *Nature, 398*, 704-708.

Trevarthen, C. (1993). The self born in intersubjectivity: the psychology of an infant communicating. In U. Neisser (Ed.), *The perceived self: Ecological and interpersonal sources of self knowledge* (pp. 121-173). Cambridge, UK: Cambridge University Press.

Trevarthen, C. (1996). Lateral asymmetries in infancy: Implications for the development of the hemispheres. *Neuroscience and Biobehavioral Reviews, 20*, 571-586.

Tucker, D. M., Luu, P., & Pribram, K. H. (1995). Social and emotional self-regulation. *Annals of the New York Academy o f Sciences, 769*, 213-239.

Tulving, E. (1985). How many memory systems are there? *American Psychologist, 40*(4).

Tulving, E. (1993). Varieties of consciousness and levels of awareness in memory. In A. Baddeley & L. Weiskrantz (Eds.), *Attention, selection, awareness and control: A tribute to Donald Broadbent* (pp. 283-299). London: Oxford University Press.

van der Kolk, B. A., Pelcovitz, D., Roth, S., Mandel, F. S., McFarlane, A., & Herman, J. L. (1996). Dissociation, somatization, and affect dysregulation: The complexity of adaptation to trauma. *American Journal of Psychiatry, 153*(7), 83-93.

van Ijzendoorn, M. H. (1995). Adult attachment representations, parental responsiveness, and infant attachment: A meta-analysis on the predictive validity of the Adult Attachment Interview. *Psychological Bulletin, 117*(3), 387-403.

van Ijzendoorn, M. H. (1992). Intergenerational transmission of parenting: A review of studies in con- clinical populations. *Developmental Review, 12*.

van Ijzendoorn, M. H., & Bakermans-Kranenburg, M. J. (1996). Attachment representations in mothers, fathers, adolescents and clinical groups: A meta-analytic search for normative data. *Journal of Consulting and Clinical Psychology, 64*(1), 8-21.

Veccio, R. P. (1988). *Organizational Behavior.* The Dryden Press.

Wada, J. (1961). Modification of cortically induced responses in brainstem by shift of attention in monkeys. *Science, 133.*

Walsh, V., Ashbridge, E., & Cower, A. (1998). Cortical plasticity in perceptual learning demonstrated by transcranial magnetic stimulation. *Neuropsychologia, 36* (1), 45-49.

Walton, M. E., & Baudonnat, M., (2012). The value of competition in the rat race. *Nature Neuroscience, 15, 9, 1182-1183.*

Watanabe, M. (1996). Reward expectancy in primate prefrontal neurons. *Nature, 382*

(6592), 629-632.

Waytz, A., Zaki, J., Mitchell, J. P. (2012). Response of Dorsomedial Prefrontal Cortex Predicts Altruistic Behavior. *The Journal of Neuroscience, 32(22):7646 –7650.*

Wenzlaff, R.M. (1993). The mental control of depression: Psychological obstacles to emotional well-being. In D.M. Wegner & J.W. Pennebaker (Eds.), *Handbook of mental control* (pp. 239-57). Englewood Cliffs, NJ: Prentice Hall.

Westbrook, C., et al., (2013). Mindful attention reduces neural and self-reported cue-induced craving in smokers. SCAN (2013) 8, 73-84.

Westphal, M., Seivert, N. H., & Bonanno, G. A. (2010). Expressive Flexibility. *Emotion, 10, No. 1, 92–100.*

Wheeler, M. A., Stuss, D. T., & Tulving, E. (1997). Toward a theory of episodic memory: The frontal lobes and autonoetic consciousness. *Psychological Bulletin, 121,* 331-354.

Whitmore, J. (1992). *Coaching for Performance: GROWing People, Performance and Purpose.* London: Nicholas Brealey.

Wike, T., & Fraser, M. (2009). School shootings: Making sense of the senseless. *Aggression and Violent Behavior, 14*(3), 162-169.

Wilber, K. (2000). *A Theory of Everything: An Integral Vision for Business, Politics, Science, and Spirituality.* Shambhala.

Wilber, K. (1982). *Eye to Eye: The Quest for the New Paradigm.* New York: Doubleday/Anchor.

Wilber, K. (2000). *The Collected Works of Ken Wilber.* Boston: Shambhala.

Wilber, K., Engler, J. Y., & Brown, D. (1986). *Transformations of Consciousness: Conventional and Contemplative Perspectives on Development.* Boston: Shambhala.

Wilber, K., Anthony, D., & Ecker, B. (Eds.). (1987). *Spiritual Choices.* New York: Paragon House Publishers.

Wilber, K. (Ed.). (1987). *Quantum Questions: Mystical Writings of the World's Great Physicists.* Shambhala.

Wilber, K., & Wilber, Treya Killam. (1991). *Grace and Grit: Spirituality and Healing in the Life and Death of Treya Killam Wilber.* Shambhala.

Wilber, K. (1995). *Sex, Ecology, Spirituality: The Spirit of Evolution.* Boston, MA: Shambhala.

Wilber, K. (1996). *A Brief History of Everything.* Boston, MA: Shambhala.

Wilber, K. (1999). *One Taste: Daily Reflections on Integral Spirituality.* Shambhala.

Wilber, K. (1998). *The Essential Ken Wilber: An Introductory Reader.* Shambhala.

Wilber, K. (1997). *The Eye of Spirit: An Integral Vision for a World Gone Slightly Mad.* Shambhala.

Wilber, K. (1998). *The Marriage of Sense and Soul: Integrating Science and Religion*. Shambhala.

Wilber, K. (1977). *The Spectrum of Consciousness*. Wheaton: Quest.

Wilber, K. (1979). *No Boundary: Eastern and Western Approaches to Personal Growth*. Los Angeles: Center Press (new edition: Shambhala, 1981).

Wilber, K. (1980). *The Atman Project : A Transpersonal View of Human Development*. Wheaton: Quest.

Wilber, K. (1981). *Up from Eden: A Transpersonal View of Human Evolution*. New York: Doubleday/Anchor.

Wilber, K. (1982). *A Sociable God*. New York: McGraw-Hill. Note: this book is currently out of print as a separate book, and only available in Collected Works, Volume 3.

Williams. W. M., & Sternberg, R. J. (1988). Group intelligence: Why some groups are better than others. *Intelligence 12*.

Winnicott, D. W. (2002). The capacity to be alone. In *Maturational Processes and the Facilitating Environment* (pp. 29-36). New York: International Universities Press, 1958.

Winston, J. S. et al. (2002). Automatic and Intentional Brain Responses During Evaluation of Trustworthiness of Faces. *Nature Neuroscience, 5*(3). Winston, R. (2003). *The Human Mind*. Bantam Books.

Witelson, S. F., Kigar, D. L., & Harvey, T., (1999). The exceptional brain of Albert Einstein, *The Lancet, 353*(9170), 2149-2153.

Wolf, N.S., Gales, M., Shane, E., & Shane, M. (2000). Mirror neurons, procedural learning, and the positive new experience: A developmental systems self psychology approach. *Journal of the American Academy of Psychoanalysis and Dynamic Psychiatry, 28*, 409-430.

Wolf, N. S., Gales, M. E., Shane, E., & Shane, M. (2001). The developmental trajectory from amodal perception to empathy and communication: The role of mirror neurons in this process. *Psychoanalytic Inquiry, 21*(1), 94-112.

Worden, J.W. (1983). *Grief counselling and grief therapy*. London: Travistock Publications Ltd.

Xue, G., et al., (2009). Functional Dissociations of Risk and Reward Processing in the Medial Prefrontal Cortex. *Cerebral Cortex, 19, 1019-1027*.

Xue, G., et al., (2008). Risk And Reward Compete In Brain: Imaging Study Reveals Battle Between Lure Of Reward And Fear Of Failure. *Science Daily*. University of Southern Califsornia. Retrieved August 7, 2013, from http://www.sciencedaily.com/releases/2008/10/081009144325.

Yong, E. (2012). The Hype About the Love Drug Is Dangerous. One Molecule for Love,

Morality, and Prosperity? *Slate.com/articles/health_and_science*

Zak, P. J., Stanton, A.A., & Ahmadi, S. (2007). Oxytocin increases generosity in humans. *PLoS ONE 2*(11), e1128, 1-5.

Zak, P. J., Kurzban, R., Matzner, W. T. (2005). Oxytocin is associated with human trustworthiness. *PLoS ONE 2(11): e1128*

Zeki, S. (2007). The neurobiology of love. *Federation of European Biochemical Societies Letters, 581,* 2575-2579.

Zeltzer, L. K., Anderson, C. T. M., & Schecter, N. L. (1990). Pediatric pain: Current status and new directions. *Current Problems in Pediatrics, 20*(8).

Zenger, J. H. & Perrin, C. (1993). *Leading teams: Mastering the new role.* Irwin Professional Publishing.

Zhu, Y., et al., (2007). Neural basis of cultural influence on self-representation. *NeuroImage, 34, 1310–1316.*

About the Author

A s an author, coach and consultant, I have been fortunate to have had a life that has enabled me to work with people, at their very best and their very worst.

When participants have attended my *NeuroPower* Transformational Leadership programs and have experienced significant breakthroughs, often they want to know a little about my story.

To this end the following thumbnail sketch of my life will give you a deeper insight into my personal and professional journey.

Let me introduce myself...

I was born on Boxing Day to two young

Peter Burow

B.Bus Comm Dip. M.MHH, NS.NLP, AFAIM

teachers in the small town of Bundaberg in Queensland, Australia. Mum was the only one in her family to have gone to university. She came from a pioneering family with eight children; times were tough, and the whole family worked and saved to send her off to be educated. She held the aspirations of her whole family. Mum taught me the power of patience and strategy. Her aspiration was to marry anyone but a farmer, which is where my father comes into the scene.

While Mum was a country girl, Dad was from town. He moved schools frequently when he was in his early teens and, in his words, never really caught up. He wanted to be an electrician but my grandfather thought that teaching was better – so he became a teacher. His only career advice to me was to try anything but teaching. Dad taught me to question everything and test the boundaries of authority. One of his sayings is 'People only seem to get upset if they know about it.' He taught me how to manage my fear in a way he has always found difficult. One of my earliest memories was when I was about three, and involved a ritual ladder climbing that took place every afternoon when Dad returned home from work. He would set up the aluminium ladder and I had to climb a step higher every day. One day I could stand on the very top. We were both very proud.

Mum, as most mums do, wanted to be the perfect mum and constantly fought with the fact that she was supposed to be using the education her family had given her rather than being at home with her child. She contented herself by giving me a full education from the moment I could talk. My first storybooks were ones that Mum thought would give me a good Christian perspective on life and introduced me to the Old Testament biblical characters. For some reason I loved Moses although Jesus was a bit of a mystery to me.

I have very clear memories of when I was three, discussing if Jesus was a normal man filled with the Holy Spirit or if he was God. I decided he was a man filled with the Holy Spirit, which meant that I too could do what Jesus did if I could work out how to be filled with the Holy Spirit. I loved Sunday School, where Mum was the Superintendent, but couldn't work out why everyone wanted to color in and not discuss the theological issues behind the stories. I quickly became a behavior management issue.

When I was five my parents bought me a keyboard. Such a thing of amazement and magic I had never seen. I started with lessons and decided that I would be the best organist in the world. I've never dreamt small. Every morning from 6.30am until 7.15am I would practise with the headphones on. It drove me mad but taught me about how to keep doing something until it's mastered.

At school I couldn't work out what the other children were doing. I couldn't see the point to 'tiggy' or any of the other games they played. I remember asking Dad what the point of tennis was; he said I'd understand when I was older.

In Year Two I wrote my first book. I proudly took it to school for show and tell. I presented my work but to my amazement I was told by my teacher that I couldn't possibly have written it and that I was obviously an attention-seeking liar. I had been so excited about showing it too!

My reaction to this was to get busy. In Grade Three I fell in love with *Dr. Who* and *The Investigators* books, both of which were banned from the school library. My response was to bond with the second in charge of the library, and create a puppet show, which ran at lunchtimes. I charged the children an entrance fee and drummed up business by volunteering for tuckshop duty and convincing the children to use their money for the puppet show rather than ice creams. Back in 1973 I made $165.00 profit over a three-month period. The money was spent on *Dr. Who* books and the entire series of *The Investigators* books for the library. For an eight-year-old this was a great victory.

Each day I had so much to do and so little time to do it. At a parent-teacher interview my Year Five teacher explained that he felt as if he was interrupting me to ask me to do schoolwork. By Year Six I had a puppet show that was taken to other schools with no less than twenty Year Six helpers – a third of the class. At lunchtime my friend Nigel and I ran a second-hand shop that sold anything kids could find from home – we made good money and donated it to the class for art materials.

When I was eleven I broke my leg at a school camp and was in hospital for 100 days. My mother says that I went in as a child and came out about forty years old. The children back at school were all put on roster to visit. Each visitor had to bring a present! This was fantastic. Imagine an eleven-year-old receiving three presents a day for 100 days! Suddenly I felt very popular.

I bonded with the nurses and the doctors, playing cards and arguing theology with the Anglican nurse and the Seventh Day Adventists who would visit me. I watched daytime television. At home I was only allowed one hour per day, but in hospital I watched TV night and day. I also discovered social politics and helped the nurses I liked get even with the nurses we didn't. For me, hospital was lonely but fantastic. It also gave Mum the opportunity to discover that I was way behind academically at school. From that day on I had after school work every day until I went to university. In the words of Jim Hacker from *Yes, Prime Minister*, I received a comprehensive education – to make up for my comprehensive education.

High school was excellent because I had the chance to start all over again. My academic results were average at best but I decided to position myself as a top student. I found out who the top students were, dressed like they did, studied harder than they did and competed at every opportunity. It was on my first day of high school that I met a curly haired chap who seemed popular and had a very endearing turn of phrase. I decided that he would also be good to get to know. Robert and I became good mates and he was good to compete with in maths and woodwork. He was always better at maths, which is just as well because today we are fellow Directors in a number of companies and for the last fifteen years he has looked after all my accounts and legal issues. I trust him implicitly.

I was fairly focused on studying at high school, although a few character forming events took place during secondary school that spring to mind. The first involved winning the state championship of Jaycees Youth Speaks for Australia. This was a national speaking competition for senior Secondary School students that focused on a seven-minute inspirational and a two-minute impromptu speech. Back then the finals were televised. For me, this involved travelling to Brisbane (about a day's trip away) and performing in a television studio. I was terrified. Much to my amazement I returned home a winner. For a fortnight after the finals Brisbane radio stations, newspapers and magazines rang me for comments about a range of topics from politics to school standards. In Bundaberg people would stop me in the street to ask my advice about how their children could grow up into a 'nice young man' like I was, or to give me advice about my hair or my clothes. I was a no-name one day and suddenly known to everyone the next.

At lunchtimes I worked with one of the church Elders down at the local piano shop. I was also President of the Young Organists' Association and was invited to be a guest concert organist by the Wurlitzer Corporation. (At the time, home organs were all the rage.) I still have a bright red (YOA) uniform blazer with sequins and diamantes on it that I wore on stage for my final eye-raising number, *The Flight of the Bumblebee*.

When I wasn't helping down at the piano shop at lunchtime, I visited elderly people from the church who had no visitors and needed the company. I helped at the local Sunday School, volunteered as an usher and ticket sales person at the local amateur playhouse (and even acted in some of their plays), MC'ed the Mayor's Concert, was on the local judging panel for baby shows, played piano at church on Sundays and for local dances and weddings on weekends for pocket money. At school I set up the drama club, the reading club in the library and was voted a School Prefect. I had an absolute ball.

At church I teamed up with a talented English girl who was a gifted mime. She taught me this engaging little skit where we mimed that we wallpapered a room over the door and couldn't find the way out. We entered the skit into the state Youth For Christ drama competition. The audience loved it and my family and I were given the funding to attend the Christian music and drama camp in Cooma down south. This is where I learned about how to play in a band, something that I didn't really use until I played keyboard in a university band called *The Surrogate Mothers*.

On Australia Day 1984, the Bundaberg City Council awarded me the Young Citizen Award. I was not expecting it at all. I was there at the invitation of the local Member of Parliament. I can remember being so amazed that I was completely speechless. I couldn't say a word. It doesn't happen often but when it does, it does. I remember receiving the award and looking at the people in the park applauding and feeling so unworthy of their applause. I had enjoyed everything I had done. I remember the local Member of Parliament saying, 'Surely you have something to say,' and me just shaking my head and his hand in silence.

I moved to Brisbane when I was eighteen and started my undergraduate degree in Business Communications. The year before I graduated I started a small communications consultancy specialising in work for not-for-profit organisations. I was the Parish Council Secretary in the Uniting Church and believed that one day I would be an ordained Minister. In the meantime, however, I would run a consultancy. It was hard. For the first two years my business partner and I survived by taking it in turns to collect the dole and split it between us for food. Our team was made up of volunteers who turned up for the coffee and biscuits and the education they could receive. I quickly learned that the moment deadlines needed to be met or the environment became too intense, they would all take the day off. This gave me great insight into the motivations of employees and the importance of having a corporate vision, to which they would commit even if only for their own reasons.

To make ends meet during this time I played piano and did stand-up comedy. This was excellent experience. It was as a stand-up comedian that I first realized that there are very different humors. Almost inevitably if I made one half of the group laugh, the other half would be offended. If the offended folk found something funny, the others would be bored. It was where I first started becoming aware of the six different ways people process information and started exploring how they combined to form personality.

About this time I started working with a Spiritual Director. In case you're wondering what a Spiritual Director looks like, mine was an eighty-four-year-old Catholic nun who didn't let me get away with anything. As I got to know her better I discovered that, while she allocated herself an allowance of just $50 per month, she had made some excellent business decisions over the years and was a multi-millionaire. Like me, she had a love of God and business. I worked with her for four years developing an awareness of emotional reactivity which was important for the professional coaching and leadership work I had ahead of me.

I built the consultancy for the following thirteen years into one of the state's largest, and most awarded marketing and media consultancies. During this time I specialized in helping leaders from all sectors, (including church leaders and State Premiers) to lead and communicate effectively during times of change and crisis.

My media training and presentation clients varied from conservative groups like Coopers and Lybrand, and Woolworths through to multi-level marketing companies and politicians. It was with the executives of these companies that I refined *NeuroPower*. Each participant in my training would complete a questionnaire before attending the course and would receive a print-out of their profile. During the training I would ask participants to cross out any information about their profile in the paragraphs I supplied them that they felt was inaccurate and add in data about their personality they felt had been left out. Over a five-year period we had more than 2000 responses, which made up the base line research for the *NeuroPower* Profiler.

During the thirteen years I ran the consultancy I also owned a travel agency, a property development firm, investment company, a disabled workshop for collation and packaging, a graphic design firm, a gardening service employing intellectually disabled folk, an IT software development company and also managed a serviced office centre.

I retired from this in my thirteenth year of operation after a nasty go-cart accident, and to recuperate financially and emotionally from a disastrous property project (and a broken heart). I also wanted to focus more on studying personality and transformation. In particular I was interested in the amazing insight held by the Maya Lenca people from Central America who conducted a 10,000 year longitudinal study into personality. This lead to four years' study of the Maya Lenca under the personal guidance of His Excellency

Leonel Antonio Chevez, the last royal Maya Lenca Prince from Eastern El Salvador, who at the time lived in Brisbane, Australia in exile. In 2004, the Maya community awarded me a Diploma in Maya Studies for my work of collating and helping to preserve the Maya Health and Personality System and in June, 2005, in the rain forest of El Salvador, the *NeuroPower* framework was blessed by Her Excellency Francisca Romero Guevara.

After leaving the consultancy in Brisbane I formed a smaller specialist team of consultants who worked in Sydney with some of Australia's largest public companies and government instrumentalities providing strategic advice in leadership development and organisational transformation.

Since 1987, my team and I have coached thousands of executives Australia-wide using the frameworks and methodologies in this book. The success of this approach has helped to change the culture and performance of some of Australia's most recognized organisations. My role, as coach or adviser, has been to focus the individual on accessing their Genius and their noble side and to help them, as leaders, bring out the nobility in others. These noble qualities are available only to those who can hold the natural tension caused by competing polarities. While this is a simple concept, it is not easy, and requires enormous discipline and determination.

Like all of us, my personal journey has had highs and lows, good times and bad times. I know what it's like to have enormous influence and power and what it's like to break down completely emotionally and physically with broken dreams and a broken heart. What this journey has provided me with has been the perfect opportunity to refine a process for converting pain to power, naivety to nobility, hell to heaven.

Today I work with teams experiencing the stress that comes immediately before success. I share the *NeuroPower* methods for converting the daily s**t that comes across their desks into fertilizer that grows nobility and power.

Looking back I would change nothing in my past. Instead I am overwhelmingly grateful for the way my life has emerged and the opportunities and privileges it has afforded me.

And of course... the best is yet to come.

Index

www.ingramcontent.com/pod-product-compliance
Lightning Source LLC
Chambersburg PA
CBHW060312030426
42336CB00011B/1017